The Handbook of

Biblical Personalities

George M. Alexander

THE HANDBOOK
OF
BIBLICAL
PERSONALITIES

THE SEABURY PRESS · NEW YORK

1981
The Seabury Press
815 Second Avenue
New York, N.Y. 10017

Printed in the United States of America

Library of Congress Catalog Number: 62-9613

ISBN: 0-8164-2316-4

Contents

Preface

IN OUR TIME IT IS UNUSUAL TO FIND MANY CHURCH PEOPLE WHO ARE THOROUGHLY ACQUAINTED WITH HOLY SCRIPTURE. For some reason, perhaps for a long list of reasons, Bible reading in the home and Bible study in the Church have become so little the custom that a whole generation has grown to maturity in basic ignorance of the biblical persons, events and places once considered knowledge necessary to people of culture, and a *sine qua non* for Christians.

Theological students and graduates of theological schools, indeed the clergy, do not have the knowledge of the Bible once expected of them. Examiners of the graduates of theological schools and seminaries report regularly that, although more than one-fourth of the curriculum of most such schools is directly concerned with biblical studies, their charges are more likely to fail examinations in the content of the English Bible than in any other subject. Yet the Bible remains at the foundation of the faith of the Church; its content and meaning provide an indispensable source of ecclesiastical authority; its portrayal of the "mighty acts of God" in history is unique; it is, as no other collection of literature can be said to be for Christians, the word of God.

The writer has tried to teach laypeople and theological students to read the Bible with pleasure as well as profit; and more than a few times he has heard the complaint, "But I don't know where to begin; I find the Bible confusing."

The following pages have been written to provide those who would read the Bible with a handbook of the important people in

Scripture and a listing and brief description of those who make the Bible interesting as well as valuable. It is intended to offer theological students a quick reference book, and the casual reader a companion to the Bible with enough facts and interpretative material to throw light on some of the more important matters which make the people significant. There is no intention to give all the facts about all the people in the Bible; rather, identification of them is the primary objective. The hope of the author is to lead the reader to the Bible, not away from it; for experience has demonstrated that an armful of books about the Bible is no substitute for the Bible itself. This book will be more useful, therefore, if it is read with a copy of the Bible, in good clear type, close at hand.

Each name listed is followed by the principal biblical references. In some cases variations in the spelling of the names will be given, together with such information as is available on their meaning— as, for example, *Bethel* means "the house or place of El, or God," and *Abraham* means "the father of many, of a multitude," perhaps "the chief of many tribes." To hold in mind such bits of information means a greater store of knowledge and, also, a better way of remembering important facts about the people. In many instances the meanings of the names are not known. In such cases the fact is acknowledged or, if possible, an inference is drawn from what seems to be a root word to which the name might be related. A note on the meanings of the Hebrew names is included.

The several forms of the name of the Hebrew God are given, for reasons of consistency and ease of handling by the reader, as "Yahweh"; and the word *El* is given as "God." It is not the purpose of the writer to sift the opinions of the critical scholars in these matters and only on occasion, where it seems necessary, will more than a few words be spent in dealing with the special problems of criticism.

Quotations, except for phrases absorbed from long acquaintance with the Authorized Version, are from the Revised Standard Version of the Bible. Acknowledgment must be made of the help received both as student and in the preparation of these pages from C. Fletcher Allen's *Who's Who in the Bible*, published by G. P. Putnam and Sons, now out of print; from Harper's *Bible Dictionary*, by Madeleine S. and J. Lane Miller; and *The Interpreter's Bible*, published by Abingdon. The *Oxford Helps to the Study of the Bible,* with its short concordance and list of proper names, was a constant companion in the early stages of this work. Such a book as this would be an impossible task without the assistance of the standard concordances, as Young's *Analytical Concordance to the Bible,* and the newer Nelson *Concordance and Companion to the Revised Standard Version of the Bible.* Frequently consulted also were Hastings' *Dictionary of the Bible* and *Dictionary of Christ and the Gospels,* and *The Jewish Encyclopedia.*

For meanings of the names reference has been made most consistently to Brown, Driver and Briggs, *Hebrew and English Lexicon of the Old Testament,* and Liddell and Scott, *Greek-English Lexicon.* Some use was made of Harper's *Analytical Greek Lexicon.* In a few instances, where none of these offered anything more than the comment "etymology unknown," the suggestions noted in Young's *Concordance* have been given. Davidson's *Analytical Hebrew and Chaldee Lexicon* was helpful in suggesting quickly many Hebrew roots.

Appreciation is gladly expressed to the Rev. J. H. W. Rhys, the Rev. W. A. Griffin, and Dr. Bayly Turlington—colleagues and learned teachers—for their patience in answering numerous questions about matters in which they are specialists, and to the two first named for reading portions of the manuscript with critical eyes and magisterial habits.

A number of people have helped generously with the progress of the work. Mrs. Ruby Peeples and Miss Charlotte Field helped with the first draft, as did my elder son Stephen. These three created a readable paper from my miserably illegible handwritten notes. My wife checked references and typed the second and third drafts. But for her interest and encouragement the work would not have been completed. My son, John, read portions of the work and contributed the title. Mrs. J. H. Hodges, my secretary, and Mr. Edward Camp, Librarian of the School of Theology, have offered time, encouragement, and expert skills to the project.

In spite of all the help received, the author sees the work as still imperfect. His first intent—to compile a book dealing with people, places and events in the Bible—was quickly seen to be a task too large for one volume. Thus the book is at the outset a compromise. Moreover, the people included from the canonical books, together with a few of the best known names from the *Apocrypha,* are only those of recognized importance or those who seem to the writer to be important, or interesting. He knows full well that in his exercise of choice he has failed to include some who might have been listed by another; that he has dealt with some who might well have been omitted. He knows, further, that the reader trained in criticism can find many a flaw in his presentation of the approximately eight hundred characters he has chosen from among the several thousand he might have considered.

It is earnestly hoped that the reader will find something of value in this work, and that the principal benefit will be a greater interest in and acquaintance with the Bible itself.

GEORGE M. ALEXANDER

Sewanee, Tennessee
Lent, 1962

A Note on The Meanings of

Hebrew Names

PRIMITIVE PEOPLE LIVED DAILY WITH WHAT SEEMS TO US AN INCREDIBLE NUMBER OF MYS-TERIES. If we remember that, enlightened as we are, we still find the origin of life and the meaning of death beyond our under-standing, we shall not be unduly complacent in pointing to the fact that primitive man found almost every aspect and incident of life shrouded within a vast cloud of mystery and ignorance. Forces seen to be at work were not understood at all; and although he de-veloped an ability to employ some of them in his service, even without knowing quite what they were or why he could use them, there were others which, beyond him in every way, aroused fear, wonder, and awe. Some were to be courted; some to be avoided if possible, or approached with utmost caution. All he could say about them was that they exhibited a power, a "spirit" perhaps, beyond himself and far beyond his ability to manipulate or control.

The early Hebrews, like their contemporaries, attributed many things they could not understand to the presence of some power, "spirit," or "god," who or which was seen to be active in the na-ture and the life around them. A god, thus, could be seen as mani-fest in the violence of a storm; his presence would be more certainly and regularly understood in one place than in another. The activity of some god was observed in the phenomena of life in a thousand different ways. It was thought that to know or to possess the name of a spirit or a god was to be provided with an intimate relationship with the deity which might insure his protection or even some control over it. Something of this is seen in the story of the revelation of the "Name" of God to Moses in the "burning bush." Thereafter Moses was intimately related to *Yahweh* and under his protection.

It is not surprising, therefore, to find that the names of early peoples are often related to the name or names of their gods, or to some unusual event taking place at the time a child was born. Nor is it strange that a man's name might be changed in consequence of some experience he might have had which could be accounted for only by an encounter with a god, a spirit, an unusual manifestation of nature.

In social patterns where family relationships were important, a child might be identified by its connections with some well-known member of the family, clan, or tribe. Any outstanding physical characteristic might be marked in the giving of a name; places, cities, countries, and so on, were often added to a person's given name as a further means of identification. A profession or a special skill could set a man apart from his fellows.

Hebrew names are found often to express a thought in a simple sentence; sometimes the thought is expressed indirectly by the use of words forming a striking phrase, or a question. Sometimes they take on auxiliary meanings from folk-lore.

As an illustration of these factors as helpful in a study of biblical personalities, the following paragraphs offer a listing of some of the more important and obvious uses of them.

The general term of reference to a god whose specific name is not given is *El,* a title common to the Hebrews and their Canaanite neighbors. If the god is referred to as the "Lord" of something or some place the word might be *Adon* or *Adoni,* very like the Greek word, *Adonis. El* was the "senior god of the Canaanite pantheon," whereas *Adon* would be the title of a minor local deity whose name was unknown or not specified. However, *El* might be referred to as *Adon,* "Lord." In later times the term *Adonai* was often used as a substitute for the name *Yahweh.* A more familiar term for "Lord" is *Baal*, in the Canaanite pantheon the son of *El*. If the name of the god is given specifically, it might work out as in the name, for example, of *Elijah*, which means: "My God (*El*) is *Jah*." *Jah* (or ("Yah") is one of several forms of the name of the God of the Israelites. Other forms used in combination with many other words are *Iah, Je, Ju*, or the letter *I*. *Adonijah* would indicate, "My Lord is *Jah*," or *Yahweh*, a form of the name accepted for use in this book. *Bealiah* states that *Jah* (Yahweh) is *Baal*, or "Lord." *Obadiah* means "servant" or "worshipper of *Jah*" (Yahweh). *Obededom* offers a good example of combinations of words which might mean several things. *Obed*, meaning "servant, slave, worshipper," adjoined to *edom*, referring possibly to a person, a place, or a god, and having some suggestion of the color red, might thus mean one or all of several things. Masculine in form, it could indicate: "A servant or slave of a man named *Edom*"; or "A servant or a slave from the land of *Edom*"; or "A worshipper of *Edom*" (the god).

The names *Jacob* and *Israel* show well the use of names to indicate events. Jacob, the twin of Esau (which means "press, squeeze, crush, compel, gnash") "struggled" with his brother at birth, and was born grasping Esau's heel. "Jacob" actually comes from a word meaning "heel," or "closely following," in much the same sense that we speak of a dog trained "to heel," to "follow closely." The term was taken in Jacob's case to mean, "supplanter," for he supplanted Esau. When, however, Jacob was on the way from Haran to Canaan with wives and children, he "wrestled" with God in the night and "prevailed." He was told that his name would not now be Jacob, but "Israel," a name meaning "god persists, perseveres," or "God strives," or even, "He who strives with God."

Bealiah, meaning "Yahweh is Baal or Lord," and *Belshazzar*, meaning "Bel protect the king or leader," are examples of uses of the familiar term "baal," or "bel," the Babylonian form of it. Baal can mean "owner, possessor," as well as "lord, master." It can mean "husband, ruler," also.

Notice the joining of words in the following designations of family relationships.

Abigail, the beautiful widow whom David married, was given a name meaning "my father is joy"; *Abimelech* means "my father is the king" (or perhaps the God Melech); *Abihu* means "he is my father." Curiously, the name *Ahab* means "father's brother," or "uncle." Why would such a name be given?

The word for father, *Ab*, is often applied to a person as associated with a thing or quality, either as something to be remembered about the father referred to or as the source of the thing or quality. Abigail's father might have been a joyful, light-hearted person, or he might have been the source of joy to his family. There is a suggestion of a sneer, or an intent to show contrast in the name of *Absalom*, "my father is peace," the very thing Absalom's life did not show.

Ahi, "brother," as in *Ahimelech* (brother of the king or the God Melech), also indicates close relationships with persons, places and things.

The word *Cain* means "a smith, artificer, craftsman." Changed to *Ken* and applied to the "Kenites" it might indicate that the Kenites were known as smiths, metal workers, or craftsmen.

Not to be overlooked is the use of animal names. Thus *Caleb* is a "dog," *Deborah* was a "bee," *Rachel* was a "ewe." Plants also were used—*Tamar*, Absalom's beautiful sister, was a "palm." *Genesis* makes some reference to the fact that Esau was "hairy," and it is possible that that fact is somehow indicated by his name.

Scholars have worked patiently and diligently over the meanings of the Hebrew words, and the findings of archaeologists have brought many hidden things to light; but still it is true that many of the words are not as yet understood. The best course to follow in many cases is to acknowledge sorrowfully with them, "etymology and meaning uncertain," meaning "doubtful." It is for this reason that in this book many of the meanings suggested are followed by a question mark or by a statement confessing ignorance of the true meaning and offering only a tentative suggestion as to what it might have meant to the Israelites. Even when the meanings might be stated with some assurance, there is no certainty as to what, exactly, the name might have meant when given to a specific person at a point in history, legend, or story. *Ahab* is a case in point. Thus, while it is true that this writer's name is a combination of two Greek words, there is no truth in the notion that he is either a Greek or a farmer. So might it have been with many an Israelite in biblical times. While we know that David was "beloved" by many at times in his career, most of all perhaps by the writer of his saga, we know also that he was hated, despised and rejected by others—hated by Saul, despised by Michal his wife, rejected by Absalom and Adonijah his sons. Yet it is interesting to know that he was called "the beloved one," even though we cannot be sure that such is the only interpretation of the word used in his name. It might be a title, "commander," or *Dodo,* the name of a sun-god.

The reader, especially one who expects to teach, will find that any amount of time spent on the meanings of the names is time well spent even though—after hours with the lexicons—one cannot say that the words from which the names are derived are precisely defined. Suggested and obscure meanings often are in themselves enough to help the student absorb some of the delightful flavor of the stories in the Bible and the people who bring them to life.

The Handbook of

Biblical Personalities

A

AARON – *Meaning of the name uncertain.*

Exodus 4:14ff.; Numbers 12, 16, 17, 20, 26; Hebrews 5:4.

The brother—or half-brother—of Moses who first appears as the one appointed to speak before Pharaoh in the place of Moses, who declared himself to be "slow of speech and of tongue." Aaron was called in later times "the Levite," and in tradition was thought of as the head and fount of the priesthood. An interesting late story shows that he was appointed to office when, in a test, the "rods" of the princes of the tribes were left before the ark of the Lord and Aaron's was the only one to produce a bud.

It was Aaron, in one strand of the story, who stood beside Moses in Egypt; but also it was he who allowed the people to build the golden calf while Moses was too long on Mount Sinai. Questioned pointedly, Aaron's explanation was that when the people put their golden objects into the fire, "There came out this calf." He and Miriam, the sister of Aaron and perhaps half-sister of Moses, combined forces to oppose Moses' leadership, saying that they as well as he had received direct revelation from God. On the other hand, although always in the background, Aaron was a strong help to Moses as he led the people against the Amalekites. In the battle with them he held up Moses' tiring arm which held his rod as a sign of victory from Yahweh.

A strange and somewhat shad-

3

owy figure (he is not mentioned at all in the "J" source of the Pentateuch), Aaron was described as sometimes strong, sometimes lacking in faith and loyalty; and, according to the later writers, he was forbidden the promised land because at Meribah in Kadesh both he and Moses lost faith in, and "murmured against," the God who had delivered them from Egypt and had promised to bring them into a good land. Thus, instead of being allowed to enter Canaan, he was publicly stripped of the robes of his office and ordered to proceed to the summit of Mount Hor where he died and was buried.

As the garments of office were stripped from Aaron they were immediately placed on his third son and successor in the priesthood, Eleazar. His two eldest sons, who should have succeeded, were killed in an effort to cense the altar with "unauthorized fire."

Many scholars think Aaron represents a cult of bull worship centered at Bethel, and a struggle for pre-eminence between the priesthood of that sanctuary and the Levitical priesthood. This means, of course, that he was neither brother nor half-brother of Moses, but rather one

who was worked into the Mosaic tradition for "political" purposes. See LEVITE, MOSES, MIRIAM, ABIHU.

ABAGTHA – *Happy, Prosperous.*
Esther 1:20.
One of the seven chamberlains sent by King Ahasuerus (Xerxes) to notify Queen Vashti of the banquet before which the king wanted her to appear. The queen refused to attend and thus opened the way for Esther to take her place on the throne. See ESTHER, MORDECAI.

ABEDNEGO   (AZARIAH) – *Servant of Nebo, Servant of Light.*
Daniel 1:6f., 19; 2:17, 49; 3:12-30.
A friend of Daniel (renamed Belteshazzar), Meshach (Michael) and Shadrach (Hananiah) who with his friends refused the favors of, and declined to worship, the image built by Nebuchadnezzar and was thrown into a furnace "seven times overheated." The king secretly sympathized with them; and when he observed the miraculous failure of the fire to burn the four faithful and apparently fearless young men, he gladly removed

them from the furnace and promoted them to honor.

The name "Abednego" was given him by the eunuch of King Nebuchadnezzar, who also called Daniel "Belteshazzar."

ABEL – *Derivation unknown.*
Genesis 4:1-15; Hebrews 11:4.
The second son of Adam who became a herdsman and whose sacrifice to God was preferred over that of his brother Cain, the farmer. Abel's sacrifice of the firstlings of his flock was costly and carefully prepared and offered, while Cain's was cheap and perhaps casually offered. The difference in attitude was, of course, known to God and finally to Cain, who killed Abel and became an outcast.

One purpose of the story of Cain and Abel was probably to account for the constant struggle between nomadic tribes and settled agricultural peoples in western Asia. Another was to show the natural tendency of man to sin and to indicate, further, the consequences of sin.

ABIATHAR – *The Great One is Father.*
I Samuel 22:20; 23:6; II Samuel 8:18; 15:24ff.; I Kings 1:7, 19, 25, 42; 2:22ff.; St. Mark 2:26.

Son of Ahijah (Ahimelech) the priest and landowner in Anathoth in Benjamin in the days of Saul. Abiathar escaped Saul's massacre of the priests who had befriended David and had given him the shewbread to eat. In the massacre at Nob Ahimelech and eighty-five other priests were put to death. Abiathar, the only one to escape Saul's vengeance, fled to David and became his close friend, confidant, and priestly advisor.

Abiathar and Zadok became very influential priests, and it was the two of them who wanted to transfer the ark to the wilderness with David when he fled Jerusalem in Absalom's rebellion. David sent them back to the city. Abiathar's son, Jonathan, carried news and messages to David about Absalom's plans. When Absalom fell, Abiathar set the stage for David's return to Jerusalem.

But Abiathar was not always completely loyal to David: in Adonijah's attempt to take the throne from David, he joined Joab in treason by taking the side of Adonijah. When the rebellion was thwarted and Solomon named king, Joab was assassinated; and Abiathar, in acknowledgement of former services to King David, was merely stripped of position and banished, by Solomon's order, to the estate at Anathoth. See DAVID, ZADOK.

ABIGAIL – *My Father is Joy.*
I Samuel 25:14ff.
The lovely, self-effacing, and sensible wife of Nabal, a foolish Carmelite, who later became the wife of David.

Nabal's herdsmen had been given the "protection" of the outlaw David's band of marauders who could have "spoiled" his flocks at will. As a feast day arrived David sent messengers to Nabal asking for provisions for himself and his men to keep the feast. Nabal treated David's men with contempt and David said to his men: "Every man gird on his sword!" With four hundred men, and wearing his own sword, David started out to destroy Nabal.

Abigail learned of the incident and of the boorishness of her husband. She also heard of David's intentions. She knew her husband well, and secretly she made careful preparations to meet David with courtesy and apologies (and with provisions for the feast, as well) in the hope of dissuading him from his purpose. Her charm and intelligence captivated David.

Later, when Abigail told Na-

bal of her actions, "his heart died within him," and about ten days later he died, no doubt from shame and disgrace. David regarded his death as the Lord's own vengeance on Nabal for his insulting manners.

"Then David sent and wooed Abigail, to make her his wife," and Abigail "went after the messengers of David, and became his wife."

Abigail shared David's adventures and his troubles in Gath. She was taken captive by the Amalekites, rescued, and lived with David in Hebron when he became king. She bore him a son, Daniel (according to I Chronicles) or Chiliab (according to II Samuel).

The story of Abigail and David is one of the great love stories in the Bible. See DAVID, NABAL.

ABIHU – *He is My Father.*
Exodus 6:23; 24:1-11; 28:1; Leviticus 10:1; Numbers 3:2-4; 26:60f.; I Chronicles 6:3; 24:1f.
The second son of Aaron who with his older brother, Nadab, was selected to be with the seventy elders and their father when, in an act of special worship, they "went up" with Moses to Sinai and "they saw the God of Israel." Abihu, with the other

three sons of Aaron, was marked for the priesthood; but he and Nadab were consumed by an unauthorized and "unholy" fire which they presumed to attempt to offer in their censers. When they offered the fire and incense, "fire came forth from the presence of the Lord and devoured them."

This story from the Priestly editors of the Pentateuch accounts for the succession of the priesthood from Aaron to Eleazar and his sons.

ABIJAH, ABIJAM – *Yahweh is My Father.*
1. I Kings 14:1ff.
Abijah was a son of Jeroboam. When he fell desperately ill his mother sought in disguise the prophet Ahijah to learn whether the child would live or die. She hoped not to be known as the wife of Jeroboam and so possibly to escape a harsh word from the near-blind Ahijah. The prophet, however, saw through the disguise and gave her the terrible word that all Jeroboam's male heirs would die; that, indeed, as soon as her feet touched the city her child, Abijah, would die. Thus in the death of Abijah was expressed the warning that Jeroboam's hoped-for dynasty could not last long in Israel.

2. I Kings 14:31-15:8;
II Chronicles 13:1ff.
In I Kings the name is spelled Abijam; in II Chronicles the spelling is Abijah. The references are to the king of Judah, the eldest son of Maachah, the favorite wife of Rehoboam. Abijah's reign was a brief three years. He was recorded as "following in the sins of his father," but also as a good man and a fighter who routed the 800,000 man army of Jeroboam, killing half of them with an army half the size. His fourteen wives produced thirty-eight children.

3. I Chronicles 24:10; 26:20; Nehemiah 10:7; 12:1-4, 12-17.
Three priests were named Abijah: a Levite in David's time; one who sealed the covenant with Nehemiah; and one who went from Babylon to Jerusalem with Zerubbabel. It is possible that the latter two are the same person.

4. II Chronicles 29:1.
A woman named Abijah was the mother of Hezekiah, king of Judah.

ABIMELECH – *My Father (Molech) is King.*
1. Judges 8:30f.; 9; 10:1.
One of the "Judges," a son of Gideon, who became king of

Shechem by assassinating all but one of his seventy brothers. Only Jotham escaped and lived to lead the Shechemites against him. In speaking to them against Abimelech, Jotham used the interesting parable of the trees (Judges 9) which in seeking a king met refusals until they came to the bramble, a mere bush, which accepted, with the proviso that all the trees would "come and take refuge in my shade," a ridiculous proposal, indeed.

Abimelech enjoyed royal position and prestige, but he had no time for royal duties in Shechem. After a rule of three years, only Zebul, his governor in Shechem, remained loyal to the absentee king. Zebul kept Abimelech informed on matters of importance. When Gaal, a natural leader, moved into Shechem and began to gain ground against the king, Zebul told Abimelech of Gaal's plans and advised the king to attack the city after lying in ambush all night. He did so and defeated Gaal, who was expelled from Shechem. Some who escaped the fury of Abimelech took refuge in the tower of Shechem; but the king burned the tower.

In following up his victory here he attacked Thebez, where a woman dropped a stone on him from the city wall. Abimelech, knowing himself to be near death, ordered his armor bearer to kill him to avoid the shame of having been killed by a woman.

2. Genesis 20; 21:22-32; 26: 1-16, 26-31.

A king of Gerar who would have taken Abraham's wife, Sarah, into his collection of concubines, because Abraham, being afraid, told the king's servants that she was his sister. Only divine intervention in the form of a dream prevented the king from keeping Sarah for himself. In this story Abraham appears in a poor light, while Abimelech seems a kind, generous man, much put upon by the lying Abraham.

Note the repetition of this story in Genesis 26, involving Abimelech with Isaac and Rebekah, instead of Abraham and Sarah.

3. Psalm 34; I Samuel 21:10ff. In the introduction to Psalm 34, Abimelech is the name given to Achish, king of Gath, before whom David in his flight from Saul feigned madness. David was afraid of Abimelech (Achish), because he knew that the king's servants were saying, "Is not this David the king of the land?" The ruse of madness caused the king to send him

away instead, possibly, of turning him over to Saul.

4. I Chronicles 18:16.

A son of Abiathar, a priest in
David's reign, was a priest
named Abimelech. See also II
Samuel 8:17.

**ABINADAB – *My Father is No-
ble, Generous.***

1. I Samuel 7:1; II Samuel
6:3f.

The man in whose custody the
ark was left for some twenty
years after its return by the
Philistines, and whose experience with the sacred box was
tragic. Abinadab's house was
"on the hill." His son was consecrated "to have charge of the
ark."

2. I Samuel 16:8; 17:13; I
Chronicles 2:13.

The second son of Jesse, an older
brother of David.

3. I Samuel 31:2; I Chronicles
8:33; 9:39.

A son of King Saul who was
killed by the Philistines in the
battle of Gilboa, in which Saul
and Jonathan also were killed.

4. I Kings 4:11.

The father of one of the twelve
administrative officers of Solomon. He was mentioned indirectly through his son, Ben-abi-
nadab.

**ABINOAM – *My Father is De-
light, Pleasant.***

Judges 4:6, 12; 5:1, 12.

A man of Naphthali whose son,
Barak, together with the "proph-
etess" Deborah, led the tribes of
Israel in a great victory over the
Canaanitish king, Jabin, and his
general, Sisera. See BARAK,
DEBORAH.

**ABIRAM – *The Exalted One is
My Father.***

Numbers 16:1ff.; 26:9; Deuteronomy 11:6; Psalm 106:17.
See KORAH.

**ABISHAG – *My Father is a
Wanderer?***

I Kings 1:3, 15; 2:17, 21f.

The beautiful Shunamite maiden
who was brought in to "wait
upon the king (David), and to
be his nurse." When David died,
Adonijah, Solomon's half-brother
and chief rival for the throne,
asked for Abishag. With her in
his harem he might have been
able to establish more firmly his
claim to the throne. Solomon's
reply was to have him killed.
Presumably Abishag remained
in Solomon's harem.

**ABISHAI – *My Father is Jesse*
(the grandfather, in reality).**

I Samuel 26:6ff.; II Samuel
2:18, 24; 3:30; 10:10, 14.

A nephew of David, brother of Joab and Asahel, and one of David's most daring and adventurous captains. Abishai went with the outlawed David to Saul's camp and would have driven his spear through the king had not David restrained him with the reminder that Saul was "the Lord's anointed." Instead they took Saul's spear and water jar, and left the king asleep and embarrassed.

It was Abishai with Joab who almost lost David's cause by murdering Abner, who had been in Hebron under the king's protection to offer help in creating a united Israel.

Abishai was given command of David's second army, or second "division," which won a battle over Edom in the valley of salt, and another over the Ammonites and Syrians. He was in command of the rebels in the revolt of Absalom.

Like David, Abishai had an encounter with a giant of the Philistines, Ishbibenob, whose spear was said to weigh 300 shekels of bronze. Abishai rescued David from the giant and killed him; whereupon David's men said to the king, "You shall no more go out with us to battle. . . ." As king, David's life was too valuable to be risked in battle.

Abishai almost made the rank of the "Three Mighty Men" of David, but not quite; for he was said to have "won a name beside the three" mighty men. Even so, he was described as chief of the thirty captains, as the most renowned and the commander of them all—a wild and daring military leader.

Abishai is called Abshi in I Chronicles 18:12. See JOAB, DAVID, ABNER, ASAHEL.

ABNER – *My Father is Ner; My Father is a Lamp, Light.*
I Samuel 14:50; 17:55f.; 26:5ff.; II Samuel 2:8-4:12; I Kings 2:5, 32.
Saul's captain of hosts was his cousin Abner, who upon the king's death tried at first to carry on the war against David. When the battles went to David's forces, however, Abner—who until this time just might have been trying to obtain Saul's kingdom for himself, as Ishbosheth claimed—negotiated with David for a uniting of the kingdom under one ruler. At the conclusion of the negotiations, while Abner was technically a guest and ally of David at Hebron, Joab con-

spired with Abishai to murder him. The murder was accomplished at Hebron's gates, a fact which made David technically responsible.

The murder upset David's plans for an immediate uniting of the tribes, almost undid them entirely; and David cursed Joab for the treachery. At Abner's funeral, an elaborate affair, undoubtedly, David delivered the eulogy. Curiously enough, when Ishbosheth was defeated and killed by David's men his head was buried in Abner's grave. See SAUL, ISHBOSHETH.

ABRAHAM (ABRAM) – Abram, *Great, Exalted Father;* **Abraham,** *Father of a Multitude.* Genesis 11:26; 12:1-28:13; 31: 42; 32:9; 49:30; St. Matthew 1:1; 3:9; St. John 8:33-58; Romans 4; Galatians 3:29; Hebrews 2:16; 6:13; 7:1-9; 11:8, 17.

Abram, as his name was at first, was the son of Terah of the city of Ur in the Chaldees, who "by faith" became the "father of many," although in his old age he as yet had no child and heir. Abraham, as his name came to be after God's promise of a son was given to him, is known as the chief of the great patriarchs of Israel.

His story begins in Genesis on two notes: First, with the account of his departure at the call of God from his home in Haran to a destination unknown, a journey which took him even into Egypt; and second, with the explanation of his childless state which was alleviated by God's gift to him and Sarai (changed with "the promise" to Sarah) of Isaac—the first of several children of promise in the Bible narratives—whose birth was regarded as God's own assurance of the foundation of Israel as a people.

Abraham responded to the call of God to go forth "not knowing whither he went," poor though possessed of great wealth; for his wealth was of no consequence to him as a childless wanderer. On the journey into the "unknown" he took with him his nephew, Lot, and his family. To Canaan they went, the land of "promise," and on the way he endured many trials. At Shechem and Bethel, Abram built altars for worship. In Egypt, where he was driven by famine after he had given Lot the choice of the better grazing lands, his wife Sarai escaped the

Pharaoh's harem only by divine intervention. The same story is given again involving Abimelech, king of Gerar, as the innocent offender. Abram's part in all of this was not altogether to his credit. Nor does he appear in a good light in his treatment of Hagar, the Egyptian slave of Sarai, who bore him a son and then was driven into the desert because of Sarai's jealousy—even though Sarai in a moment of self-pity gave Hagar to Abram for the very purpose of providing him with a child.

If, as the Genesis story indicates and as the Epistle to the Hebrews states, Abraham's faith was manifested in his departure from Haran and was tested in his trials along the way to Canaan, it was undoubtedly pressed almost beyond endurance by the further response to his understanding of the call of God to "take your son, your only son Isaac, whom you love, and go to the land of Moriah and offer him there as a burnt offering." Yet again he obeyed, even to the point of taking up the knife to kill Isaac for sacrifice. This is perhaps one of the most poignant stories in all literature and one of the most dramatic scenes in the pages of the Bible. With knife in hand, with Isaac

bound and laid on the wood on the stone altar, Abraham heard again the command of God not to offer his son. Herein is not only a great story but also a profound expression of religious conviction; namely, that one offers to God only that which is best and dearest to oneself. This theme carries over into the New Covenant in the blood of Christ, into practical, working Christianity.

Abraham was certainly a man great in his own times, for he was well received by Pharaoh and many of the chieftains of the areas through which he travelled. With some of them he allied himself to defeat the Elamites who had captured Lot. He scorned his share of the spoils of battle. He made a treaty with Abimelech, king of Gerar, whose respect he earned; and it is said that he resided at Hebron in peace.

As the story of Isaac is heartwarming and elevating, so, by contrast, is the story of Hagar and her son Ishmael disturbing and depressing.

When Sarah died, Abraham was said to have married Keturah who bore him six sons. These became the legendary patriarchs of the tribes of Arabia. Thus, Abraham, the father of many, was considered the source of the Israelites, the Ishmaelites and the Arabians.

Abraham died at the age of "one hundred seventy-five" and was buried in the cave at Macpelah "with Sarah his wife," a spot he had purchased many years earlier from Ephron the Hittite. See SARAH, ISAAC, LOT, REBEKAH, ISHMAEL, HAGAR.

ABSALOM – *My Father is Peace.*

II Samuel 13:1-19:10.

Absalom's name, suggesting "peace," is quite in contrast with the facts of his life. The third son of David, he first appears as the avenger of Ammon's rape of Tamar, Absalom's beautiful sister, Ammon's half-sister. In plotting the murder of Ammon he showed himself to be clever, determined, and ruthless; although he did show some feelings for the indignity heaped upon the unfortunate Tamar.

Having murdered Ammon he fled to take refuge for three years with Talmi, his grandfather and king of Geshur. David, however, had a peculiar love for his charming son, and Joab, being aware of it, arranged for the return of Absalom through the allegorical words of a "wise woman of Tekoa." David saw the "hand of Joab" in all this but sent him, nevertheless, to bring Absalom home, although he would not allow Absalom in the king's house or his presence for two years.

When, again through Joab, Absalom was restored to the king's presence he began to use his charm to undermine David's place among the people. He employed a personal guard and acquired chariots of his own and began to suggest, especially to the northern tribes, that he would give a better brand of justice than that of his father. In so doing he was carefully setting up a revolt against the king, and in time—when "the hearts of the men of Israel" were stolen—Absalom sent out messengers to have himself declared king. This was the signal for revolution, and David was forced to flee from his city; yet when the decisive battle with Absalom's rebels was about to begin David told Joab and Abishai to "deal gently with the young Absalom." In his attempt to escape after the defeat of his armies Absalom's mule ran under a thick branched oak, and the rider's head was caught in the branches. Joab, hearing this, quickly ran three darts into his heart and ten of his young armor-bearers "struck him and killed him."

So ended the revolt and the story of the clever and handsome son of David; but the disharmony exposed by him lasted on and eventually resulted in the division of the kingdom.

ACHAN – *Meaning unknown, but association with the Valley of Achor might indicate "trouble."*

Joshua 7:1ff.

When in the battle for Canaan Jericho fell to the Hebrews, orders were given by Joshua that all spoils were to be "utterly devoted," that is, sacrificed to God. Achan, the son of Carmi of the tribe of Judah, however, hid out certain items which he desired for himself and so broke a vow taken by the whole of the people. The result was the disastrous defeat at the town of Ai, where Israel was repulsed and 36 men were lost. Since Ai, according to all calculations and signs, should have fallen to the forces of the Israelites without difficulty, the leaders knew something was wrong internally; someone had not kept faith. Lots were cast to see whose was the fault, and Achan was found to be the culprit. He confessed; the secreted spoils were found

buried under his tent; he and all his household were killed and the whole outfit, part and parcel, were later buried in the Valley of Achor. The name Achan is considered synonymous with a curse arising from greedy treachery. See JOSHUA.

ADAM – *Of the Ground, "Created."*

Genesis 1:26-31; 2:15-5:5; Job 31:33; Romans 5:14; I Corinthians 15:22, 45; I Timothy 2: 13.

Then God said, "Let us make man in our own image, after our likeness; and let them have dominion over the fishes of the sea, and over the birds of the air, and over the cattle, and over all the earth . . ."

The first man, Adam (the name means also, merely, "man," and might well be spelled adam, until the story has progressed to Genesis 3:20), was placed in the garden of Eden and given everything in it to keep and use; except, according to the second and later story, the tree of the knowledge of good and evil "in the midst of the garden."

The first of the two stories states flatly that "male and female he created them"; but the second portrays Adam (adam) as a lonely creature needing companionship. Thus Eve, meaning "woman" or "mother of all living," was created from one of his ribs to be his companion. It was Eve, beguiled by the serpent, who persuaded Adam to disobey orders and to eat of the fruit of the forbidden tree. The two, having eaten and having become aware of the difference between good and evil, were thrust from the garden in consequence of their disobedience and to prevent their eating of the fruit of the tree of life. They were then "alienated" from God and "doomed" to toil, pain, and death. "You are dust, and to dust you shall return."

Notice that until the end of the poem (Genesis 3:14-19) in which "the Lord God" rebukes the serpent and the "man" and the "woman," no proper names have been used. In the next verse "the man" called his wife "Eve"; and in verse 21 the Lord God calls the man "Adam."

At this point the authors of the interwoven stories begin to tell their principal story—how it happened that "the Lord God" was concerned about the people of Israel from the days of the first man until their own times.

Later theologians have pored over these stories, and in them they have found Adam to be representative man. In Adam's image, they find all men to be created in the image of God, enlivened by the "breath" of God and haunted by consciousness of alienation from God. They find "in Adam's sin" a story which seems to fit the condition of life which all men share. Thus, in the story of the first man there might be seen the germs of the great biblical doctrine of man which culminates in the statement about man in the Epistle to the Romans. In this story may be seen also the seeds of the story of the relationship of God to man which culminates in the doctrine of the Incarnation in the New Testament.

The early writers were not concerned about these things, of course. Having told their primitive stories about first man and first woman, they moved on to say that Adam and Eve were the parents of Cain, Abel and Seth, who, in turn, were the progenitors of the people of Israel for whom their God Yahweh had performed such mighty acts. In doing so, however, they expressed an astonishing concept of both God and man, and of the relationship of initiative and response between them which is the essence of the highest forms of religious understanding.

ADNAH – *Pleasure.*

1. I Chronicles 12:20.

"Some of the men of Manasseh deserted to David when he came with the Philistines for the battle against Saul" on Mount Gilboa. One of them was Adnah, a chief of "thousands" and a mighty man of valor. Adnah and the other deserters helped David recover his wives and his goods from the "raiders" of the Amalekites who had razed Ziklag while he was away.

2. II Chronicles 17:14.

A commander of three hundred thousand "mighty men" in the armies of Jehoshaphat, king of Judah. The Chronicler states that "some of the Philistines" brought presents to Jehoshaphat and that none of the kingdoms made war on him. Perhaps it was because of the size and efficiency of his armies, of which that commanded by Adnah was said to be the largest.

ADONI-BEZEK – *Lord of Bezek, My Lord is Bezek.*

Joshua 10:1ff.; Judges 1:5ff.

When Judah and Simeon were fighting their way into Canaan, they battled the Perizites at Bezek and defeated an army led by Adonibezek. The Israelites caught Adonibezek and his four

ally kings and stored them in a cave until the pursuit after the battle was over. Then they arraigned Adonibezek and the others "and cut off his thumbs and his great toes," an especial indignity, since without thumbs he could not wield the bow and without great toes he could not run well. In the Judges story he died in Jerusalem in disgrace; in Joshua they were re-sealed in the cave to die.

ADONIJAH – *My Lord is Yah-*(*weh*).

II Samuel 3:4; I Kings 1:5-2:28.

The son of David and Haggith, "a very handsome man . . . born next after Absalom." He "exalted himself," saying, "I will be king." David, in his old age, indulged his arrogance and failed to check his gathering of a personal guard, a small army in fact.

When Adonijah, having "conferred with Joab and Abiathar the priest," assembled his brothers and many officials of Judah to make his move toward the throne, Nathan the prophet revealed the plan to Bathsheba whose son, Solomon, was said to have been promised the throne. Bathsheba went to David saying, "Adonijah is king, although you, my Lord the king, do not know it," and reminded the king of his promise to her and to Solomon. As she said these things Nathan entered the king's chamber and confirmed her words.

Then and there David renewed his promise to Bathsheba and Solomon and ordered Nathan and Zadok the priest to have Solomon, riding on the king's mule, go to Gideon and there be anointed and declared king by joint royal and priestly authority.

News of this caused Adonijah's supporters to go "each his own way," leaving the rebel to seek refuge on the horns of the altar until he was given Solomon's word of mercy.

After David's death Adonijah, through Bathsheba, asked Solomon for Abishag, the beautiful maiden who had nursed and warmed David in his last days. He thought thereby to establish his claim to the throne. Instead of granting the request, Solomon had Adonijah put to death and so removed a source of certain discontent and probable rebellion. See DAVID, ABSALOM, SOLOMON.

AENEAS – Probably from the Greek verb, "to praise."

Acts 9:33f.

At Lydda Peter found Aeneas who was paralyzed and had been bedridden for eight years. Peter called his name and said: "Jesus Christ heals you; rise and make your bed." Aeneas arose immediately.

AGABUS – *A Locust? A Wonder Worker?*

Acts 11:27-30; 21:10.

Agabus was a prophet of the Church in Jerusalem who went with other prophets to Antioch and, "by the spirit," foretold the coming of a world-wide famine which "took place in the days of Claudius." In response to the work of Agabus the disciples at Antioch sent relief "to the brethren in Judea" by Barnabas and Saul.

It was probably this same Agabus, a prophet from Judea, who went to Caesarea to warn Paul not to go to Jerusalem. He gave his warning by symbol and sign, taking Paul's girdle and binding his own hands and feet with it to show what the Jews at Jerusalem would do to "the man who owns this girdle . . ."

AGAG – *High, Warlike.*
Numbers 24:7; I Samuel 15:8-33.
As the poem in Numbers 24 shows, Agag is a poetic name for the tribe of Amalek. Possibly it is a "standing" title for the chief.

Agag was a king of the Amalekites whom Saul spared from the sword when he had been instructed by the Lord, through Samuel, to destroy "utterly" the Amalekites. This disobedience in saving Agag and "all that was good" in Amalek elicited from Samuel the words, "Behold, to obey is better than sacrifice," and the proclamation that as Saul had not carried out the "ban" against Amalek, so the Lord would reject Saul "from being king."

Thus Agag was the indirect cause of Saul's decline.

AGRIPPA I (37-44 A.D.) – *One Who Causes Pain at His Birth?*
Acts 12.
This Agrippa is known as Herod in Acts 12.

Agrippa was the grandson of Herod the Great. By court influence at Rome and friendship with the mad Emperor Caligula he was given the estates of Philip the Tetrarch in Galilee. When Caligula was murdered, Agrippa helped to place Claudius on the throne and was given other estates in Galilee and Judea, together with the title "king." The second set of properties was taken from Herod Antipas and Herodias who were banished. Agrippa and all his Herodian kin were more Roman than Jewish. The book of Acts reports that it was Herod Agrippa who "killed James the brother of John with the sword" and, "to please the Jews," he put Peter in prison. When Peter was miraculously delivered from the prison Agrippa ordered a search for him and the death of the commanders of the prison garrison.

While speaking to the people of Tyre and Sidon, Agrippa was striken by "the angel of the Lord," and was "eaten of worms."

AGRIPPA II
Acts 25-26.
The vassal king of Judea, last of the Herods, to whom Paul was sent after he had "appealed to Caesar" on the ground of his rights as a citizen of Rome. Paul's appearance before King Agrippa and his sister Bernice was an empty gesture, since the puppet king had no jurisdiction

in a case appealed to Caesar. His comment on hearing Paul's story was that he "might have been set free if he had not appealed to Caesar."

AHAB – *Father's Brother, Uncle.*

I Kings 16:29-17:1; 18:1-19: 18; 20:1-22:53.

King of Israel, son of Omri, one who "did more to provoke the Lord, the God of Israel, to anger than all the kings of Israel who were before him." Such was the judgment on Ahab of the editor of the Book of Kings. Not the least of his errors as presented by that writer was the fact that "he took for wife Jezebel . . . and went and served Baal, and worshipped him."

Idolatry brought him into conflict with Elijah the Tishbite whom Ahab called the "troubler of Israel." But Elijah's answer— "I have not troubled Israel; but you have"—was, in the mind of the writer, nearer the truth. It was before Ahab and Jezebel's priests that Elijah staged the famous contest on Mount Carmel.

Ahab was a courageous man, however, and a good military leader and strategist. He defeated a large army of Ben-hadad, king of Syria, and later as an ally of Ben-hadad and

others, he checked the power of Shalmaneser III of Assyria in the battle of Karkar, 853 B.C. In spite of a bitter, three-year famine, Ahab's reign was a time of expansion and prosperity for Israel. He seemed able to accomplish and to have his way except for the peace and harmony he desired for his own kingdom and household. With his mind on "larger issues" he was not much concerned about Elijah's demand for exclusive worship of Yahweh. He ignored the prophet's warning and failed to do away with Ben-hadad, as ordered, and the prophet's word, "Your life shall go for his life," came in time to be true. His was a "live and let live" attitude in these matters and, although he was probably a worshipper of Yahweh, he did not hesitate to use his own judgment when it ran contrary to the word of the prophet.

The editor of Kings was careful to show that the prophet's word prevailed. Indeed, Ahab's end was the worst one imaginable for, as Elijah had predicted, the king of Israel was killed in battle and "In the place where the dogs licked up the blood of Naboth (whom Jezebel had caused to be murdered in order to satisfy Ahab's whim to have the poor man's inheritance) shall dogs lick your own blood." Worse still, at the hands of Jehu (whom the prophet had caused to be anointed king in Ahab's stead) all Ahab's male heirs, 70 in number, were killed, so that the kingdom of Israel was eventually relieved of his entire household.

Ahab's reign, from c. 869 to 850 B.C., was roughly parallel to that of Jehoshaphat of Judah. See OMRI, JEZEBEL, ELIJAH, JEHU, OBADIAH, NABOTH, ATHALIAH.

AHASUERUS – King, Mighty Man, Mighty Eye.
Esther 1ff.
The Persian king, Xerxes (476-465 B.C.), who "reigned from India to Ethiopa" and who figured in the story of the Book of Esther as benefactor to his favorite wife's captive people. See ESTHER.

AHAZ – He (Yahweh) Has Grasped.
II Kings 15:38-16:17; I Chronicles 3:13; 9:42; II Chronicles 27:9-28:27; 29:19; Isaiah 1:1; 7:1ff.; 14: 28; 38:8; Hosea 1:1; Micah 1:1.
Son of Jotham, king of Judah, who being advised by Isaiah to ignore both Israel and Assyria, chose to ally himself with the latter rather than to yield to the pressure of Israel to join in a common alliance with Syria. His treaty with Assyria was on such terms as to make Judah not an ally but a tribute-paying subject. Ahaz actually was forced into the humiliation of a journey to Damascus to pay the tribute in person.

On that journey he learned of the Assyrian religion which, as a vassal, he was forced to introduce as an accepted religion at home, with the result that he built an altar like the one he had seen in Damascus and set it in the place of the "bronze altar which was before the Lord." With the new altar there came cultic acts as well, and Ahaz was said to have "burned his sons as an offering."

The strength he expected from Assyria proved to be disastrous in every way, and his reign of sixteen years was considered a complete failure.

Hosea, Micah and Isaiah prophesied during his reign (c. 735-715 B.C.) which was approximately co-terminous with the reigns of Pekah and Hosea, kings of Israel.

AHAZIAH – Whom Yahweh Upholds.
There were two kings who bore this name, neither of very great

importance, though the stories of both are interesting.

1. I Kings 22:40-53; II Chronicles 20:35-37; II Kings 1: 2ff.

The son of Ahab, king of Israel, who "walked in the way of his father, and in the way of his mother (Jezebel). . . . He served Baal and worshipped him." His was a short two year reign (c. 850-849), which ended when he "fell through the lattice in his upper chamber in Samaria," and died because—according to Elijah—he sent "to inquire of Baalzebub, the god of Ekron," instead of the God of Israel concerning his condition.

Ahaziah tried to join an expedition of Jehoshaphat of Judah in sending ships made in Tarshish to Ophir for gold. The enterprise was a failure from the point of view of either king. Jehoshaphat declined Ahaziah's offer to join the effort; and the ships were "broken" at Eziongeber without delivering a cargo. Thus the peace that existed between the two kings was qualified by suspicion.

2. II Kings 8:24f.; 9:16-29; 10: 13; 12:18; 13:1; 14:13; II Chronicles 22.

A king of Judah, Ahaziah was the youngest son of Jehoram. His older brothers were carried away by the Philistines and he,

at the age of twenty-two, was made king by acclamation. He lived one year as king, c. 842 B.C. Ahaziah's tragedy lay in the fact that his mother was a daughter of Ahab (the Authorized Version gives it as the daughter of Omri), which in the eyes of the writers of Chronicles and Kings put him under the curse on the house of Ahab. This was thought a sufficient cause for his untimely death under somewhat unusual circumstances.

King Jehoram of Israel had been wounded in battle with the Syrians and had gone to Jezreel to recuperate. Ahaziah went to Jezreel to visit Jehoram. While they were visiting, the watchman on the tower saw a company of horsemen approaching and Jehoram sent two sets of messengers to learn who they were. None of the messengers returned. This was reported by the watchman who then observed that the oncoming horsemen were driving "like the driving of Jehu the son of Nimshi; for he drives furiously." The two kings then went to meet Jehu, not knowing that he had been anointed king of Israel by Elisha (or was it Elijah? See I Kings 19:16; II Kings 9:3), and that he had come to kill Jehoram, the son of Ahab and Jezebel. When Jehoram understood the situation he turned to run, and warned Ahaziah, who started to run in the opposite direction. Jehoram was shot in the back as he fled; and when Jehu saw Ahaziah he said, casually, "Shoot him also." Ahaziah died of his wounds.

Ahaziah is also known as Azariah and Jehoahaz. See JERORAM, JEHU.

AHIJAH (AHIAH) – *Brother of Yahweh.*

Only two of the nine men of this name are of significance.

1. I Samuel 14:3; 22:9.

A priest who cared for the ark when, in the days of Saul, it was carried with the armies to the battle camp, and who cast the lot to find the culprit when Jonathan had innocently brought Saul's curse on the army by eating against a vow of fasting of which he was unaware.

The ark was kept by him in the sanctuary at Nob to which it was moved after the destruction of Shiloh. Ahijah, son of Ahitub, was called Ahimelech in I Samuel 21:1 and 22:9.

Ahijah was the priest whom David encountered at Nob as he fled from the jealousy of Saul. It was from Ahijah that he received both counsel and help. Ahijah was remembered as having given David "provisions" of "holy bread" (shewbread), and as having armed him with the sword of Goliath which was held as a trophy, probably behind the Ark. For these courtesies to David, observed by Doeg the Edomite sheepherder of Saul's household, Saul had Ahijah (Ahimelech) and eighty-four other "persons who wore the ephod" slain; and the city of the priests at Nob was "put to the sword."

2. I Kings 11:29ff.

Ahijah the Shilonite, a prophet, who foretold the rise and fall of Jeroboam, son of Nebat (Jeroboam I, c. 922-901 B.C.), to whom ten of the twelve tribes of the United Kingdom were to be given as Solomon's reign came to an end. The prophet gave his word to Jeroboam by tearing a new garment into twelve pieces and presenting ten of them to that "very able" young man.

When Jeroboam achieved his ambitions in drawing the ten tribes into his orbit, he forgot the warning of Ahijah that he must "walk . . . as David my servant did"; indeed, hoping to wean the people from the temple at Jerusalem, he set up two golden calves at Bethel and at Dan. In time, Jeroboam's son became ill and he had his wife disguise herself to seek out the old prophet, Ahijah, to ask "What shall happen to the child?" Ahijah, almost blind, yet saw through the disguise, greeted the woman by name and gave her the sad news that because of Jeroboam's evil ways the Lord would "cut off from Jeroboam every male"; and he told her that the child would die just as she returned to the city. As she "came to the threshold of the house, the child died."

AHIMAAZ – *My Brother is Wrath.*
1. I Samuel 14:50.
The father of Ahinoam, the wife of Saul and mother of Jonathan.
2. II Samuel 15:27, 36; 17:17-21; 18:19ff.
A son of Zadok the priest. Ahimaaz, with his father and Abiathar the priest and his son, Jonathan, was sent back to Jerusalem when David fled the city in the rebellion of Absalom. This group of loyal supporters of David was charged with the care of the ark and also with the duty of taking news to the king. It was Ahimaaz who, running ahead of a Cushite appointed by Joab, gave the news to David of the failure of the uprising; but he did not tell David of the death of Absalom, intending no doubt to spare the king's feelings as long as possible.

Some scholars think Ahimaaz might have been the author of "the early source" of Samuel, which is considered by them as possibly "mankind's first written history," and a masterpiece.
3. I Kings 4:15.
An officer in Solomon's organization who was responsible for food in the king's household for one month. He was in charge of the territory of Naphtali.

AHIMELECH – *Brother of Melek* (the God Melek?), or *Brother of the King* (Melek also means king).
1. I Samuel 14:3; 22:11; II Samuel 8:17.
See AHIJAH.
2. I Samuel 26:6.
A Hittite warrior in David's band. He must have been one of the more reliable and courageous of the band; for when David proposed to enter the camp of the sleeping Saul, it was to Ahimelech and Abishai that he said, "Who will go down with me into the camp of Saul?" Abishai went, but the question was put to Ahimelech as well, and by name, as if he was highly regarded by David.

AHITHOPHEL – *My Brother is Folly?*

II Samuel 15:12; 16:23; 17:23.
A highly respected advisor and counselor to David who turned traitor to him in the revolt of Absalom. He advised Absalom to attack David immediately, in the night, as he fled. Had the rebel done so, he probably would have won out in his purpose. Absalom, however, chose to hear the words of Hushai, the clever Archite, whom David had sent back into the city as an "infiltrator" of Absalom's conspirators. The result was that David's prayer, that the counsel of Ahithophel might be "turned to foolishness," was answered. Ahithophel, knowing now that Absalom's cause was lost, and his own with it, went to his home city, "put his house in order," and hanged himself. See AB-SALOM, DAVID, HUSHAI.

ALCIMUS – *Strong, Stout.*

I Maccabees 7.
Alcimus was a high priest much hated by the Jews because he was sympathetic to the Greeks. In 160 B.C. he was leader of "all the lawless and ungodly men of Israel" who appealed to King Demetrius to send a trustworthy man to "see all the ruin which Judas has brought upon the land

of the king," and to punish him. Demetrius then made Alcimus high priest and sent him to "take vengeance on the sons of Israel." Alcimus and his men "did great damage in Israel," more evil indeed "than the Gentiles had done." Failing to gain complete control over the country Alcimus returned to Demetrius and "brought wicked charges" against Judas and his followers.

ALEXANDER – *Leader of Men.*

1. Daniel 7:7; 11:3.
It is possible that these verses make cryptic reference to Alexander the Great.

2. St. Mark 15:21.
A son of Simon of Cyrene, the man who, passing by as the Lord bore the cross toward Calvary, was "compelled" to carry it for Jesus. Alexander was further identified as having a brother named Rufus.

3. Acts 4:6.
Alexander was among those of the "highpriestly family" who gathered in Jerusalem to question Peter and John about their preaching and healing in the name of Jesus. Alexander was apparently a Jew of wealth and position.

4. Acts 19:33.
A Jewish companion of St. Paul when in Ephesus the crowd was

aroused to an uproar by Deme-trius the silversmith. Alexander was pushed forward by the crowd and he motioned as if to "make a defense," but the crowd seeing he was a Jew, shouted all the more.

5. I Timothy 1:20.
Alexander and Hymenaeus were "certain persons" who had made "shipwreck of their faith"—that is, had turned apostate. They were thus regarded as blas-phemers, and were "delivered to Satan" by the Apostle, without further ado.

6. II Timothy 4:14.
Alexander the coppersmith to whom Paul referred as having done him "great harm." It is possible that this Alexander is the same as the one mentioned in I Timothy. See above.

ALPHAEUS – Chief, a Thou-sand, Transient?
St. Matthew 10:3; St. Mark 2: 14, 3:18; St. Luke 6:15; Acts 1:13.
The father of James, one of the disciples of Jesus. It is possible that the same Alphaeus was fa-ther of Levi whom Jesus met at the tax office, and into whose home he went to dine with "tax collectors and sinners."

AMALEK – War-like,   Dweller in the Valley.
Genesis 36:12; Exodus 17:8-16; I Samuel 15.
Traditional leader of a tribe which fought against Israel at Rephidim.
It was in the battle with the Amalekites that Moses held the rod in his hand and so brought victory to Israel; but his arm would tire, and in order to keep the battle going in Israel's favor Aaron and Hur sat Moses on a large stone and held his arms up and steady, "until the going down of the sun," while "Joshua mowed down Amalek and his people . . ." Perpetual war was declared against Amalek, a tribe which by the decree of the Lord to Moses was to be completely "blotted out from all remem-brance." The Amalekites con-tinued nevertheless to be a thorn in Israel's flesh. In the first days of Saul's reign the city of Amalek was ordered "by the Lord" to be utterly destroyed. Saul defeated the Amalekites and destroyed the city; but he kept Agag, the king, "and the best of the sheep and of the oxen . . . and all that was good . . ." For this diso-bedience Saul was "rejected . . . from being king over Israel." Samuel's words on the subject were spoken in a striking, poetic

oracle given him doubtless when the night before he had "cried to the Lord all night." He said: "Behold, to obey is better than sacrifice, and to hearken than the fat of rams." Fitting actions to words, Samuel himself "hewed Agag in pieces before the Lord . . ." Saul's disobedience led to the anointing of David.

Saul's victory was not, thus, complete. The Amalekites raided David's city, Ziklag, and carried off "all who were in it," including two of David's wives. David then gathered his band of six hundred, caught the Amalekites in their victory celebration, and killed all "except four hundred young men." Amalek paid tribute to David after he became king.

Little is known about Amalek, but the name "valley-dwellers," and the area of their operations, suggests associations with the regions of the Dead Sea.

AMASA – *Burden, Load?*
II Samuel 17:25; 20:4ff.; I Kings 2:5, 32.

Amasa was appointed captain of the host of Absalom. His ascendency was of short duration, for with the collapse of the revolt he was killed by Joab who "took him by the beard to kiss him," and struck him with a sword concealed in the left skirt of his soldier's garment.

AMAZIAH – *Yahweh is Mighty.*
1. II Kings 12:21; 13:12; 14:1-23; 15:1, 3; II Chronicles 24: 27; 25:1-26:4.

The son of Joash, king of Judah, who became king after his father was killed by two of his "servants" (c. 800-783 B.C.). Amaziah liquidated his father's killers and otherwise strengthened his position, then took the town of Sela from the Edomites in a battle in the Valley of Salt. Having done so he sent to Jehoash to ask for a face to face encounter in battle, or for some sign of recognition of equality or superiority. Being scorned by Jehoash, the new and arrogant king of Judah forced a battle which was fought at Beth-shemesh, where Amaziah was badly defeated. Indeed, Amaziah was captured and Jehoash attacked Jerusalem with such force as to break through the wall of the city. The treasures of the temple and of the king's house were taken, with hostages, to Samaria. A conspiracy against Amaziah caused him to flee to Lachish where he was murdered.

2. Amos 7:10-14.

A priest of Bethel who in response to the prophecy of Amos said: "O seer, go, flee away to the land of Judah, and eat bread there . . ." It was to Amaziah that Amos declared that he was "no prophet, nor a prophet's son . . . ," but a herdsman to whom the Lord had said, "Go, prophesy to my people Israel." Amaziah wanted Amos to prophesy almost anywhere else, for, he said, "The land is not able to bear all his words."

3. I Chronicles 4:34 and 6:45 refer to two other men named Amaziah who are of no significance.

AMMON, AMMONITES – *A Fellow-countryman.*

Genesis 19:38; Numbers 21:24; Deuteronomy 2:19, 37; 3:11, 16; Joshua 12:2; 13:10, 25; Judges 3:13; 10:6-12:3; I Samuel 12:12; II Samuel 8:12; 10:1-12:31—etc.

Ammon was the legendary name of the descendants of Ben-ammi, son of the younger son of Lot. Although thus related, there was long and bitter strife between Israel and Ammon. In their trek from Egypt the tribes of the Israelites took lands from the Ammonites after being refused free passage through their lands. Jephthah defeated them once after an attempted talk of peace failed. Saul defeated them. David got on well with one Ammonite king, but had to fight the next one who hired an army of Syrians. This king, Hanun, David intended to deal with as he had dealt with his predecessor, but Hanun disgraced David's messengers by cutting off half their beards and their garments "up to the hips." David's armies under Joab took the capital city of the Ammonites.

To defeat the Ammonites in battle was not, however, to dispose of the influences of these kinsmen of Israel; for it appears that there was considerable intermarriage with them, and their religious practices, known as "abominations," crept into Israel's patterns of life over a long period. The prophets Amos, Ezekiel, Jeremiah and Zephaniah, foretold the doom of the Ammonites; and the Ammonites taunted Nehemiah as he rebuilt the walls of Jerusalem. See HANUN.

AMNON – *Faithful.*

II Samuel 3:2; 13:1ff.

David's oldest son who was killed by Absalom because Amnon had raped the beautiful Tamar, Absalom's sister. Amnon's passion for Tamar was such as to make him lose his reason. Had he asked his father for her, as Tamar herself suggested, all might have been well; but to force her with trickery was in Tamar's words, "A thing not done in Israel . . . a wanton folly." Having raped Tamar he then hated her and threw her out. The scene she created aroused the wrath—and the jealousy—of Absalom, who doubtless saw in the incident an excellent means of disposing of his chief rival for the throne. Amnon's rape of Tamar set the stage for Absalom's rebellion.

AMON – *Workman.*
II Kings 21:18-23; II Chronicles 33:20-23.
A king of Judah, son of Manasseh, who was remembered as "idolatrous," having not been affected at all by the repentance of his father. He served and worshipped all the strange images once set up by Manasseh and might have gone so far as to offer human sacrifice. Amon was killed by the members of his own household, the courtiers, after a reign of only two years (c. 643-641). The murderers were themselves killed by the people. His successor was his son, Josiah.

AMORITES – Possibly *Mountain-dwellers, Mountaineers?*
Genesis 10:16; 14:13; 48:22; Exodus 3:8; Numbers 21:13, 21-31; 32:33; Judges 1:34; 3:5; I Samuel 7:14; II Samuel 21:2; I Kings 4:19; 9:20f.; 21:26; II Kings 21:11; etc.
A tribe of Canaanites said to stem from the fourth son of Canaan, according to the late source in Genesis 10. Some of the chiefs of the tribe were at one time allies of Abraham and, later, the Amorites were opposed to Jacob who took lands from them and at his death assigned these lands to Joseph.

The land of the Amorites was a "hill country," part of the promised land to which Moses was instructed to lead the people, a "good and broad land . . . flowing with milk and honey." As the Israelites left Sinai for the invasion of the land, Sihon was king of the Amorites and Heshbon was his principal city. Israel asked first for the right of free passage through the land; but Sihon refused and attacked them, with the consequence that Sihon was killed and his city and surrounding villages taken and occupied. The area is often referred to as "Gilead." Treatment of Sihon seems to have struck terror in the minds of the surrounding tribes.

Og, king of Bashan, was an Amorite.

In the distribution of lands, the former kingdom of Sihon was assigned to "Gad," to "Reuben" and to the "half-tribe of Manasseh."

The Amorites were not easily disposed of, in spite of the alleged terror the defeat of Sihon aroused; for Judges speaks of their driving "the Danites back into the hill country," and of the Israelites as dwelling amongst them, as taking their daughters for wives and as worshipping their gods. In the period of Samuel there was peace between the Amorites and Israel. In David's time few Amorites were left and those under Solomon were in a state of servitude. Even so, they were influential, for their god, Chemosh, was still worshipped in the time of Ahab and Manasseh; and in Ezra's day, also, it was said that the people had not "separated themselves" even yet "from the peoples of the lands with their abominations."

AMOS – *Burden, Burden-bearer.*

The Book of Amos.

The herdsman of Tekoa, a dresser of sycamore trees, to whom the command of the Lord was, "Go, prophesy to my people Israel." Amos was a prophet who refused the title, saying of himself, "I am no prophet, nor a prophet's son."

The judgment of history about him is, however, that he was a prophet who saw the signs of the times more clearly than most and who spoke so directly to those to whom he was sent that they were ready to do almost anything to stop his words. History has given him the title of prophet.

From Judah Amos went to Bethel in the kingdom of Israel and began his words of prophecy in what must have been a welcome tone: by pointing the finger of doom at Damascus, Gaza, Tyre, Edom, Ammon, Moab and Judah. Suddenly, however, he turned on Israel, using the same formula, "For three transgressions of Israel, and for four, I will not revoke the punishment. Thus says the Lord!"

In Israel, he said, they "sell the righteous for silver, and the needy for a pair of shoes"; they "trample the head of the poor"; they are immoral in many ways and hypocritically religious. They "turn justice into wormwood" and "abhor him who speaks the truth"; they take bribes and "turn aside the needy at the gate."

In recompense for these things, cried Amos, Israel will find that the "day of the Lord" is a day of "darkness and not light . . . and gloom with no brightness in it." His plea was, "Let justice roll down like the waters and righteousness like an everflowing stream."

The Book of Amos contains many phrases often quoted by those concerned with social evil and the need for social reform, phrases striking to the mind, easy to remember and readily applicable to almost any society. Powerfully illustrative of the righteousness of God are the descriptions of the Lord "forming locusts" to destroy the "latter growth"; of the "Lord standing beside a wall built with a plumb line, with a plumb line in his hand" to measure the uprightness of Israel; of the Lord showing a basket of summer fruit to signify the end of good times.

Amos was accused by Amaziah, the priest at Bethel, of conspiracy against Jeroboam the king. Certainly his words which, said Amaziah, the land was "not able to bear," were likely to stir up the poor and were disturbing to the complacent well-to-do; for Amos stated that the king would

die by the sword and Israel would go into exile. He was asked to leave Bethel, to go to Judah to speak his terrible words. In answer, Amos spoke his words of doom and destruction more thunderously; and having done so, since he was not a prophet or a prophet's son, it is likely that he returned to his home and other duties. He is not mentioned elsewhere in Holy Scripture. There is no doubt, nevertheless, that with the raising of his voice at some point in the time of Jeroboam II (c. 786-746) a new note was sounded in prophecy amongst the Hebrews.

ANANIAS – *Yahweh is Gracious.*

1. Acts 5:1.

Ananias the husband of Saphira, members of the Church in Jerusalem, sold a piece of property and made a gesture of giving all the proceeds to the apostles for the use of the Church. In fact, however, Ananias withheld part of the money he had received. Peter rebuked him, saying that what he had was his own and that there was no need for the gift; but that since the gift had been made falsely, Ananias had lied to God. On hearing this Ananias "fell down and died."

Later, Peter questioned Saphira about the matter, confronting her with his knowledge of the deception she shared with her husband, and she died also.

2. Acts 9:10; 22:12.

A disciple of Jesus at Damascus who was sent by a vision to inquire for "a man of Tarsus named Saul." It was this Ananias who ministered to Saul in his blindness, who baptized him and by the laying on of hands restored his sight.

3. Acts 23:2f.; 24:1.

Ananias the high priest before whom Paul was brought and to whom Paul referred as a "whited wall." Later he appeared against Paul in the court of Felix.

ANDREW – *Manly.*

St. Matthew 4:18ff.; St. Mark 1:29; St. John 1:40; 6:8; 12:22; Acts 1:13.

The brother of Simon Peter who was called to be a disciple of Jesus while fishing in the Sea of Galilee. Probably, as indicated in St. John's Gospel, Andrew was a follower of John the Baptist. In any case, he is acknowledged to be one of the first two of Jesus' disciples, and story-tellers have liked especially the account in the Fourth Gospel in which Andrew, the first disciple to be

called, "found his brother Simon . . . and brought him to Jesus." The Lord visited in the home of Peter and Andrew and healed Peter's mother-in-law there.

Andrew it was who told Jesus about the boy with the loaves and fishes at the feeding of the thousands, and he assisted in the distribution of the food blessed by the Lord.

Andrew and Philip brought to Jesus "some Greeks" who came to the group wishing "to see Jesus."

Tradition suggests that he worked in Scythia and so became the patron-saint of Russia. Tradition is strong in asserting his crucifixion in Patrae in Achaia and, to prolong his sufferings he was bound, not nailed, to the cross.

ANNA – *Grace.*

St. Luke 2:36-38.

An elderly prophetess of the tribe of Asher who gave herself to prayer, "night and day," not departing from the temple in Jerusalem. It was she who gave testimony of Jesus on the occasion of the Purification as "the redemption of Israel," after Simeon had uttered his song of blessing.

ANNAS – *Grace of Yahweh.*
St. Luke 3:2; St. John 18:13, 24; Acts 4:6.

Annas was high-priest, with Caiaphas, "in the fifteenth year of the reign of Tiberius Caesar," when John the Baptist began his ministry. Caiaphas was his son-in-law.

It was before these two, in the year of the high-priesthood of Caiaphas, that Jesus was brought for questioning after he had been betrayed by Judas. The soldiers took Jesus first to Annas who sent him to Caiaphas, who in turn sent him to Pilate.

These two also questioned Peter and John about their preaching and healing after the Resurrection, and warned them not to preach again or heal in the name of Jesus.

ANTIOCHUS IV (Epiphanes) –
The Opposer.
II Maccabees.

King of Syria (c. B.C. 175), whose relation to biblical matters is to be found in the apocryphal book of II Maccabees.

Palestine came into Syrian hands after the victory of Antiochus III, the "Great," over Egypt in 198 B.C. Antiochus IV visited Jerusalem to see Jason, the simoniacal high priest who was in time replaced by one Menelaus, whose primary qualification for the position was a greater sum of money to offer for it. Jason was driven to take refuge with the Ammonites.

Jason heard rumors that Antiochus was dead, and he raised an army to attack Jerusalem. He took the city and held it for a very short time; but, having slaughtered his own citizens he did not get the office he sought and was forced into exile.

Antiochus IV took Jerusalem again and spoiled both the city and the Temple. Another attack was made later—for no good reason. This time he burned the city, massacred the Jews, sold off the women into slavery and set up his own religion which he tried desperately to impose on the Jews.

Judas Maccabaeus was one of the few who escaped from this attack. He led an opposition which eventually took from Antiochus all the territory of Judah, except the city of Jerusalem itself.

In 164 B.C. Antiochus died in madness, a horrible death, which the writer of the apocryphal book regarded as quite proper for one so cruel and debased.

ANTIPAS (Antipater) – Possibly a shortened form of Antipater, from a Greek word meaning "to suffer" or to "endure in turn."
1. St. Matthew 14:1, 3, 6; St. Mark 6:14ff.; St. Luke 3:1, 19; Acts 4:27; 13:1.

Herod Antipas, the son of Herod the Great, who was a Samaritan and Tetrarch of Galilee and Perea. He was banished in 41 A.D. Herod Antipater, also known as Antipas the Idumaean, was the father of Herod the Great.
2. Revelation 2:13.

A member of the Church in Pergamos who was "my witness, my faithful one," and who died a martyr's death.

APOLLOS (Apollonius) – From a Greek word meaning "to drive away, evil, disease"?
Acts 18:24; I Corinthians 1:12; 3:3f., 22; Titus 3:13.

A man "eloquent and mighty in the Scriptures." Apollos was an Alexandrian Jew who was converted and came under the influence of Priscilla and Aquila at Corinth. Having been enlightened by them in the faith, he used his abilities to refute the Jews, "showing by the Scripture that Christ was Jesus."

So successful was he that some in Corinth thought themselves to be "of Apollos," that is, of the "party" of Apollos. Factions or "parties" began to develop in the Church there. Paul wrote sharply against these in his first Epistle to the Corinthians. In time Apollos went to Crete.

It is significant of him that Paul acknowledged his work in Corinth: "I planted, Apollos watered." Some think that Paul and Apollos were together at Ephesus.

AQUILA – *An Eagle.*
Acts 18:2, 18, 26; Romans 16:3; I Corinthians 16:19; II Timothy 4:19.

A Jewish convert of Pontus who migrated to Corinth when Claudius expelled the Jews from Rome. It was his custom to speak in the synagogue, and in so doing he "persuaded many Jews and Greeks." Paul found him and his wife, Priscilla, to be cordial hosts and fellow tentmakers. The Apostle stayed with them in Corinth. Later Aquila went with Paul to Ephesus where his home became a center of Christian activity.

Aquila and Priscilla were hosts also to Apollos and his tutors in the faith.

When Paul was in prison in Rome, Aquila visited him, "risking his neck," in defiance of the edict of Claudius.

ARAM – *Be High, Exalted?*
1. Genesis 10:22f.; 22:21; Deuteronomy 26:5.

A son of Shem, who was said to be the father of all the children of Eber, Aram was regarded as the father of the Syrians. On the other hand, he is seen as a grandson of Nahor, Abram's brother. The Aramaeans and the Syrians are identified in the Old Testament; sometimes they were enemies, sometimes friends and kinsmen. In Deuteronomy Jacob is labelled an Aramaean.

2. I Chronicles 7:34; St. Matthew 1:3f.

Aram here is listed as a son of Shamar, of the tribe of Asher; and although in St. Matthew the name is spelled simply Ram, he is regarded as of the lineage of David.

ARAUNAH – *Yahweh is firm.*
II Samuel 24:16-24.

Araunah, a citizen of Jerusalem, owned a threshing floor which must have been on a bit of high ground, for it was said that while at his work, presumably, he "looked down" and saw David and his servants coming toward him. He learned that the king wanted to buy his threshing floor for use as a spot for an altar. He offered to give the king the floor, the oxen, and the threshing sledges and the yokes to use for wood; but David insisted on paying, saying that he would not "offer burnt offerings to the Lord . . . which cost me nothing." The place and the oxen were purchased for fifty shekels, an altar was built, sacrifice was offered, and the plague which had beset the people was "averted." The Chronicler (I Chronicles 21) calls this man Ornan. See ORNAN.

ARCHELAUS – *Chief of the People, Ruler.*
St. Matthew 2:22.

Ruler of Judaea, Samaria and Idumaea, 4 B.C.-6 A.D. He was son of Herod the Great, but stripped of office by the Emperor Augustus. It was fear of him that caused Joseph, in bringing the Holy Family back from Egypt, to turn to Nazareth in Galilee.

It was in the time of Archelaus that direct Roman authority— and taxation and rebellion— came to Judaea.

ARCHIPPUS – *Chief Groom.*
Philemon 2.

One whom Paul regarded as a "fellow soldier" in the Church in the house of Philemon.

ARIOCH – Meaning of the name not known. Possibly *Venerable, Ruler*.
1. Genesis 14:1, 9.
A King of Ellasar, one of the "four kings" who fought against "five kings," including the kings of Sodom and Gomorrah. Having defeated the "five kings," the "four kings" took Lot captive. Abram gathered "three hundred and eighteen" of his "trained men" and rescued Lot.
2. Daniel 2:14f., 24f.
Arioch was the name of a captain of the guard of Nebuchadnezzar mentioned in the story of Daniel as the one who told the king of Daniel and his special talent as an interpreter of dreams.

ARISTARCHUS – *The Best Ruler*.
Acts 19:29; 20:4; 27:2; Colossians 4:10; Philemon 24.
A Macedonian who, with Gaius, travelled with Paul to Ephesus and was there imprisoned when Demetrius, the silversmith, stirred up a riot, saying that because of Paul's persuasiveness the silversmiths and the "great Goddess Artemis" might come

into disrepute. Aristarchus was with Paul in Rome, and tradition avers he was killed in the persecution of Nero.

ARTAXERXES – The name is derived from a misunderstanding of Artakhshatra, a king of Persia. The Persian name means *He Whose Empire is Perfected*.
Ezra 4:7ff.; 6:14; 7:1ff.; 8:1; Nehemiah 2:1; 5:14; 13:6.
The books of Ezra-Nehemiah present an enigma to scholars. Discussions among them as to the proper way to solve the riddles are long and complicated. The reader should see one of the books listed in the bibliography for an account in detail of the several kings mentioned in the Ezra-Nehemiah stories.

Suffice it to say here that the writer was confused about the person to whom he referred as Artaxerxes. The reference in Nehemiah 2:1, etc., is probably to Artaxerxes I; those in Ezra are probably to Artaxerxes II.

Artaxerxes I (465-425 B.C.) was called "the Longhand," because his right hand was longer than the left. He came to the throne after his father had been murdered. Discovering the murderer, he killed him by hand-to-hand fight in the palace. He was said to be mild, kind, not a very strong king; one who would be very likely to hear the cries of his cupbearer, Nehemiah, and help him in the reestablishment of his religion, as indeed he did in 445 B.C.

Artaxerxes II (c. 404-359 B.C.) lived in a faltering empire, constantly beset by rebellion. The several uprisings opened the way for the Greek armies and alliances between the satraps and leaders of the Greek city states. The empire was saved by the mistrust between the satraps themselves. It was in his reign, probably c. 398 B.C., that Ezra appeared in Jerusalem. See EZRA, NEHEMIAH.

ASA – *Physician, Healer?*

I Kings 15:8ff.; II Chronicles 15-16:10.

A king of Judah who reigned forty-one years (c. 913-873 B.C.), Asa was one of the few kings of whom it was said, "He did right in the eyes of the Lord." He is credited with having removed all the idols introduced by his predecessors, even the image of Asherah belonging to his mother. He also did away with male prostitution.

Asa was at war with Baasha, king of Israel, "all their days." The latter king built Ramah as a fortress against Judah. Whereupon Asa sought and received the help of Ben-hadad of Syria, and having conquered five of his cities, put Baasha in his place. Asa then appropriated the stones of Ramah to build two cities of his own.

The Book of Chronicles speaks of a war with the Ethiopians won by Asa, and of a rigid death penalty for any who refused to accept his religious reforms. Reformer though he was, he was reprimanded by Hanani "the seer" for putting his faith in Benhadad instead of in the Lord.

ASAHEL – *God Has Made.*

1. II Samuel 2:18-32; 3:26-30; 23:24; I Chronicles 11:26.

A brother of Joab and Abishai, the son of Jeruiah, David's sister. Asahel was a fleet runner, "as swift of foot as a wild gazelle." When after the death of Saul, Ishbosheth and Abner fought a last and losing battle against David's attempt to unite the kingdom under himself, Abner fled the field of battle, pursued by the fleet-footed Asahel. When he knew his pursuer was Asahel he tried to divert him by suggesting that much spoil was available—"to your right hand or your left"—but Asahel was not to be turned from his purpose. Abner knew he could not outrun Asahel; but being a better spearman, probably more powerful as well as more experienced, and not wanting to kill the young man, he did everything possible to avoid a meeting. Overtaken finally, Abner killed Asahel "with the butt of his spear."

Asahel's death at Abner's hands, though in self-defense, was avenged with savagery by Joab. See ABNER, JOAB.

2. II Chronicles 17:8.
A Levite named Asahel was sent by Jehoshaphat "through all the cities of Judah" to teach the people the law.

3. II Chronicles 31:13.
Another Levite named Asahel was appointed by Hezekiah as an officer of the tithes, offerings and the "dedicated things."

4. Ezra 10:15.
Asahel was the father of Jonathan who was displeased at the idea of delaying (because of heavy rains) final decisions for the separation of the people from their foreign wives.

ASAPH – *Collector, Gatherer.*
1. I Chronicles 15:17; 25:1; 26:1; Psalms 50, 78-83.
Asaph was accounted a descendant of Levi and Kohath, whose sons were gatekeepers for the tent of meeting and were "set apart" to "prophesy with lyres, with harps, and with cymbals" in the service of the tabernacle. They were to serve under the special orders of David, the king. Some of them were "trained in singing," and "to raise sounds of joy."

2. II Kings 18:18, 37; Isaiah 36:3, 22.
This Asaph was father of Joah, who was recorder for King Hezekiah of Judah.

3. I Chronicles 9:15.
A Levite listed with the priests as being among the "first to dwell again in their possessions in their cities" after the exile to Babylon.

4. Nehemiah 2:8.
Asaph was "the keeper of the king's forest" (King Artaxerxes) in Judah, who was ordered to prepare for Nehemiah's use "timber to make beams . . . of the temple, and the wall of the city, and for the house" to be occupied by Nehemiah on his return to Jerusalem.

ASHER – *Fortunate, Happy,* possibly related to the god, *Asshur.*
Genesis 30:13; Joshua 19:24; Judges 5:17; Ezekiel 48:2, 34.
Asher was the son of Leah's maid, Zilpah, Jacob's eighth son.

He was titular founder of the tribe of that name, as indeed the names of all of Jacob's sons were given by tradition to the tribes of Israel.

In the assignment of territories to the tribes Asher's lot was fifth, including twenty-two cities and their villages. The Song of Deborah in Judges speaks lightly of the tribe of Asher, which "sat still at the coast of the sea, settling down by his landings." Asher was too far away and too much engaged with affairs on the coasts to be much concerned with the struggle going on inland. The tribe was not, therefore, known for daring adventures. In whatever way it arrived at the coast, the tribe was soon dominated by the Phoenicians.

ASHTORETH (Astarte) – *She Who Enriches, a Wife*. The great Mother Goddess of the Near-East.
I Samuel 31:10; I Kings 11:5.
A goddess of the Phoenicians whose popularity extended to the Babylonians and Assyrians, and to the Israelites as well. In various forms she is mentioned some forty times in the Old Testament. In the area of Palestine she was worshipped as the wife of Baal, and the cult involved fertility rites and sacred prostitution. It was in her temple that the armour of the dead Saul was placed as a trophy, for war was also her business. Solomon in his later years succumbed to her popularity through one of his many wives. He built an altar in honor of "Astarte," at the request of the new wife and probably attended some of the ceremonies. Ahab's wife, Jezebel, was a devotee of this goddess and it was against Ashtoreth, as the consort of the Tyrian Baal, that Elijah fought so desperately.

ASSHUR (Assur) – *Level, Plain*. Although this name is sometimes left untranslated and is used as a reference to Assyria and the Assyrians—as in Numbers 24:22, 24—it is also employed as a name for persons.
1. Genesis 10:11.
One of the descendants of Ham, who according to tradition built the city of Nineveh. The Revised Standard Version uses "Assyria," dropping Asshur altogether.
2. Genesis 10:22; I Chronicles 1:17.
A son of Shem who was the "father of all the children of Eber." Here the name appears to be the same as Asher.

ATHALIAH – *Whom Yahweh has afflicted, Yahweh is Strong, Exalted?*
II Kings 8:28; 11:1f.
Athaliah was the granddaughter of Omri, daughter of Ahab and Jezebel, and mother of Ahaziah, king of Judah. When she saw that Ahaziah was dead she succeeded in having her grandchildren destroyed, with the exception of Joash, who was hidden away in a bedchamber when the murderers were about their work. Thinking the way was now clear, Athaliah took the throne for herself. Needless to say she was idolatrous as well as murderous.

Jehoida the high priest contrived with the captains of the army to dispose of her on the ground that Joash, the rightful king, was still alive. After seven years of hiding Joash was quietly brought forth and crowned. Carefully guarded, he was then brought into the house of the Lord and anointed.

Athaliah heard the shouts, "Long live the King!", and in reply shouted, "Treason"; but she was conducted firmly via the horse entrance from the temple to the palace, and there she was assassinated.

She was the only non-Davidic ruler of Judah from the establishment of the united kingdom to the fall in 586, and the only woman ruler of Judah or Israel. Her reign is dated c. 842-837 B.C. See JOASH, JEHOIADA.

AZARIAH – *Whom Yahweh Helps, Keeps.*
More than twenty persons named Azariah appear in the Bible. Many were priests; some were captains of the armies; one was known as Abednego, the friend of Daniel. The name is very like Zerahiah, Seraiah and Ezra. We shall attempt here to concentrate on men who seem to have been of some importance, listing only a few.

    1. II Kings 14:21ff.; 15:1-27; I Chronicles 3:12; Isaiah 1:1.

Azariah, the son of Amaziah, who became king of Judah at the age of sixteen, after the assassination of his father, reigned for fifty-two years (c. 783-842? B.C.). He was known also as Uzziah. Although he was so long the king, he was a leper and he "dwelt in a separate house," so that his son Jotham was in charge of the royal household, "governing the people" during the latter part of his tenure. Prior to his leprosy, however, Azariah (or Uzziah) did rather well as king. I Chronicles states that he was successful in war against the Philistines and Arabs, and that he was respected "even to the border of Egypt." The Chronicler explained his leprosy as the result of pride, which led him to attempt to usurp the office of the priesthood in burning incense in the sanctuary. A priest named Azariah with eighty other priests "withstood the king," whose leprosy was revealed to all the priests in the course of his raging against them.

The rule of this king was, on the whole, a time of growth and prosperity for Judah. See UZZIAH.

2. I Chronicles 6:9f., 13, 36; II Chronicles 29:12; 31:10.

Several members of the priestly family of Aaron named Azariah are listed. One was the son of Hilkiah the priest in Josiah's reign (c. 640-609 B.C.). Two Azariahs, Levites, are mentioned in the list of those at work in cleansing the temple in the time of Hezekiah, and one was high priest under Hezekiah.

3. II Chronicles 23:1.

Two men named Azariah, captains of "hundreds," helped Jehoiada bring Joash to the throne of Judah in defiance of his grandmother, the murderous Athaliah.

See JOASH, JEHOIADA.

4. II Chronicles 15:1, 8.

Azariah, son of Oded, was a prophet sent to Asa, king of Judah, to encourage him to "put away the abominable idols" in Judah, Benjamin, and the Ephraimite cities he had taken. Thus supported by Azariah's prophecies, Asa destroyed the Asherah of his mother, and removed her "from being queen."

5. Nehemiah 3:23f.; 8:7; 10:2; 12:33.

Azariah, "son" of Amariah, who after the exile helped repair the wall of Jerusalem. His house must have been a landmark of a sort, for it is said that he "repaired beside his own house," and the next section was described as "from the house of Azariah to the Angle."

An Azariah, along with several others, explained the law to the people as it was read to them by Ezra (All references in this paragraph are to Nehemiah). "They gave the sense, so that the people understood (8:7); and an Azariah set his seal to the "firm covenant" (10:2). An Azariah, described as a "prince of Judah," was brought by Nehemiah to the procession on the wall of Jerusalem at the time of its dedication (12:33).

B

BAAL, BAALIM – *Lord, Owner, Possessor, Husband.*

Judges 2:11-14; 6:28; I Kings 18:40; etc.

Baal is the generic name for the local deities worshipped by the people with whom the Israelites came into contact in their wanderings. In their attempt to settle in the land of Canaan they found a powerful, well established cult of Baal, the fertility god who was known by several names. Amongst the Canaanites he was Hadad; elsewhere he was Marduk, Molech, Melkarte, Bel, etc. Each cult was different in detail, but in time they began to be confused with each other and fused into a like set of practices and referred to by the Hebrew leaders under the name Baal.

Surrounded as they were by Baal worship, there was often in Israel a temptation to "forsake Yahweh," thought to be a god of the storm and the desert. Israel was not always sure whether Yahweh could protect his people in the new lands. Sometimes, too, Israel was led from its austere worship of Yahweh to favor the more colorful, more sensual practices of the neighboring peoples with their important seasonal fertility rites, or to drift easily into the ways of the people immediately at hand. Often Israel tried to worship at once Yahweh, the dominant Baal, and the local deities; and there seemed to be a tendency to tack the name of Yahweh to the cult of Baal, saying "Yahweh is Baal."

Elijah's famous "battle of the prophets" on Mount Carmel and his famous words of challenge, "How long will you halt between two opinions?" had to do with such a situation. He meant to prove once for all that Yahweh was indeed more powerful than the "local owners," or even than the gods of Tyre and Sidon (Melkarte and Astarte), and that Yahweh must be worshipped to the exclusion of all others and in the way proper to him only. His victory, however, dramatic as it was, did not stamp out the worship of Baal; for not only did Ahab continue to have devotees of Baal as counselors, but also the later prophets inveighed against Baal as did he.

The student should look into some of the recent studies of the "Ras Shamra Texts," from the ancient Ugarit, for further information on Baal worship.

BAALZEBUB(BEELZEBUB) –
Lord of Flies, Prince of the Devils (in the N. T.).
II Kings 1:2f., 6, 16; St. Matthew 12:24; St. Mark 3:22; St. Luke 11:19f.
Beelzebub, referred to in the Synoptic Gospels as "prince of devils," is the same as Baalzebub, "Lord of the flies," who

was consulted by Ahaziah, king of Israel, when he fell through the lattice of his upper chamber. Elijah rebuked Ahaziah: "Is there no God in Israel that you go to inquire of Baalzebub, the God of Ekron?"

BAASHA – *Wicked? Boldness?*
I Kings 15:16-16:13.
King of Israel for twenty-four years (c. 900-877 B.C.) after he killed Nadab, son of Jeroboam I and all the latter's descendants. Since Baasha was the son of Ahijah, "of the house of Isachar," an humble house, Baasha was said to have been "exalted out of the dust."

And since he "walked in the sins of Jeroboam"—continued, that is, to support calf worship —Jehu the prophet said that his house would be utterly swept away, eaten by dogs or by birds of the air. Baasha fought against Asa, king of Judah, and was completely routed. He died a natural death and his son Elah succeeded to the throne; but Elah and "all the house of Baasha" were killed by Zimri, a captain of the chariots, bringing Jehu's prophecy to reality.

BALAAM – *Lord of the People, a Pilgrim?*
Numbers 22-24; 31:8, 15f.; Jude 11; Revelation 2:14.

Balak, king of Moab, having seen the complete destruction wrought by the Israelites on the Amonites, sought the protection of a curse on the Israelites. He thus engaged Balaam, a "soothsayer" of the Midianites—whose leaders had been gathered to look out on the devastation of the Amorites—to place a curse on "this horde" of the Hebrews.

Balaam, with fees in sight, "sought the Lord," who said to him: "You shall not curse the people, for they are blessed." Whereupon Balaam informed Balak's messengers of this disquieting word of the Lord, and they returned to Balak. Again Balak sent messenger princes to Balaam to offer Balaam even greater fees in exchange for a proper curse on Israel; and again Balaam refused to speak until he had received the word of the Lord ordering him to go with Balak's envoys and to do as the word would bid him further.

While en route to Moab, the ass on which Balaam rode saw an angel with drawn sword standing in the way, and the ass turned aside to go around the apparition. But the angel blocked the way and no amount of beating would make her proceed; indeed, she "lay down under Balaam," and he, now thoroughly angry, beat her with his staff. Then the ass spoke, saying, "Was I ever accustomed to do so?" Balaam's answer was a bewildered "No!" Then Balaam himself saw the angel, who told him to go on and to speak as he would be told to speak.

Balaam, quite willing to employ divination to curse Israel, found himself blessing instead, saying, "He has blessed and I cannot revoke it . . . God brings them out of Egypt." Hearing this, Balak was beside himself and begged Balaam to withdraw the blessing. But of course Balaam could not do so, and Balak refused to "honor" the seer, to pay the fees agreed upon. Balaam then placed a curse on Balak and Moab!

Israel must have become too intimate with Balaam and his religious practices at Baal-Peor; for when the "plague" struck Israel after the war with the Midianites, in which Balaam was killed, Balaam was accused of having given the people "treacherous" counsel and therefore of being responsible for the "plague." See BALAK.

BALAK – *Void, Empty, a Waster.*
Numbers 22:2-24:25; Joshua 24:9; Judges 11:25; Micah 6:5.

King of Moab who, worried about the invasion of the Hebrews and the havoc they had created among the Amorites, employed Balaam to produce a divine curse on the people of Israel. See BALAAM, above.

BANI – *Posterity.*
1. II Samuel 23:36.
One of David's thirty valiant men, a Gadite.
  2. Ezra 2:10; 10:29, 34; Nehemiah 7:15.
Bani was the name of the father of some who left Babylon with Zerubbabel to return to Jerusalem. In Nehemiah the name is also spelled Binnui. Bani was also one whose descendants had taken foreign wives.

  3. Nehemiah 3:17; 8:7; 9:4f.; 10:13f.; 11:22.
A Levite whose son, Rehum, helped repair the wall of Jerusalem.

A Levite who helped the people understand the law as read by Ezra.

Several other people named Bani are mentioned, all with two exceptions listed in Ezra, Nehemiah. The exceptions are found in I Chronicles 6:46; 9:4. None of these others is of any importance.

BARABBAS – *Son of Abba, Father's Son.*
St. Matthew 27:15ff.
Both Jesus and Barabbas were held for the judgment of Pilate. It was in Pilate's power, according to custom, to release a prisoner at the time of the Passover. He asked the mob which of the two prisoners before him they wanted released, Barabbas who was held for robbery, or Jesus, in Whom Pilate could find no wrong. The answer was the cry, prompted by the high priests, "Barabbas!"

BARAK – *Lightning, Thunderbolt.*
Judges 4:6-5:15; Hebrews 11:32.
Barak, the son of Abinoam, was a warrior-chief of the tribe of Naphtali. At the prompting of Deborah, a prophetess and a mother in Israel, Barak gathered the warriors of the tribes to defeat Sisera, general of the armies of Jabin, king of Canaan, into whose hand the lord had "sold" the Israelites.

When Deborah proposed the uprising against Jabin, Barak's response to her urging was: "If you will go with me I will go." She agreed and prophesied: "The Lord will sell Sisera into the hand of a woman." Defeated by Barak's armies in a battle in which it seemed that the "stars in their courses" favored Israel, Sisera fled afoot to the tent of Heber the Kenite, whose wife, Jael, pretending to give him refuge, drove a tent peg through his head.

Barak's victory was an important one, for prior to his success in assembling "ten thousand men" on Mount Tabor, Israel's tribes had been badly disorganized and discouraged.

See Judges 5 for the "Song of Deborah," a remarkable and very ancient poem memorializing the victory of Barak. See DEBORAH.

BARNABAS – *Son of Encouragement or Consolation.*
Acts 4:36; 9:27; 11:22, 30; 12:25; 13-15; I Corinthians 9:6; Galatians 2:13.
Barnabas was a Levite of Cyprus whose name originally was Joseph. The apostles gave him the name Barnabas, because he was among the first to sell his land and give the proceeds for the benefit of the "company of those who believed." It was Barnabas who commended Saul to the Church and who took him to Antioch. He was a suc-

cessful evangelist, both on his own and in company with Paul. He persuaded the Antiochene Christians to send relief funds to the Church at Jerusalem at the time of impending famine.

Barnabas was called an "apostle," though not of course one of The Twelve. Today he is classed with the "apostolic men," one of the first to receive special authority at the hands of the apostles. He was companion to St. Paul on his first missionary journey; but he did not go on the second journey because of a difference with Paul with regard to John Mark, whom Paul did not want in his company.

Barnabas and Paul made a good team. At Lystra they were thought to be gods "in the likeness of men." Barnabas they called "Zeus," and Paul, "Hermes," because he was the chief speaker.

After the separation from Paul, Barnabas and Mark went from Antioch to Cyprus.

In I Corinthians (9:6) Paul refers to Barnabas as a self-supporter, like himself.

BARSABBAS – *Son of Saba.*
1. Acts 1:23.
Joseph, called Barsabbas, was

nominated with Matthias to "be put forward" to fill the vacancy left by Judas in the apostolic rank. Matthias was chosen by lot.

2. Acts 15:22.

Judas called Barsabbas was sent with Paul, Barnabas, and Silas to deliver a message to the Church at Antioch.

BARTHOLOMEW – Son of Tolmai.

St. Matthew 10:3; St. Mark 3:18; Acts 1:13.

One of The Twelve, named sixth in the list in St. Mark 3. Sometimes he is thought to be the same person as Nathanael. Tradition makes him the Apostle of Armenia and the writer of a Gospel.

BARTIMAEUS – Son of Timaeus (honored, highly prized). St. Mark 10:46.

The blind beggar healed by Jesus at the gate of Jericho. Jesus, hearing his cry, asked, "What do you want me to do for you?" The answer came quickly: "Let me receive my sight!" Having received his sight, Bartimaeus "followed him on the way." He is not mentioned elsewhere in the New Testament.

BARUCH – Blessed.

1. Jeremiah 32:12-16; 36; 43:3-7; 45.

Baruch, son of Neriah, was secretary and "scribe" for the prophet Jeremiah. Barred from the temple area prior to the fall of Jerusalem, Jeremiah called Baruch to write down messages being received from the Lord. The prophet asked Baruch to read what he had written in the presence of the people gathered in the temple area on a day of fasting. Having done so, he was then told to read the same warnings to a gathering of the princes, who, being afraid, yet wanted King Jehoiakem of Judah to hear. Baruch and Jeremiah were advised to hide from the wrath of the king. The king, in a gesture of contempt, cut off sections of the scroll as the reader finished his reading and tossed them into the fire. He ordered Baruch and Jeremiah seized, but "the Lord hid them."

Another scroll was now written in which warnings and threats were expressed against the stubborn king.

To Baruch was entrusted the deed to the "field of Anathoth," which Jeremiah purchased as a sign from the Lord that at some time the Lord would bring his people back from captivity to reside again in their own land.

When Baruch reported the words of Jeremiah warning the people against "going to Egypt," the scribe was called a liar and was accused of turning the prophet against the people of Judah. The statement was that because of Baruch's influence Jeremiah would "deliver us into the hand of the Chaldeans."

Baruch and Jeremiah were taken with the remnant of Israel into Egypt. It is said that Baruch remained there until the death of Jeremiah and left thereafter for Babylon to live out his days.

In former times the apocryphal book of Baruch was attributed to him as well as some lesser works. It is possible that he was author of some of the passages in Jeremiah.

2. Nehemiah 3:20; 10:6.

Baruch the son of Zabbai "repaired another section (of the wall of Jerusalem) from the Angle to the door of the house of Eliashib the high priest." He also "set his seal" to the "firm covenant" prepared by Ezra to express the intention of Israel to walk once again "in God's law."

3. Nehemiah 11:5.

A descendant of Perez the "Shi-lonite" who was in Jerusalem after the exile.

BARZILLAI – *Strong, Iron.*

II Samuel 17:27; 19:31-39; I Kings 2:7.

A friend of David, a Gileadite, who brought beds, basins, food, and other comforts of life to the king when he was in flight from Absalom. Barzillai was a very aged man, eighty years old, and very wealthy. David asked him to remain with him in Jerusalem, but Barzillai declined the honor —and perhaps the responsibility—preferring to be in his own home and away from the excitement and intrigue surrounding the court.

BATH-SHEBA – *Daughter of an Oath? of Opulence?*

II Samuel 11:2ff.

The wife of Uriah the Hittite whom David saw as she was bathing and took her for himself. Having taken another man's wife, and finding her pregnant, the king tried to cover by bringing Uriah home. Uriah did not cooperate with the king's plans and David had him sent to the front of the battle to be killed. With Uriah dead, David then acquired Bath-sheba as his wife. Bath-sheba was beautiful and clever. After her one indiscretion, which after all was David's fault, she was a faithful and helpful wife. She was level-headed enough in those days of political uncertainty to secure the throne for her son, Solomon.

It was because of David's affair with Bath-sheba that Nathan the prophet tricked him into declaring what he would do to a rich man who had taken a poor man's one ewe lamb. When Nathan heard the king's words of indignation at such a business, he pointed to David and said: "Thou art the man!" See DAVID, URIAH, SOLOMON, NATHAN.

BEERI – *My Well.*
Hosea 1:1.
The father of the prophet Hosea.

Another Beeri, a Hittite, was the father of one of the wives of Esau. The Hittite wife was one of two belonging to Esau to whom Rachel referred, saying that they made her "weary of her life." The experience with Esau's Hittite wives was given as the reason for sending Jacob into Padan-aram for a wife. See Genesis 26:34.

BEL – *Lord, Owner, Possessor.*
Isaiah 46:1; Jeremiah 50:2.
The Babylonian form of the name "Baal." This is the god mentioned in the apocryphal story of "Bel and the Dragon."

BELSHAZZAR – *Bel Protect the King.*
Daniel 5; 7:1; 8:1.
In Daniel Belshazzar is called the "son" of Nebuchadnezzar. He was not, in fact, at all related to the king. He was a general in the army, son of one Nabonidos. Nabonidos became king after a palace revolution, and the reference to Belshazzar as "son of the king" has to do with Nabonidos. The thought that he was the last of the Chaldean kings may be attributed to the fact that he died shortly after the fall of Babylon. The banquet given by him as king is, therefore, quite fictitious; but the dramatic qualities of the story are splendid. The words, "You have been weighed in the scales and found wanting," written on the wall by "the fingers of a man's hand" are memorable indeed. The "handwriting on the wall" is widely understood as a sign of doom.

BELTESHAZZAR – *(Bel)* *Protect His Life.*
Daniel 1:7; 2:26; 4:8f., 19.
The name given to Daniel by the chief eunuch of the king of Babylon. In renaming Daniel, it

was thought that he would be given the power and the "spirit of the holy gods."

BENAIAH – *Yahweh Has Built Up.*
II Samuel 8:18; 23:20-23; I Kings 1:26, 32; 2:25-46; I Chronicles 11:22-24.

Benaiah was one of David's captains, a "valiant man," a "doer of great deeds." He "was a name beside the three mighty men," and was in charge of the Cherethites and the Pelethites, and chief of David's body-guard. It was he who proclaimed Solomon king and was made commander of the army of Solomon.

When Solomon determined to assassinate Adonijah, Benaiah was ordered to kill him; it was Benaiah also who reluctantly obeyed Solomon's command to "strike down" the mighty Joab who had taken refuge on "the horns of the altar." These unpleasant jobs Benaiah did out of loyalty to David's house and his appointment of Solomon to the throne.

Several other men of the same name are mentioned. One was a priest under David, according to I Chronicles 15:18-24; one was an overseer in the Temple under Hezekiah, II Chronicles 31:13; several are mentioned in Ezra 10:25, 30, 35, 43; Ezekiel 11:1, 13.

BEN-HADAD – *Son of Hadad.*
The name of three kings of Syria.
1. I Kings 15:18, 20; II Chronicles 16:2.

Ben-hadad I was the Syrian king used by Asa, king of Judah, as a buffer against Baasha, king of Israel.

2. I Kings 20; II Kings 6:8ff. Ben-hadad II, succeeded his father, above. He was not very successful in his wars against Ahab. He was defeated by Ahab at Aphek, and c. 853 B.C. he was an ally of Israel against Assyria. He was forced to grant Ahab trading rights in Damascus, and approached him in sack cloth, saying, "Pray, let me live!" A prophet declared that the Lord had marked Ben-hadad for death. Ill and worried he was killed by Hazael who took the crown as well as his life.

3. II Kings 13:3-25; Jeremiah 49:27; Amos 1:4.
Ben-hadad III, son of Hazael, was defeated three times by Joash, who recovered from him all "the cities of Israel."

BENJAMIN, BEN-ONI – *Benjamin, Son of the Right Hand;*

Ben-oni, *Son of My Sorrow.*
Genesis 35:18, 24; 42:4, 36;
43:14-34; 44:12-45:22; 46:19,
21; 49:27; Joshua 18:11, 20f.;
Judges 1:21; 5:14; 20:3-21:23;
I Samuel 9:1; II Samuel 2:31;
3:19; Romans 11:1.

Rachel died as her second son,
Benjamin, was born. She gave
him the name Ben-oni, meaning
"Son of my sorrow"; but Jacob
called him "Son of the (my)
right hand," Benjamin. As his
last son and, further, as the son
of his favorite wife, Jacob allowed Benjamin to take the place
in his feelings once held by the
lost Joseph. Benjamin, however,
is a character not clearly exposed
in the stories of the sons of Jacob.

When Jacob sent his sons into
Egypt during the great famine
"he did not send Benjamin, Joseph's brother . . . for he feared
that harm might befall him." But
Joseph, accusing his brothers
(whom he recognized) of being
spies, demanded that Benjamin
be brought to him as a testimony
of their integrity. Jacob was
overwhelmed at the thought of
losing Benjamin, but, having no
alternative, he sent him with his
brothers as they fearfully made
their way back to Egypt to redeem Simeon, left as hostage,
and to buy more grain.

In the presence of Joseph, Ben-

jamin was greeted warmly, indeed was fed with five times as
much (thus a "Benjamin portion") from Joseph's table as
were the others, and in due time
the mystery of Joseph's identity
was cleared. As the story builds
up to its moving climax it is evi-
dent that Joseph, Benjamin's full
brother, intended to use "the
lad" as a means of discovering
whether the "brothers" would be
now as callous toward Benjamin
and their father as once they had
been in selling him into slavery.
In allowing the men to return
to Canaan he put his own silver
cup and grain money into Benjamin's sack and then had the
sacks searched, thus threatening
"the lad" and frightening the
brothers. The brothers this time
stood firm, and Judah, their
spokesman, offered himself to go
into slavery if only Benjamin
might be allowed to return to
his father. This was the very
thing Joseph needed to hear.
Overcome with emotion "he
could not control himself," with
the result that Benjamin was sent
to Canaan with the brothers to
bring their father to Egypt.

In the blessing of Jacob on his
sons Benjamin was described as
"a ravenous wolf"; in the Song
of Deborah (Judges 5) the tribe
is mentioned as a leader. Some

Benjamites of Gibeah ravished the concubine of a "Levite" from Ephraim (Judges 19-21), and killed her. The Ephramite cut her body into twelve pieces and "sent her throughout all the territory of Israel." In retaliation men chosen by lot from all the tribes were formed into an army to oppose Benjamin. Having asked the men of Gibeah to give up the culprits in their midst, and having been refused, the army of Israel engaged the Benjamites in a three day battle, disastrous to both sides, from which only "600 men" of Benjamin emerged alive. Then Israel, further punishing Benjamin, vowed not to give their daughters to the Benjamites—evidently intending to eliminate the identity of the tribe. Relenting however, Israel took wives for the 600 from Jabesh-gilead and helped the Benjamites steal women from Shiloh.

Perhaps because of this bloody series of incidents, Benjamin was regarded as a small, if war-like and powerful, tribe (I Samuel 9:21). Whatever its size, Benjamin was influential. Saul, the first king of Israel, was of Benjamin; and the Benjamites were faithful to him and his heirs. They did support David, though somewhat uncertainly; but they refused to follow Jeroboam after the death of Solomon.

Saul of Tarsus, who became Paul the Apostle, was a Benjamite. See JACOB, JOSEPH.

BERNICE – Probably from Greek words meaning *Bearer of Victory.*
    Acts 25:13, 23; 26:30.

A daughter of Herod Agrippa, sister of Agrippa II, who was present when Paul was brought before Festus to defend himself against the charges of the Jews that he was a "pestilent fellow, an agitator." All present agreed that the Apostle could have gone free had he not appealed to Caesar. Bernice must have added to the "pomp and splendor" of the occasion.

BETHUEL – *Man of God.*
    Genesis 22:22f.; 24:15ff.; 25:20; 28:2, 5.

A son of Nahor, the brother of Abraham, and father of Rebekah. He received Abraham's servant and emissary with great courtesy and gave Rebekah the right to choose whether she would or would not go with the man to become Isaac's wife.

BEZALEEL (Bazalel) – *In the Shadow (protection) of God.*
    Exodus 31:2; 35:30; 37:1; I Chronicles 2:20.

Israel's first architect, Bezaleel was the son of Uri, of the tribe of Judah. Yahweh filled him with "ability and intelligence, with knowledge and craftsmanship, to devise artistic designs," and authorized him to build the tent of meeting, the ark of the covenant, the altars of incense and burnt offerings. He was also ordered to fashion the holy garments for Aaron. His appointed helper was Oholiab.

BILDAD – *Son of Contention.*
Job 2:11; 8:1; 18:1; 25:1; 42:9.
One of Job's three friends, a Shuhite, who argued that Job must somehow be held responsible for all his troubles; he must have sinned in some way. For, said he, "God does not pervert justice," and, "God will not reject a blameless man." If therefore Job were really blameless, God would soon set things right

for him. To Bildad Job answered, "How can a man be just before God?" See Job.

BOANERGES – *Sons of Thunder, Rage.*
St. Mark 3:17.
The "surname" given by our Lord to James and John, sons of Zebedee, who were quick-tempered, overly zealous.

BOAZ – *Swiftness, Strength.*
Ruth 2:1-4; 4:17.
A Bethlehemite of wealth and distinction, relative of Mahlon the deceased husband of Ruth the Moabitess. As an act of kindness Ruth was allowed to glean from his fields. Kindness and his sense of responsibility blossomed into marriage. From this marriage came Obed, the father of Jesse who was the father of David. See RUTH, NAOMI.

C

CAIAPHAS – *Depression.*
St. Matthew 26:3, 57; St. John 11:49; 18:14, 24, 28; Acts 4:6.

The high priest whose trust in false witnesses made the trial of Jesus a mockery. Caiaphas was a Sadducee who was disturbed at the teaching and rising popularity of Jesus, who had performed many "signs." The chief priests and Pharisees gathered the council and deliberated what to do about Jesus; for, they said, "If we let him go on thus, everyone will believe in him, and the Romans will come and destroy both our holy place and our nation."

In the council Caiaphas suggested that it might be "expedient" that "one man should die for the people," and, further, that Jesus should die. From that time on, reports the Fourth Gospel, they tried to find a way to put him to death.

When Jesus was taken by the collusion between Judas and representatives of Caiaphas, the latter called the infamous night meeting of the Sanhedrin to deal with the situation immediately. Caiaphas was afraid to wait longer. Jesus, of course, gave no answer to the charges trumped up against him, until finally Caiaphas put to him the question, "Are you the Christ, the Son of the Blessed?" To this Jesus, knowing well the consequence, answered, "I am."

This to Caiaphas was sheer blasphemy and relieved him of

53

the need to hear the witnesses further or to work out an agreement in their conflicting testimony. Now, with this confession in hand, he had only to turn to the others and say, "You have heard his blasphemy." The decision was, as Jesus knew, inevitable.

Caiaphas was the son-in-law and successor of Annas. He was in office between 18-36 A.D.

Caiaphas and Annas were involved in the questioning of Peter and John about their authority in healing the lame man at the temple gate.

CAIN – *Possession, Smith, Artificer.*
Genesis 4:1ff.; Hebrews 11:4.
Cain was the first son born to Adam and Eve; he was the "first" farmer, the "first" to be guilty of fratricide, the "first" fugitive from the consequence of murder, the "first" builder of a city.

His offering to the Lord of the fruits of the earth was not acceptable as was the animal offering of Abel, his brother; and in jealousy and disappointment he lured Abel into a field and killed him. Abel's blood "cried out from the ground" and Cain fled to the land of Nod, "east of Eden," where he is said to have built the city of Enoch, named after his first son. See ABEL, ADAM.

CALEB – *Impetuous, a Dog.*
1. Numbers 13:6, 30; 14:6; 26:65; Joshua 14:6; 15:13; Judges 1:12-20; I Samuel 25:3; 30:14.
Caleb was one of the scouts sent out to spy on the promised land of Canaan. Only he and Joshua thought that the land could be taken. The others were so fearful that they said the land was not worth having, even if it could be captured. For this report Caleb and Joshua were saved from a stoning only by the appearance of the "glory of the Lord." These two were rewarded by being the only ones of those "numbered at Sinai" permitted to enter the land. In the assignment of territory, Caleb claimed and received Hebron and its adjacent country in the hills; and his clan was a very important part of Judah.

Of him, in response to his own claim to have done so, Moses said, "You have wholly followed the Lord my God." See JOSHUA, RAHAB.

2. I Chronicles 2:18, 19, 42.
It must be admitted that the story of this Caleb, such as it is, is not clear. He seems to have

been the father of Hur and grandfather of Caleb the spy. It appears that he had a son, also named Caleb, mentioned in I Chronicles 2:50.

CANAAN – Etymology uncertain. Canaan = Phoenicia, and came to mean *Trader*.
Genesis 9:18-27; 10:6, 15; I Chronicles 1:8, 13.
The name is used to designate both a son of Ham, grandson of Noah, the people who were thought to stem from him, and the land these people occupied. The Canaanites, however, were only one of several peoples living in the land invaded by the Israelites. Although Israel was "promised" the land of Canaan repeatedly, and regarded the territory as a natural heritage, the Israelites never fully conquered the "descendants of Canaan"; nor is Israel's debt to the "Canaanites" as yet fully assessed. See one of the books dealing, for example, with the "Ras Shamra" texts.

CEPHAS – *A Stone.*
See PETER.

CHEMOSH – *Subduer?*
Numbers 21:29; Judges 11:24; Jeremiah 48:7, 13, 46; I Kings 11:7; II Kings 23:13.
The god of the Moabites with which the devotees of Yahweh struggled for centuries. This deity was first encountered when the Israelites "journeyed through the wilderness and went around the land of Edom and the land of Moab." The rites of Chemosh probably included the sacrifice of living children as burnt offerings. Solomon "built a high place for Chemosh the abomination of Moab," and worship of this god was still strong in the days of Jeremiah, who prophesied that "Chemosh shall go forth into exile, with his priests and his princes . . ." The altar built by Solomon was not destroyed until the reform under Josiah.

CHILEAB – *Etymology unknown.*
II Samuel 3:3; I Chronicles 3:1.
The second son of David, who was also the son of Abigail. Chileab, called Daniel in I Chronicles, was born at Hebron.

CHILION – *Pining, Wasting Away?*
Ruth 1:2, 5; 4:9.
The second-named son of Elimelech and Naomi, Chilion married Orpah, the Moabitess. While still in Moab and not long after his marriage he died, pos-

sibly of tuberculosis—as his name might imply.

CHLOE – *Fresh Green, Young, a Shepherdess.*
I Corinthians 1:11.
A woman at the place from which this Epistle was sent who informed the Apostle of "quarreling" in the Church at Corinth.

CLAUDIA – Feminine of Claudius. *Lame?*
II Timothy 4:21.
A woman disciple at Rome who was named in the second letter to Timothy as remembering him gladly.

CLAUDIUS – From the Latin *claudus, Lame?*
Acts 11:28.
The Emperor of Rome who ruled from A.D. 41 to 54. Although physically weak and ill, he was nevertheless a good ruler in his earlier years. In his reign the Empire was extended northward to Britain.

In his time the Jews, a quarrelsome lot, were expelled from Rome, and a great famine "over all the world" occurred. It is to these events that the Book of Acts refers in 11:28f. and 18:2.

Claudius died very suddenly in A.D. 54 and it is generally supposed that he was murdered, possibly poisoned by Agrippina, his wife.

CLAUDIUS LYSIAS
Acts 23:26; 24:7, 22.
Paul the Apostle was involved in a riot in Jerusalem, stirred up by Jews who accused him of all sorts of things, not the least of which was that he brought Greeks into the temple. He was arrested and brought before the tribune, Claudias Lysias, who discovered to his embarrassment that Paul was born a Roman citizen. He then had Paul meet with the council of the Jews. This meeting produced an uproar and St. Paul was returned to the barracks. During the night the Jews resolved to kill Paul, some of them swearing on oath not to eat until he was dead.

Paul's nephew heard of the plot to kill him from ambush as he was to be led from the barracks to the council chamber for a period of further questioning. This knowledge was passed on to the tribune who had Paul moved under guard to Caesarea and to the jurisdiction of Felix, the governor. A letter of explanation was sent with the guard.

CLEMENT – *Mild, Kind, Merciful.*
Philippians 4:3.

Clement was a fellow-worker with Paul at Philippi, one whose name was said to be "in the book of life," a responsible man. In the early Church it was commonly thought that this was the Clement known as Clement of Rome, but scholars now have decided otherwise.

CLEOPAS – *The Whole Glory, Full of Glory.*
St. Luke 24:18.
A disciple who with another met the Risen Lord on the road to Emmaus. It was to these two that Jesus revealed himself "in the breaking of the bread."

CLEOPHAS – A form of Cleopas; see above.
St. John 19:25.
This man was the husband of one of the Marys who stood at the foot of the Cross. The name is also spelled "Clopas."

CORNELIUS – *A Spear* or a *Beam of the Sun.*
Acts 10:1ff.
A Roman centurion at Caesarea, devout and generous, who was instructed in a vision to have Simon Peter brought to his city. Peter was also given a vision in which he was instructed to eat food not properly prepared, and a second vision in which he was told to follow the men sent for

him by Cornelius. On arriving at Cornelius' home he found a gathering of Gentiles. Peter, feeling and saying that he should not be in such company, asked why he had been sent for. The result of his visit was that the Gentiles were converted and baptized—to the astonishment of the strict Judaising party in Jerusalem before whom Peter was called to give an account of himself. Cornelius and his party were thus the first Gentiles converted through the efforts of Peter.

CUSH – *Black?*
Genesis 10:6-8; I Chronicles 1:8-10; Isaiah 11:11; 18:1.
Grandson of Noah, eldest son of Ham. The name "Cush" also refers to the descendants of Cush, who are known variously as Ethiopians or Abyssinians.
An enemy of David—a Benjamite—was named Cush. See Psalm 7—the title.

CUSHI – *Black?*
II Samuel 18:21-32; Zephaniah 1:1.
The messenger from Joab to David, with the news of the battle in which Absalom was defeated, was named Cushi, though the Revised Standard Version uses simply, "the Cush-

ite." This runner was instructed to tell the king the truth that Absalom had been killed.

The father of the prophet Zephaniah was named Cushi.

CYRENIUS (Quirinius) – Meaning uncertain, *Governor?*
St. Luke 2:2.

The real and full name of the Governor of Syria when Caesar Augustus decreed that all the world should be "enrolled" was Publius Sulphicius Quirinius. The enrollment and need to pay taxes are given as the reason for the presence of Mary and Joseph in Bethlehem at the time of Jesus' birth.

CYRUS – *Sun? An Heir?*
II Chronicles 36:22f.; Ezra 1:1-8; 3:7; 4:3-5; 5:13-17; 6:3, 14; Isaiah 44:28; 45:1; Daniel 1:21; 5; 6:28; 10:1.

Cyrus II was king of Persia (c. 559-530 B.C.), head of the greatest Empire yet to be formed in the ancient world. Although his armies conquered many peoples, Cyrus was known far and wide for his wisdom in managing the diverse elements subject to him and for his clemency. It was he who stated in writing, for example, that "the Lord . . . has charged me to build him a house at Jerusalem . . ." He assisted the Jews in returning to their own land from Babylon, which he captured c. 539 B.C. Because of his kindness he was called "Yahweh's anointed," "Yahweh's shepherd."

One of the books on biblical archaeology should be read concerning the cylinder which gives many interesting facts about Cyrus II and his times.

D

DAGON – *Corn? Fish?*

Judges 16:23-30; I Samuel 5:1-7; I Chronicles 10:10.

An ancient deity of the Canaanites who might have been worshipped in the area long before the peoples associated with the Israelites arrived. Dagon seems to have been adopted by the Philistines after their invasion of Palestine—a local god which became their national idol. Some think the idol was half-man half-fish in form; others that it was in the form of a man and was an agricultural, a corn, deity. I Samuel would suggest the latter, since Dagon was embarrassed by the mice sent by Yahweh to destroy the crops, to "ravage the land."

In the rustic story of Samson the Philistines were said to have offered Dagon sacrifices of rejoicing for the capture of that powerful man by the wiles of Delilah.

When the ark of God was captured by the Philistines (I Sam. 5) it was placed beside the Dagon idol in Ashdod. The next day when attendants entered the temple they found Dagon "fallen face downward before the ark." Dagon was set up again and the next day was found face down as before—but this time its hands and feet were "lying cut off upon the threshold." The ark was then considered to be a heavy burden on the people and Dagon, and it was sent from Ashdod to Gath, from Gath back to Israel.

After the battle in which king Saul was killed at Mount Gilboa,

59

his head was fastened "in the temple of Dagon."

DAMARIS – Possibly derived from the Greek word meaning *Heifer?*
Acts 17:34.

"A woman named Damaris," with Dionysius the Areopagite, and others with them," was converted in Athens when Paul preached there "in the middle of the Areopagus," the "hill of Ares."

DAN – *A Judge.*
Genesis 30:6; Joshua 19:40f.; Judges 5:17; 18:1-31.

Dan was the son of Jacob and Bilhah, Rachel's maid, and was known as founder of the tribe bearing his name.

In the assignment of territories during the invasion of Palestine, the Danites were given rather a small inheritance which apparently they were not able to hold against the Philistines. Judges 18 gives a series of stories about the Danites in search of a place to live. Moving northward, they found a pleasant place at the town of Laish. They conquered the town and renamed it Dan. On the way a group of the Danites found a Levite serving as priest to a man named Micah, who had made a "sacred box" for himself and family. The Danites persuaded the Levite to join them in their northward trek, taking Micah's box and other sacred objects along for use in Laish.

Dan was considered the northern boundary of the land of the Israelites. With Beer-sheba as the southern boundary, the phrase "from Dan to Beer-sheba" was intended to indicate the whole country, much as Americans use the phrases "from Maine to Florida," or "from coast to coast."

DANIEL – *God is Judge.*
The Book of Daniel, 1-6; I Chronicles 3:1; Ezra 8:2; Ezekiel 14:14, 20; 28:1-8.

The Old Testament includes four men known as Daniel.

1. David's second son is called Daniel in Chronicles; in II Samuel he is called Chileab. Abigail was his mother.

2. A king of ancient Tyre seems to be mentioned in Ezekiel 28:3. The oracle was directed to "the prince of Tyre" and stated, "You are indeed wiser than Daniel . . ."

3. Daniel, the son of Ithanear, who went with Ezra from Babylon to Judaea.

4. In the Book of Daniel, Daniel, Hananiah, Mishael and

Azariah were presented as captives brought from Jerusalem to
Babylon and carefully trained as
young nobles in the palace of
King Nebuchadnezzar. There
the king's eunuch called them,
respectively, Belteshazzar, Shadrach, Meshach and Abednego.

As favorites they were
royally treated; but Daniel, a
natural leader, refused to "de-
file himself" with the rich foods
and wines of the king's table and
asked to eat the plainest food,
vegetables with water. Daniel
and his friends fared well on the
simple diet and did equally well
in their appearances before the
king and in competition with
the local magicians and en-
chanters.

Daniel was called upon to interpret the king's strange dream,
indeed to reveal the dream itself, after the wise men of Chal-
dea had failed. He confessed
that he could not tell or interpret
the dream, but that his God
would do both. This was the
dream of the image of many sub-
stances. Daniel was given high
honors and rule over Babylon;
then was thrown into the fiery
furnace for refusing to worship
the image which the king created.

Nebuchadnezzar died and
King Belshazzar, his successor,

was a dreamer. Daniel unrav-
elled for him the riddle of the
"handwriting on the wall" which
appeared as the king and his
court made merry, using for their
pleasure the vessels from the
temple of Jerusalem. Again
Daniel was honored, made now
the "third ruler of the kingdom,"
even though the message on the
wall spelled disaster for King
Belshazzar.

Darius, the third king under
whom Daniel is said to have
served, made him "president,"
one of three in the kingdom.
Jealous "presidents" and satraps,
however, plotted against him,
knowing he was faithful to his
religious heritage. Their conniv-
ings brought Daniel to the den
of lions. Again he was delivered by the hand of God and
his enemies were given his place
therein—without divine protection.

These stories are found in
Daniel, chapters 1-6. The next
six chapters deal with visions of
Daniel himself, adding little if
anything to the story. The
apocryphal book, the Song of
the Three Holy Children, is associated with the Book of Daniel, as is the story of Susanna.

The reader should consult a
good commentary—one from
those suggested in the bibliog-

raphy appended hereto—for help in dealing with special problems raised in the Book of Daniel. See DARIUS, BELSHAZZAR, NEBUCHADNEZZAR.

DARIUS – *King?*

The name of two, possibly three, kings appearing in the Old Testament.

1. Ezra 4:5, 24; 5:5ff.; 6:1, 12-15; Haggai 1:1, 15; 2:10; Zechariah 1:1, 7; 7:1.

Darius I, the Great, king of Persia (c. 522-486 B.C.), continued the lenient policy of Cyrus toward captive peoples in the Empire and encouraged the Jews to proceed with the rebuilding of the temple in Jerusalem. Protests from Tattenai, governor of "the province beyond the River," brought the work to a halt until a search of the archives in Babylonia produced a scroll showing that Cyrus had authorized the restoration of the temple. Darius then issued a new decree on the subject and Tattenai and his associates gave every assistance possible to the project, which was "finished . . . in the sixth year of the reign of Darius the king."

2. Nehemiah 12:22.

There is no certainty as to the identity of this "Darius the Persian." The reference could point to one regarded as Darius III, or "Codomannus," the last king of Persia (c. 336-330 B.C.), or possibly to Darius II, otherwise known as "Ochus."

3. Daniel 5:31; 6:1, 6, 9, 25, 28; 9:1; 11:1.

Darius the Mede, about whom also there is no little uncertainty; it is probable that he is a "story-book character" rather than an actual, historical person. It was this Darius, nevertheless, who in the story is credited with having made Daniel, the Hebrew captive in Babylon, the first of three "presidents" in the kingdom. It was in the reign of this Darius that Daniel's popularity aroused the jealousy of other "presidents" and satraps to such a degree that they persuaded the king to throw Daniel to the lions. Daniel's deliverance from the lions by the power and care of his God caused Darius to legalize worship of Yahweh in the kingdom.

DATHAN – Possibly from a word meaning *Law, Usage?*

Numbers 16:1ff.; 26:9; Deuteronomy 11:6; Psalm 106:17. See KORAH.

DAVID – *Beloved.* The word

"David" means "beloved"; but

it might be a title rather than a name.

Ruth 4:17, 22; I Samuel 16:13-I Kings 2:11; I Chronicles 10:14-29:30; Psalms 60, 110 (e.g.); Isaiah 9:7; 22:22; 55:3; St. Matthew 1:1; 22:41; Acts 2:25.

David, shepherd boy, youngest son of Jesse, who became the darling and the king of united Israel, is one of the most important—and most interesting—characters in the Bible.

His story begins with Samuel's dissatisfaction with Saul as king. Once in power, Saul seemed to deteriorate under the pressure, and Samuel, the great priest-judge in Israel, began to look around for a likely prospect to succeed Saul. Samuel was led by divine guidance to the house of Jesse and to young David who at the time was tending sheep in the hills. David was "ruddy," had "beautiful eyes and was handsome." Samuel, having called him in and laid eyes on him, anointed him without hesitation.

Another story introduces David as having been called to Saul's court, as a player of the lyre, to soothe the king's frayed nerves and to serve as an armour-bearer to the king.

Still another story brings David to Saul through Goliath, the giant champion of the Philistines, whom David challenged to battle over the protests of Saul. After telling the king of his experiences with lions and bears, David went out to kill Goliath with a stone from his sling.

In any case, David as a young man was attached to Saul's court, and soon the news got around that David was "the man to watch." Stories of his might, of his successes in battle and, perhaps, of the anointing by Samuel aroused Saul's suspicion and jealousy. He sent David unnecessarily to battle with the Philistines, hoping to have him killed. Each foray, however, only added to David's reputation. Everybody but Saul loved David, it seems, including Saul's son and daughter Jonathan and Michal. In time David was married to Michal and formed with Jonathan a remarkable pact of friendship. The latter, to Saul's disgust, quite gladly recognized David as the next king and asked only to be second to him.

Saul tried to kill David on several occasions, drove him into outlawry and tried to hunt him down. Saul's efforts to murder David were thwarted once by Michal, twice by Jonathan. In retaliation Saul gave Michal to another man and made a mad attempt on Jonathan's life. David could have killed Saul at least twice; instead, he simply clipped Saul's skirt on one occasion, took his spear and water jar on another. David would not lay his hand on "the Lord's anointed."

These stories, of course, only added to David's prestige and to Saul's chagrin.

While still an outlaw David acquired Abigail and Ahinoam as wives, together with a considerable following of seasoned warriors and much spoil of war. He lived with the Philistines and provided a sort of bodyguard for Achish, king of Gath, who hoped to hold him permanently in that capacity. Achish gave him the town of Ziklag in recognition of his services, and, perhaps, as a means of having him out of the limelight at Gath. The stories say that during this time David continued to prey on the Philistines, leaving no survivors of attacks to give him away to Achish. Except for the protests of other Philistine commanders, David might have been involved with Achish in the battle of Mount Gilboa, in which Saul and Jona-

than were killed. The commanders could not believe that David would fight against the Hebrews and refused to countenance his presence with them in the battle. They might have been right.

Having been sent away from the battle, David found Ziklag burned by the Amalekites, whom he pursued and defeated and from whom he recovered his wives and his goods. He took also the cattle of the Amalekites and their goods. Wisely, he sent gifts from the spoils to the elders of Judah and to other chiefs who had befriended him in his days of wanderings.

On learning of the death of Saul and Jonathan, David mourned a proper time and then went to Hebron where he was anointed king by those men of Judah who had recently received his gifts. As king of Judah he still had to deal with Abner, Saul's commander, who held out as leader promoting Ishbosheth (Ishbaal), Saul's son, as king of Israel. After seven years, David's men finally defeated Abner decisively; but a quarrel between Ishbosheth and Abner over one of Saul's concubines sent Abner to David's camp and served to break the power of the house of Saul.

Abner was the key to that power.

Abner's murder by Joab, avenging the killing of Asahel, almost spoiled the new and tenuous unity of the tribes. David was able to prove he was not responsible for the murder and cemented the new arrangement by exceptional kindness to Mephibosheth, the crippled son of Jonathan. Resistance was completely broken when two of Ishbosheth's raiders murdered him in his bed and brought his head to David, who, of course, had them mutilated and hung for their trouble.

A united Israel accomplished, David cleared out the Philistines in a guerilla type warfare; made a few astute alliances; took Jerusalem, the erstwhile impregnable city of the Jebusites, by storm and called it Zion, the city of David; and "David became greater and greater."

The Philistines recouped and attacked in force, only to be defeated again. Now David brought the ark of God, the "sacred box," into the city. As he danced in joy before the ark, Michal, once again his wife, thought him undignified and "despised him." She said as much; and David, not one to take lightly either her talk or the sorry implications of it had her relegated to a sort of unnatural widowhood. "She had no child to the day of her death."

Now that a time of relative peace and prosperity had come, the king began to plan for the building of a house, a temple, "for the ark of God." He called Nathan the prophet for consultation. Nathan at first agreed that it should be done, but later a vision indicated that the temple should be built not by David but by his son and successor.

Under David's generalship, with Joab, Abishai and Benaiah as field commanders, the military organization of Israel was so successful that some of the lesser princes began to submit and to pay tribute without further ado. Indeed, David needed no longer to take the field, for his "mighty men" without his active participation were fully capable. During the years David avoided the mistake of Saul in pitting his forces in large numbers against the enemy in pitched battles. His were the "hit and run" tactics learned so well in the days of his exile.

It was during a war with the ravaging Ammonites that David remained in Jerusalem and got himself involved with Bath-sheba, the wife of Uriah the Hittite. There was nothing to do, thought David, but to get rid of Uriah, and quickly, in that Uriah declined to cooperate with the king's schemes to have him at home for awhile. Get rid of him he did by having Uriah, an honorable man, sent to the thick of battle and left to be killed. The stratagem worked, and in due time Bath-sheba moved into the king's house as his wife. Her child died, as Nathan the prophet in his forth-right words to the king said it would. But David's confession of sin was accepted and Bath-sheba later became the mother of Solomon.

As David grew older, his sons became wild, arrogant and rebellious under his indulgent eye. Ammon ravished Tamar his half-sister, who took refuge in Absalom's house. The latter held his resentment for two years, biding his time, and then had Ammon killed. Of course Absalom fled the country until he could have Joab arrange his return some three years later. Back in Jerusalem he decided there was no good reason not to take the throne for himself, and after four years of preparation he went to Hebron (where

David was crowned and where now there was apparently some dissatisfaction with David) and had himself called king. He succeeded in forcing David out of Jerusalem, but his army was no match for the king's forces under Joab, Abishai, and Ittai. The result was Absalom's death, a rebellion crushed and a father sad at the tragic end of a beloved but wayward son.

Shortly after this a Benjamite named Sheba rebelled. Joab and Abishai put him down and killed Amasa, Absalom's commander, in passing.

Somewhat later, when David was quite old, his son Adonijah tried what Absalom failed to do. He conferred with Joab and Abiathar, the erstwhile faithful priest, and won them to his favor against the prospect of the ascendency of Solomon. But Nathan the prophet and Bath-sheba, hearing of the claim of Adonijah to be king, went to David and persuaded him to abdicate and to have Solomon crowned immediately. News of this action caused the movement of Adonijah to deteriorate.

"Then David slept with his fathers," a king whose unusual qualities have captured the imagination of many generations.

He may be regarded as hero, adventurer, outlaw, vicious and savage warrior, faithful friend, cunning adversary, shrewd trader, winsome lover and husband, philanderer, wise and popular king, lax and poor administrative officer, over-indulgent father. Studied from any point of view he is an interesting personality to whom all Israelites look with some awe and no end of affection. Although the kingdom existed with many problems in his times, yet his reign has been considered as possibly the best period in Hebrew history; and, when in later times he was idealized beyond his just deserts, all kings were measured beside him as model. Indeed, so overwhelming a person did he become that in the early days of the Christian era much was made of the fact that Jesus was "of the house and lineage of David," the most illustrious house in all Israel. See SAMUEL, SAUL, JONATHAN MICAH, JOAB, ABSALOM, ADONIJAH, BATH-SHEBA, NATHAN, SOLOMON, etc.

DEBORAH – *A Bee.*
Judges 4:4-5:31.
A well-known prophetess and "judge" in Israel who "sat under the palm of Deborah between Ramah and Bethel in the hill country of Ephraim."

In the twelfth century B.C. Jabin, a king of Canaan, with Sisera, his commander-at-arms, had for twenty years oppressed the Israelites "cruelly." No doubt Deborah, hearing the complaints of her people as they came to the site of her palm tree, became more and more disturbed over their plight and decided to do what she could to help them break out of an intolerable situation. She sent for Barak, a Naphtalite, and suggested that he assemble Israel at Mount Tabor to do battle with Sisera "by the river Kishon." Barak, thinking of Sisera's nine hundred chariots of iron and his well organized army, agreed to call Israel to Mount Tabor provided Deborah would go with him and support him in his effort. This she agreed to do. She assured Barak that the Lord was on their side, that therefore Israel would gain a victory; but she warned him that the victory would not add to his prestige because, she said, the Lord intended to "sell Sisera into the hand of a woman."

Inspired by Deborah, the Israelite army under Barak defeated Sisera's 900 chariots of iron and Sisera fled afoot to the tent of Jael, the wife of Heber the Kenite, who lured him inside with soft words and gave him curds "in a lordly bowl." Then she crushed his head with a mallet and drove a tent peg through it.

In the battle with Sisera the Israelites might well have been routed had not a storm come up out of the desert, "from the region of Edom," with heavy rain and thunder, to turn the brook Kishon into an "onrushing torrent," and the floor of the valley into a morass which trapped the heavy iron chariots of Sisera. Thus did it seem to the Israelites that the Lord came in the storm from Sinai to take a hand in the battle and to bring victory to his people.

Judges 5 contains the "Song of Deborah," an ancient and fascinating victory song which, primitive though it is, nevertheless attributes the victory to the Lord. "Lord, when *thou* didst go forth . . ." This song is one of the oldest portions of the Bible and a remarkably clear and excellent example of Hebrew poetry. See BARAK, SISERA, JAEL.

DELILAH – *Traitor? Faithless One? "Hetaera," Coquette?*

Judges 16:1ff.
The Philistinian siren who "enticed" Samson into giving away the secret of his great strength, thereby bringing about his capture and downfall as a champion in Israel, and his death, as well.

DEMAS – *Popular, Ruler of the People, the "Peoples' Choice"?*
Colossians 4:14; II Timothy 4:10; Philemon 24.
In the reference to him in Colossians Demas is linked with Luke "the beloved physician" as a co-worker and companion of Paul in Rome. In II Timothy, however, he is described as a "deserter." "Demas, in love with this present world, has deserted me."

DEMETRIUS – *Belonging to Demeter* (the earth goddess in Greek Mythology who was the mother of Proserpene).
Acts 19:24-41.
A silversmith in Ephesus who, seeing that Paul's preaching was winning enough attention to cut into his trade of making idols for the shrine of Diana, incited a riot against the Apostle.

DIDYMUS – *Twin.*
See THOMAS.

DINAH – From a Hebrew Root meaning *Judge*.
Genesis 30:21; 34:2, 25.
Jacob's daughter by Leah. Dinah "went out to visit the women of the land," and was raped by Shechem, a Hivite, who then wanted to marry her. But Jacob's sons, with revenge in mind, would not allow the marriage unless Hamor and his son Shechem and all his tribe would agree to submit to circumcision. The Hivites gladly agreed, for Shechem's "soul was drawn to Dinah"; but while "they were sore," after the operation, Jacob's sons killed them all and plundered their city. Jacob warned his sons that by their treachery they had exposed the smaller tribes of the Hebrews to the vengeance of the Canaanites. The incident of the rape of Dinah, followed by double revenge, might well account for the homelessness of the tribes of Simeon and Levi.

DIONYSIUS – Derived from Dionysius the Greek God of the vine and of wine.
Acts 17:34.
The "Aeropagite," who with Damaris and "others," was converted when Paul preached in the Aeropagus in Athens. The Aeropagus, the hill of the Greek God Ares, was the meeting place of the ancient Athenian court which regulated public morals and was still in existence in the time of S. Paul. The title, "the Aeropagite," implies that Dionysius was a member of the court and thus a "leading citizen."

DIOTREPHES – *Cherished by the God* (Jupiter).
III John 9, 10.
Diotrephes was a self-important member of the Church to which this Epistle was addressed. The writer spoke of him as not acknowledging proper authority in the Church, and said that if he should go to that Church he would bring up for discussion the things being done by Diotrephes, namely, of being overly ambitious and of trying to exclude itinerant preachers and teachers from the fellowship of the Church and of saying slanderous things about them. Could it be, as it has been suggested, that Diotrephes is the first bishop whose name is known, and that he represents a time of significant change in the life of the Church, a change which "the Elder" saw and felt but did not understand? Perhaps, with the growth of the Church, the "settled ministry"

was taking control and the travelling "evangelist" was not as welcome as in former times.

DIVES – From the Latin *dives*, meaning *Rich*.
St. Luke 16:19-31.
The name given to the rich man in the story involving such a man and a beggar named Lazarus. Having had his good things in this life, he was "in torment" in the next, and asked that the beggar who once sought crumbs at his table be sent with a drop of water to cool his tongue; but Lazarus could not do so, however he might want to do.

DOEG – *Anxious, Concerned.*
I Samuel 21:7ff.
Doeg the Edomite, chief of Saul's herdsmen, was at Nob when Ahimelech the priest gave David the holy bread from the altar and provided him with Goliath's sword, which was, no doubt, regarded as an important trophy. Doeg observed all this quietly, and in due time reported to Saul what he had seen. Saul was furious with Ahimelech and summoned him and all the priests who were at Nob to appear before him and answer to the charge of treason. To the king's accusation that he

had befriended David, Ahimelech answered, "And who among all your servants is so faithful as David . . . ?" At this rebuke Saul demanded that all the priests be slaughtered; but his bodyguard would not touch them. Saul then ordered Doeg to kill them. He did so, eighty-five of them. All, indeed, but one were killed, and the sanctuary at Nob and everything in it were destroyed. The one escapee was Abiathar, son of Ahimelech, who found refuge with David and served him well for many years. See ABIATHAR.

DORCAS – *Gazelle,* so called from its large, "bright eyes."
Acts 9:36.
Also known as Tabitha, Dorcas was a woman disciple at Joppa. She was especially charitable, "full of good works." She fell sick and died; and the other disciples, hearing that Peter was nearby at Lydda, sent for him. When he arrived he sent everyone out from the upper room where Dorcas lay ready for burial, and after earnest prayer, he commanded: "Tabitha, arise!" She did rise. He took her then by the hand, lifted her up, and calling the "saints and widows" he presented her to them alive.

E

EBED – *Servant (of God), Slave.*

Judges 9:26-35.

Ebed was the father of Gaal who was governor of Shechem under Abimelech.

EBEDMELECH – *Servant of the King.*

Jeremiah 38:7ff.; 39:16.

A eunuch captive from Ethiopia who informed King Zedekiah of the fact that Jeremiah had been thrown into a cistern to die of starvation and exposure. With the permission of the king and the use of ropes and old clothes, Ebedmelech lifted the prophet out of the cistern and so effected his release both from the cistern and from prison.

EBER (Heber) – From a word meaning *the region beyond, the other side.*

Genesis 10:21, 24; 11:14-17; I Chronicles 1:18f.

Several men named Eber are to be met in the Scriptures. Only one is of real importance, and that mostly by implication. Eber the son of Shem was the imaginary, the patronymic ancestor of some of the tribes of Hebrews, Arabs, and Aramaeans which lived "on the other side" of the Euphrates River, tribes which might be described as "off-shoots" of the better known groups.

EDOM, EDOMITES – *Red.*

Genesis 25:30; 36:1, 8, 19.

Edom was the elder son of Isaac. His name given at birth was Esau, but when he sold his birthright to Jacob he came upon him in the act of boiling "pottage" and asked, "Let me eat some of that red pottage . . ." Genesis states the name "Edom" was derived from the color of the pottage. The descendants of Esau, or Edom, were known as Edomites and they inhabited an area to the south and east of the Dead Sea, consisting mostly of mountains and plateaus. The ancient unpleasantness between Jacob and Esau was revived when the tribes of Israel were refused passage through the lands of the Edomites and had then to fight their way through. Strife between the two groups was never ending, for as both copper and iron were to be found in their lands, and as the great "King's highway" crossed the country, the possessions of the Edomites were much in demand. It is thought that the original "home" of the God Yahweh might have been on Mount Seir in Edom.

EGLON – *Circle, Round, a Wheel.*
Joshua 10:3ff.; 12:12; 15:39; Judges 3:12ff.
Eglon was a king of Moab, a fat man; Ehud was a judge in Israel, a left-handed man. Eglon with the Amalekites and Ammonites took Jericho from the now idolatrous Israelites and held them and the city for eighteen years.

Ehud, a Benjamite, pretended to take presents, tribute really, to Eglon. But being left-handed and clever, Ehud concealed a specially made two-edged sword under the right side of his clothing. He delivered the tribute, made a start for his home and then turned back alone, asking for a secret audience with the king. When the king's courtiers departed Ehud drove the dagger into Eglon "beyond the hilt" and left it there. The regicide then slipped out, quietly locked the doors behind him and escaped before the king's people knew what had happened.

With this initial success Ehud then defeated the Moabites in battle and "subdued" them.

EHUD – *Strong.*
See EGLON, above.

ELAM, ELAMITES – *Young, (Mature, Vigorous), Ancient, Enduring?*
Genesis 10:22; 14:1, 9.
The son of Shem, grandson of

Noah whose name was given to a group of ancient people who lived east and north of the Tigris River, north of the Persian Gulf. Tradition among the Hebrews said that the Elamites were a wild, hard-fighting people who were especially dangerous with the bow. Elamites were among those who captured Lot in the sack of Sodom. The chief city of the Elamites was Susa, which figured in the empires of the Babylonians, the Assyrians, and the Persians; yet the Elamites remained a distinct people. Cyrus the Great, for example, was an Elamite, although he preferred to think of himself as a Persian. Elamites were allies of Assyria in the invasion of Judah (cf. Isaiah 22:6, e.g.) and of Egypt (cf. Ezekiel 32:24). A tough and spirited people.

ELDAD, MEDAD – *God is a Friend, God has Loved.*
Numbers 11:26f.
While Moses and the elders were away from the camp "inquiring of the Lord," two men, Eldad and Medad, who should have been with Moses and the "seventy," remained in the camp. The Spirit was given to Moses and the elders and they prophesied; but the Spirit came also to Eldad and Medad, who "prophesied" in the camp. Joshua asked Moses to forbid such prophesying, for he thought it might undermine Moses' authority; but Moses replied: "Would that all the Lord's people were prophets . . . !"

ELEAZAR – *Whom God Helps.*
1. Deuteronomy 10:6; Numbers 3:2, 4, 32; 4:16; 16:37, etc.
The third son of Aaron and Elisheba. Eleazar was a priest and successor to Aaron. The duties of Aaron's sons are given in Exodus 28-29.
2. I Samuel 7:1.
Eleazar, the son of Abinadab, was consecrated to have charge of the ark of God after it was returned by the Philistines, whose experience with it had been disastrous. The ark was said to have been in the custody of Eleazar for twenty years.
3. II Samuel 23:9ff.
Eleazar the son of Dodo was one of David's captains, but probably not one of the "mighty men" as stated in this reference.
Four other men named Eleazar are mentioned.

ELHANAN – *God is Gracious.*
1. I Chronicles 20:5.
The son of Jair who killed Lahmi, the brother of Goliath.

2. II Samuel 23:24.

A son of Dodo who was one of David's thirty captains.

ELI – *Yahweh is High.*

I Samuel 1:9-3:21; 4:4, 11-22;
I Kings 2:27.

From one point of view Eli was a kindly judge and priest at Shiloh; but his evil sons, Hophni and Phinehas, brought ruin to his house and shrine, though they, too, were priests. It might be said that Eli did not understand his sons and could not control them; but he could comfort Hannah in her trouble and later he was able to guide her son of promise, Samuel, who as a very young lad was given under vow into his custody.

The sons of Eli—seen from this point of view—were rough, crude, and greedy. Moreover, they were contemptuous of the services at which they assisted. They took more than they were entitled to have; they were arrogant; and they used their office to create intimacies with the women who "served at the entrance of the tent of meeting." In view of all this it was prophesied that they and their father would all die in one day. The Philistines attacked the Israelites who had taken the ark into their camp, attended by Eli's sons. The ark was captured and the sons of Eli were killed—in just punishment for their sins. Eli waited at the gate of Shiloh for news of the battle. When he heard the news of the tragedy he was so overcome that he fell from his seat and broke his neck.

While, from another point of view, the sons of Eli were just as rough and greedy, Eli might be regarded as merely a weak and ineffective judge, and his sons, who died in battle on the same day, died the death of heroes attending to their duty in defense of the sacred ark of God. With the same set of facts, essentially, the two points of view are suggested in the story of Eli the priest of Shiloh.

Whatever the point of view, the fact is that Shiloh did not survive Eli and his sons, for the Philistines razed it and took the ark as a prize of battle, and found it too burdensome a trophy to keep. See HOPHNI, PHINEHAS, SAMUEL.

ELIAB – *God is Father.*

1. Numbers 1:9; 2:7; 7:24, 29; 10:16.

A son of Helon who at the time of the numbering in the wilderness was made captain of the tribe of Zebulun.

2. Numbers 16:1, 12; 26:8f.
The father of Dathan and Abiram, Reubenites. See ABIRAM.

3. I Samuel 16:6; 17:13, 28.
Eldest brother of David whose daughter, Abihail, became the wife of Rehoboam. This Eliab is also known as Elihu.

4. I Chronicles 12:8ff.
A Gadite warrior, "mighty and experienced, expert with shield and spear," who with his band "went over" to David at Ziklag.
Two others named Eliab need not be mentioned.

ELIAKIM – *My God Establishes.*
1. II Kings 18:18ff.; Isaiah 22:20; 36:3ff.
Eliakim was steward or manager of the household of king Hezekiah of Judah.

2. II Kings 23:34.
King Jehoiakim's name originally was Eliakim.

ELIAM – *My God is Kinsman.*
1. II Samuel 11:3.
Bath-sheba's father was named Eliam.

2. II Samuel 23:34.
One of David's mighty men was Eliam, a Gilonite.

ELIEZER – *My God Is Helper.*
1. Genesis 15:2-6.
The Damascene slave whom Abram, childless, thought would be his heir. Eliezer was born in Abram's house. It was as Abram was complaining about this poor state of his affairs that the Lord promised him a son and heir.

2. Exodus 18:4; I Chronicles 23:15f.
The son of Moses by Zipporah. There were two sons born to this daughter of Jethro, the priest of Midian. The other was Gershom. See ZIPPORAH.

3. II Chronicles 20:37.
A prophet who opposed the alliance of Jehoshaphat, king of Judah, with Ahaziah, king of Israel, "in building ships to go to Tarshish." Jehoshaphat had been a "good king," but in joining interests with Ahaziah, who walked "in the ways of Ahab," he brought misfortune to himself. The ships built by the two kings were wrecked and "were not able to go to Tarshish." Eliezer felt that the curse on the "house of Ahab" would fall in some measure on all associated with Ahab's descendants. See JEHOSHAPHAT, AHAZIAH.

ELIHU – *He is My God.*
1. I Chronicles 27:18.
The eldest brother of David, also called Eliab.

2. I Chronicles 12:20.
A "chief of thousands" of Manasseh who joined David at Ziklag.
3. Job 32-37.
Elihu was a man younger than the three friends of Job. As the older men talked Elihu sat quietly by until they had finished speaking. He became angry at Job because he "justified himself rather than God." He was equally angry at the friends who could think of nothing more or better to say in refutation of Job's arguments. Elihu made quite a long speech in reproof of the friends, of Job's self-righteousness and impatience, and then declared God's justice, power, and mercy. He begged Job to consider the wondrous works of God; "For he does not regard any who are wise in their own conceit." After Elihu's speech the Lord began to speak to Job out of the whirlwind.

ELIJAH – *Yahweh is My God.*
I Kings 17-21; II Kings 1:3ff.; St. Matthew 11:14; 16:14; 17:3; St. Mark 9:4; St. Luke 1:17; 9:8, 19; St. John 1:21.
Elijah the Tishbite! Even if only half of what is said of him in the Books of Kings is true in the literal sense—and there are strange inconsistencies in the stories about him which indicate, of course, different sources—Elijah stands out as one of the most exciting personalities in the Bible. The meaning of his name is in itself a commentary on his life and work; he was God's man. He appears first before King Ahab to warn him of an impending drought which could be ended only by God's word to his prophet. The prediction did not please the king and by divine direction Elijah went to hide, "east of Jordan," by the brook Cherith. Here he was to have water for himself and be fed with bread and meat by ravens.

When the brook dried up Elijah went to Sidon to be cared for by a poor widow whose "handful of meal in a jar and little oil in a cruse" were all she had for herself and her son. But Elijah assured her that these would be enough, and in good faith she took him in; and the "jar of meal was not spent, neither did the cruse of oil fail." While Elijah was with the widow her son died and was brought to life again by the Lord who "hearkened to the voice of Elijah" as he pleaded for the widow and her son.

After three years of the drought the Lord sent Elijah again to Ahab to tell him that the rains would soon come. On the way to Ahab the prophet met Obadiah, the king's chief steward, who had been sent in one direction while Ahab searched in another for grass and water. Obadiah was afraid to obey the prophet's command to find Ahab and tell him, "Behold, Elijah is here!" He feared, he explained, that Ahab would kill him, for the king had searched every nation and kingdom for the prophet and any mention of him made the king unreasonable. Elijah demanded that he go anyway, saying, "I shall surely show myself to him today." With that assurance given, Obadiah went to the king.

Ahab's greeting was, "Is it you, you troubler of Israel?" And the prophet's response was a blistering one in which he took Ahab to task for worshipping the Baals. Jezebel, Ahab's wife from Sidon, had brought in her own religion with a host of priests, had cut off the priests of Yahweh from their usual sources of income and their customary services, and had been responsible for the death of a number of them. The inference is that only a hundred priests of Yahweh were left, and that these were alive only because Obadiah had hidden them in caves "by fif-ties" and had fed them secretly.

Having had his words with Ahab, Elijah demanded that he assemble the priests of Baal and Asherah (850 of them) at Mount Carmel for what we might refer to as a showdown. Ahab brought up the priests on schedule and Elijah asked of the people assembled with them his famous question as a way of showing the significance of what he was about to do: "How long will you go limping with two different opinions? If the Lord be God, follow him; but if Baal, then follow him!" This would indicate that the people were confused, trying perhaps to worship both.

Elijah then claimed to be the only one left of the prophets of the Lord in the kingdom. Yet he was willing to initiate a contest between himself and the four hundred fifty appointed prophets and priests of the Baalim. He and they were to have each a bull for sacrifice—but no fire. The god of power, he said, would provide the fire; and all would see his power, once for all, and follow him with confidence.

How Elijah enjoyed the futile, ludicrous and pitiful efforts of the prophets of Baal to produce fire! All day long he mocked them. As they danced and performed their rites, finally slashing themselves in their frenzy and frustration, Elijah jeered, suggesting that the Baalim were asleep or looking elsewhere.

When his turn came, Elijah first repaired the broken down altar of Yahweh, dug a trench around it and prepared the bull for sacrifice. He had quantities of water poured over the bull (some sceptics say it might have been mixed with naphtha) until even the trench was filled. In response to his prayer the "fire of the Lord fell," consuming everything, the bull, the water and the stones. At this Elijah cried: "The Lord, he is God, he is God!" The contest was over. Having won it, Elijah had the prophets of the Baalim seized and killed. Elijah was not one to lose the fruits of victory.

After this event, Elijah prophesied the coming of the rains, which fell in accord with his promise.

Jezebel was not pleased with the disposition of the priests of her gods, and she threatened Elijah's life. He, essentially a practical man, went into hiding again, bitterly discouraged that Ahab refused to return to the strict worship of Yahweh. Elijah felt he had failed and ought

to die. A "still small voice" from the Lord aroused him. This vision informed him that he should anoint Hazael to be king in Syria, Jehu to be king in Israel, and appoint Elisha as prophet in his own place. He was told also that all was not lost, that seven thousand of the faithful would be left in Israel.

Elijah then left the cave in which he had hidden himself from the wrath of Jezebel. Shortly thereafter he found Elisha behind an ox-plow. On him he cast his mantle and Elisha left the farm to follow Elijah as his master.

Jezebel, still a power in Israel, acquired for her husband the vineyard of one Naboth, who had refused to sell his inheritance to the king. Jezebel's method was cunning and deadly. She simply had Naboth falsely accused of treason and put to death, so that his lands and goods could be confiscated. When news of this got out, Ahab found himself once again confronted by Elijah, the man of God, who now told the king that for this and other crimes too numerous to mention, he and his whole house were to be destroyed, that Jezebel would be eaten by dogs within the bounds of the city. Ahab "repented" and "humbled himself," and the curse on him was postponed, briefly, in the sense that his son would be allowed to succeed him. But Ahab was killed in battle and the dogs licked his blood from the chariot in which he died and from the pool in which it was washed.

Ahaziah, his son, died after falling through the lattice in his upper chamber. Before he died he sent a messenger to consult Baalzebub, god of Ekron, about his condition. Elijah heard about this and prophesied the death of the new king, making it seem that his death was caused not by the fall but by the king's apostasy in consulting Baalzebub, the "god of the flies," instead of Yahweh.

Elijah and Elisha went by stages to the Jordan river, making preparation along the way for the great prophet's death. At the river Elisha asked to inherit a "double portion" of the prophet's spirit. Then the two were separated by a chariot of fire which came between them, and Elijah was carried by a whirlwind to heaven. Elisha saw the ascension and so knew he had received the prophet's mantle and spirit.

Like Abraham, Moses, **Samuel**, and David, Elijah's memory was strong in Israel. It was thought that before the Messiah should come Elijah would return to earth as his herald. Some thought that John Baptist was he, and so strong was the notion that John had to deny it. It is significant that in the vision of the disciples of Jesus on the mount of the Transfiguration Elijah and Moses were seen as companions of the Lord; and further that at the Crucifixion the words of Jesus, "Eloi, Eloi," were misinterpreted as a call for help from Elijah, the great prophet of Israel. See AHAB, JEZEBEL, ELISHA.

ELIMELECH – *God is King.*
Ruth 1:2f.; 2:1, 3; 4:3, 9.

A man of Bethlehem, husband of Naomi, who in a time of famine took his family to Moab, where his sons married women of the land. His son Chilion married Ruth. He and his two sons died in Moab.

ELIPHAZ – *God is Dispenser.*
1. Genesis 36:4, 10-16.

The son of Esau and Adah. Tradition said that the son of Eliphaz was Amalek, founder of the people, the Amalekites.

2. Job 2:11; 4:1; 15:1; 22:1; 42:7, 9.

Eliphaz was the first named of

the three friends of Job, described as a Temanite, and therefore associated with the Eliphaz above, whose son was Teman. See JOB, BILDAD, ZOPHAR.

Eliphaz was more gentle in his criticism of Job than were the other two friends, but he was nonetheless insistent that Job's own words had condemned him.

ELISHA – *My God is Saviour, Salvation.*
I Kings 19:16f.; II Kings 2:1-8:14; 13:14ff.
For several years after Elijah found him plowing with a team of twelve oxen, Elisha was disciple and minister to the great prophet. Although a farmer of the tribe of Issachar, Elisha's duties as prophet made him become a friend and counselor for kings in Israel and Judah, and in Moab and Syria as well.

His first act as prophet in his own right was the cleansing of the waters of Jericho. This he did by putting salt in the spring. Elisha was not above the use of his "powers" for private vengeance. While on a journey to Bethel some small boys ridiculed him, calling him something like "old baldy." He cursed the boys in the name of the Lord, and soon two angry she-bears emerged from the woods to tear

forty-two of the boys to shreds. Elisha made no attempt to stop the carnage.

Jehoram, Jehoshaphat and the king of Edom, in need of water while marching to battle against the Moabites, called for help from Elisha. At first he demurred, but on the appeal of Jehoshaphat he reconsidered and agreed to help. Under the influence of a minstrel he saw the vision of a dry stream-bed fill up with water from no visible source, the work of the Lord; and the next morning water came "from the direction of Edom, till the country was filled with water." The kings defeated Moab.

A wealthy Shunamite woman built for Elisha's convenience a small roof chamber in her home. He had his servant, Gehazi, ask what might be done for her in return for her kindness. Her answer was, "Nothing," but Gehazi observed that she had no son. Elisha promised her a son; and when later the son died, Elisha's prayers were the means of new life for him. In this story is one of the most poignant conversations to be found in literature. Elisha saw the woman riding toward his place on Mount Carmel. He sent Gehazi to ask: "Is it well with you? Is it well with your husband? Is it well with the child?" She had come to tell Elisha of the death of the child; but her answer was: "It is well."

A variety of signs and wonders were performed by Elisha, including a feeding of a hundred men with twenty loaves of barley bread; the healing of Naaman the Syrian leper, by having him bathe seven times in the Jordan; the floating of the lost axe head; his own deliverance from a whole army of Syrians by having them stricken blind and led by him into Samaria, where they were at the mercy of Israel. He also prevented the sale of a poor widow's sons by miraculously providing enough oil for her to use in payment of her debts.

Elisha moved into Damascus and anointed Hazael to be king of Syria and the scourge of the Lord on Israel for the sins of Ahab. He arranged also for the anointing of Jehu as king of Israel, this time as the scourge of the Lord on the house of Ahab itself, in fulfilment of Elijah's prophecy.

Just before his death Elisha encouraged Joash to fight valiantly against the Syrians, assuring him of at least a partial victory over them.

Elisha was a great prophet, but not of the stature of his predecessor. It is interesting to observe that whereas Elijah seemed to work alone, Elisha worked with a company of prophets on occasion, lived with the group from time to time and conferred with them when he chose to do so. The likeness between some of the narratives concerning Elisha to those about Elijah arouses suspicions in the minds of the critics, for it seems that some of Elijah's greatness is deliberately made to apply to the man on whom his mantle fell. See GEHAZI, ELIJAH.

ELIZABETH – *God is Swearer.*
St. Luke 1:5ff.
Elizabeth, "of the daughters of Aaron," was the wife of Zechariah the priest and a cousin of Mary the mother of Jesus. In her old age she bore her first child, whose conception was announced by the angel Gabriel. Before the child was born, the angel also announced to Mary the fact that she would bear a son conceived of the Holy Spirit and told her of Elizabeth's condition. Mary visited Elizabeth "in the hill country of Judah," and found it was so with her. It was in response to Elizabeth's words that Mary uttered the

song now known as the *Magnificat.*

Elizabeth's child was named John. It was he who became the "Baptizer," the prophet who was the forerunner of Jesus.

ELKANAH – *God Owns, God Possesses.*
I Samuel 1:1-2:21.

Although eight men named Elkanah are biblical figures, only one is of any special significance —Elkanah whose wives were Peninnah and Hannah. He was kindly, patient and understanding, especially so with Hannah, who had no children. When she wept because she was barren, he asked: "Why is your heart sad? Am I not more to you than ten sons?" But Hannah, taunted by Peninnah, was desolate, and she sought the Lord in her misery. Her prayer was answered with the birth of Samuel, and Elkanah readily assented to his being taken to Eli the priest at Shiloh in accord with Hannah's vow to "devote" her son to the Lord who had answered her prayer.

Elkanah is thus important chiefly as the father of the great Samuel.

ELYMAS – *Sorcerer, Magician, the "Devious One"* (From a Greek verb meaning "to twist").
Acts 13:8.

Barnabas and Saul were summoned by Sergius Paulus, the proconsul at Salamis and "a man of intelligence," to speak before him "the word of God." Resisting the efforts of Barnabas and Saul was the magician Elymas. At this point in the story in Acts Saul becomes Paul, and Paul boldly called Elymas a "son of the devil . . . full of deceit and villainy." He said Elymas would be made temporarily blind. He was blinded, and the proconsul believed.

EMIM – *The Terrible.*
Genesis 14:5; Deuteronomy 2:10.

A tribe of very large people who were defeated by the "four kings" in the days of Abram and who were absorbed into the Moabite groups, but the memory of whose stature lingered in the minds of neighboring peoples. They were also known as Rephaim, or "the strong ones."

ENOCH – *Teacher.*
1. Genesis 4:17f.

The first son of Cain. The first city, built by Cain, was named Enoch in honor of Cain's firstborn.

2. Genesis 5:18ff.; St. Luke 3:37; Hebrews 11:5; St. Jude 14.

A son of Jared who was a descendant of Seth. Hebrew tradition held that because Enoch pleased God he did not die, but was translated directly to heaven.

EPAPHRAS – Short form of Epaphroditus, *Charming, Handsome.* Devoted to Aphrodite, thus "lover boy"?
Colossians 1:7; 4:12; Philemon 23.

Friend, fellow-worker of St. Paul, resident of Colossae and founder of the Church there. In Colossians 4:13 it is suggested that he might have had a part also in the founding of churches in Laodicea and Hierapolis. Epaphras visited Paul in prison at Rome to consult him about the problems disturbing the Church at Colossae. The Epistle is the result of that conference.

EPAPHRODITUS – *Charming.*
Philippians 2:25; 4:18.

"Brother in Christ," fellow-worker, fellow-soldier of St. Paul, who was appointed a messenger from the Philippians to Paul during his Roman imprisonment. Paul says that Epaph-roditus "nearly died for the work of Christ, risking his life to complete your service to me." Apparently he had been sent to Paul with gifts from his good friends at Philippi and became ill on the way. Paul sent him back to reassure the people of the Church there, and probably he delivered the Epistle when he arrived.

EPHRAIM – *Fruitful? Double Fruitfulness?*
Genesis 41:52; 48:1ff.; Joshua 21:20; II Samuel 2:9; 18:6; Isaiah 7:2; Hosea 5:3ff.

The younger son of Joseph who was born in Egypt and whom his grandfather, Jacob, blessed as if he were the first-born son of Joseph instead of Manasseh. The tribe of which Ephraim was titular founder was a large one and the strongest of the tribes subdued by David in his effort to create a united Israel. Judges 1:29 places Ephraim in the area of Gezer and states that the tribe simply settled in the territory without driving the Canaanites out of the country. In the division of the kingdom on the death of Solomon, the tribe of Ephraim became prominent in the kingdom of Israel. The name "Ephraim" was, in fact, often used to speak of the whole of Israel. The Ephraimites were allied with Syria against Ahaz of Judah, and both Hosea and Isaiah spoke harshly of the idolatry and immorality of the Ephraimites, predicting catastrophe for them. Ephraim was made captive c. 722 B.C., by Shalmaneser V. and Sargon II, Kings of Assyria.

ERASTUS – *Beloved, Loveable.*
Acts 19:22; Romans 16:23; II Timothy 4:20.
Erastus was with Timothy a helper of Paul, who sent the two of them into Macedonia to check on the progress of the Church there. Romans 16:23 refers to him as "city treasurer" of Corinth, from which city the Epistle was dispatched. In II Timothy it is said that "Erastus remained at Corinth" when Paul departed.

ESARHADDON – *Conqueror.*
II Kings 19:37; Ezra 4:2; Isaiah 37:38.
The son of Sennacherib, king of Assyria (c. 681-669 B.C.), who took Manasseh, King of Judah to Babylon as a captive, Esarhaddon was one of the great kings of the Assyrians.

ESAU – From a word meaning, *Press, Squeeze, Gnash* (the teeth).

Genesis 25:25f.; 27:42; 28:5-9; 32:3-33:16; 35:1ff.; Joshua 24:4; Malachi 1:2f.; Deuteronomy 2:4ff.; etc.
The son of Isaac and Rebekah who sold his birthright for a mess of "red pottage." Esau and Jacob were twins, but since Esau was, precisely speaking, the first-born he was Isaac's proper heir. Isaac loved Esau, a hunter and man of the field; but Rebekah loved Jacob, a "quiet man, dwelling in tents." Esau was generous, and as a young man not concerned about his right of birth, which he tossed off to Jacob for a not too good meal. He was concerned later, however, when he realized that Jacob was serious about the whole thing and that Jacob and Rebekah had actually tricked him out of the birthright, and with it the blessing of his father.

Isaac had asked Esau to bring him a meal of game, his last one, and promised his blessing. While Esau was away on the hunt, Rebekah urged Jacob to bring kids from the flock which she prepared to pass off on Isaac as Esau's meal of game. She clothed Jacob in Esau's garments and put the skins of the kids on his hands and neck to make him seem "hairy," and brought him to Isaac as Esau.

Jacob received the blessing promised and rightfully Esau's. When the latter discovered the trick he was enraged and swore to kill Jacob after their father's death. Rebekah rescued Jacob by sending him to her brother, Laban, until Esau could see the situation in better perspective.

Jacob feared Esau and was a fugitive from his wrath for many years, until, finally, an uneasy peace was effected between them on the initiative of the anxious Jacob as he returned from Laban in Haran. When an agreement between them had been sealed, Jacob went his way to Shechem and Esau returned to "the land of Seir, the country of Edom."

It is well to remember that Esau and his descendants are often called Edom. See EDOM, JACOB (ISRAEL).

ESTHER (Hadassah) – *Star.*

The Book of Esther.

Queen Vashti's refusal to attend the banquet of King Ahasuerus, her husband, brought about her dismissal as queen and created an opportunity for Esther, a Jewish maiden, to become queen in her place. Ahasuerus was the Persian king, Xerxes I, who was ruler c. 486-465 B.C.

Esther was wisely counselled for her duties by her cousin, Mordecai, and carefully trained in court protocol and queenly beauty by Hegai, the king's eunuch in charge of the royal harem. When Esther's turn came to appear before the king, she won his favor immediately and completely.

Mordecai, out of interest in Esther, frequented the gate of the palace and overheard a plot on the king's life. This he reported to the queen who saved the king in Mordecai's name and gained favor for him. In all this, however, she did not reveal her Jewish origin.

Meanwhile a certain Haman was promoted to high place and expected everyone to do obeisance before him, as, indeed, the king commanded. Mordecai did not bow down before him and Haman plotted to destroy the Jews to get at Mordecai. Word went out that all the Jews should be annihilated on a certain date.

When Esther learned of this she went, unbidden and against Mordecai's wishes, to the king's court to reveal her identity and to appeal for her people. Being received graciously by the king she invited him and Haman to a special banquet. Haman by now had prepared a gallows for

Mordecai. At the banquet Esther revealed herself as a Jewess and turned the tables on Haman, so that Mordecai received the honors Haman had planned for himself and Haman was hanged on the gallows he had constructed to accommodate Mordecai. The Jews were saved and were allowed to take vengeance on their enemies.

The occasion of the turning of the tables was the alleged origin of the Feast of Purim. In the keeping of the Feast each year Jews everywhere remember and honor the beautiful, courageous—and fictitious—Esther, who offered herself for the safety of her people.

The Book of Esther is fiction, not history, intended probably to promote the Feast of Purim. Records do not show a queen named Esther or a Jewish queen by any name at the court of Xerxes. It is thought that the book was written c. 125 B.C., and that the chapters in the Apocrypha known as the "Additions to the Book of Esther" were written somewhat later.

EUNICE – *Glad, Happy Victory.*
II Timothy 1:5; Acts 16:1.
The mother of Timothy, whose faith had been observed with pleasure. The writer of II Timothy felt certain that the same faith found in her and in Lois, Timothy's grandmother, would "dwell in" him also.

EUODIAS – *Good, Prosperous, Happy Way* or *Course.*
Philippians 4:2.
A woman in Philippi who must have been a cause of trouble in that Paul remembered to "entreat" her to "agree in the Lord" with Syntyche. He thought that because "they have labored side by side with me in the Gospel," they should be able to settle whatever difference lay between them—if the Church would help them to do so.

EUTYCHUS – *Happy, Fortunate.*
Acts 20:9f.
A young man who sat in a window during one of Paul's sermons. Falling asleep, he tumbled from the third storey and was "taken up dead." The Apostle went down to him, embraced him, and declared that "his life is in him."

EVE – *Life, Life-giving, Mother of all Living* (men).
Genesis 1:27; 2:18ff.; 3; 4:1; II Corinthians 11:3; I Timothy 2:13.

In the first reference to the creation of Adam's female companion she is called simply a "female" and "helper," or a "woman." She was called "woman, because she was taken out of man," having been fashioned from Adam's rib.

In Genesis 3:20 the woman is identified as Eve, because "she was the mother of all living." (Josephus was first to call her "Eva," or "Eve.")

She it was who, beguiled by the serpent, first ate of the fruit of the tree of knowledge in Eden and then persuaded Adam to do so. This act of disobedience brought about the expulsion from the Garden of Eden and to it was attributed the woman's pain in childbirth and her desire for children, together with woman's "vassalage" to her husband.

Eve's association with the serpent suggests an echo of the ancient theory that all life came from some sort of "primeval serpent."

Yet Adam was held responsible also; for, being expelled from the paradise of Eden, he was told he would have to work for his living in an earth which was cursed and which would bring forth "thorns and thistles" in spite of all his efforts.

Further, Adam and Eve were now to be identified with the earth, for "out of it you were taken; you are dust, and to dust you shall return."

EZEKIEL – *God is Strong.*

The Book of Ezekiel.

Ezekiel was a priest-prophet among the exiles who lived by the river Chebar in Babylon. He was the son of Buzi, a priest of Jerusalem, born in that city during the time of Jeremiah the prophet, and was carried into captivity with Jehoiakin of Judah, in 598 B.C.

In Babylon Ezekiel had a wife and the privilege of a house of his own, together with religious freedom. About five years after the captivity began he was called to prophecy and to a ministry of some sort for his people, for he felt himself to be a "watchman" over the congregation beside the Chebar. He preached to the people and shared his vivid visions with them. Some of the group must have objected strenuously to what he said, for he called them rebellious, stubborn, impudent, and he was told that he should not be afraid of them, "though briers and thorns are with you and you sit on scorpions."

His sermons, addressed to his

immediate congregation and to Israel-at-large, especially to the people still in Jerusalem, were at first warnings pointing to moral and spiritual shortcomings which had brought disaster to the people and which would surely lead to the collapse of Jerusalem. Because Israel had not been brought to repentance there could be little, if any, hope for Jerusalem. Ezekiel felt this so deeply that it brought him to a symbolic silence, to a Vision of God in which he saw a storm and from it emerging a "likeness of the four living creatures," "wheels within wheels," the "likeness of the glory of the Lord," and a hand with a roll containing "lamentations, and mourning, and woe." From a seven day "stupor" after the vision he emerged with a series of "signs" which were given him from time to time to use as warnings of doom to come unless the people could be brought to turn to righteousness. The prophet felt himself compelled to use these signs and to speak such words as the Lord gave him, for in the vision he had been warned that unless he did so the blood of the unwarned, unrighteous men "I will require at your hand." The import of the signs was that for their sins the Lord

would "spend my fury upon them," producing "disaster after disaster," and death by sword, famine and pestilence. Thus with symbol, riddle, allegory and apocalyptic did Ezekiel give the warning; and he made it clear that every man was responsible—"the soul that sins shall die," said the Lord, and no man shall die "for his father's iniquity." Thus, even in the midst of the disaster of Jerusalem some would bear the "mark" of the righteous and would escape the death all around them. A "remnant" would be left, and any who would repent might have a place therein, for, said the Lord through Ezekiel, "I have no pleasure in the death of the wicked; but that the wicked turn from his way and live; turn back, turn back . . . for why will you die, O house of Israel?"

When Jerusalem fell, after the revolt of Zedekiah, the depression in which the prophet had lived so long seemed to be relieved and he became now a "watchman" in another sense. The day Jerusalem was attacked, his beloved wife died; but he did not mourn for her. Nor should he mourn for the falling city, he was told. He remained indoors and "sighed," but "not aloud."

In time news of the fall of the city came to him, and his silence was broken. Broken also was the old tone of his prophecy. A watchman he still was, but now the news he called out from his post was good news, news of hope and happy expectation.

Ezekiel's great visions and powers of expression were turned now to descriptions of the Lord, as a Good Shepherd, searching for, finding and bringing home his sheep. He spoke of the restoration of Israel with Yahweh at its head, of a new relationship between God and his people who would be sprinkled "with clean water." "A new heart will I give you, and a new spirit will I put within you; and I will take out of your flesh the heart of stone and give you a heart of flesh."

Ezekiel's visions now are of the new temple, of the new, clean and holy worship taking place in it, of a new and more glorious Jerusalem with a new prince of the house of David as king and a restored line of priests and Levites dominating the scene. The city will now be God's city, and the "glory of the Lord" will brood over it. The new kingdom will be, in his eyes, not just another kingdom, but a theocracy, a religious community, a "holy nation," whose real king is Yahweh.

Ezekiel was much concerned with holiness, righteousness. To him this was not some abstraction or a matter of the following of a code of ethics alone. While he was concerned with the "law in the heart," he was also definite in his belief that the outward expression of inner conversion was necessary. In the new Jerusalem there would be every outward and visible manifestation of the inner holiness now characteristic of the people. The law would be kept in strict detail.

It is to be observed that Ezekiel's vision of the new life for Israel gave small place to other peoples. Israel was to be holy, the people of the holy God whose glory would rest upon them; but no place was offered to the Gentiles.

Ideas and phrases from Ezekiel were picked up and developed in many later writers. In his parable Jesus used the picture of the Good Shepherd. Later writers developed to a high degree Ezekiel's use of the "apocalyptic," and he contributed greatly to the development of angelology. His exclusiveness and rigidity were also to become part of the thinking of later Judaism, and his insistence on purity of worship, with emphasis on ceremonial correctness, became a strong factor in the life of the later Israel. The "city four square," the "river of life," the "likeness of the glory of the Lord," and the "four living creatures" are phrases made current by later writers.

The Book of Ezekiel makes good reading taken by itself, but read with a commentary at hand it makes both good reading and better sense.

EZRA – *Help.*

The Book of Ezra, especially 7:27-9:15; 10; Nehemiah 8-10. Ezra was a Jewish exile in Babylon in the reign of Artaxerxes II (c. 405-359 B.C.). His father was Seraiah, of the priestly family of Aaron. Ezra was himself a scribe and priest "skilled in the law," who went from Babylon to Jerusalem with letters patent from the king giving him authority to refurbish the Temple and to set up a community under the law of the Israelites. A generation before the time of Ezra an attempt was made under Nehemiah to restore Jerusalem and to create such a community there as Ezra intended, but that effort had been only partially successful. The Temple had been restored somewhat and the walls repaired, but Nehemiah's efforts to create a proper Jewish community had failed.

In permitting Ezra to go to Jerusalem, Artaxerxes, aware of the need for some action to settle the unhappy situation existing in Judah, was glad to have Ezra try to produce some sort of order there. If Ezra's purpose to establish the Jewish law with all the reforms the law would demand could actually be accomplished, the king's purposes for the land could also be served.

Thus, encouraged by the king, Ezra took with him priests, certain souls from the representative house of David, and a large group of "plain citizens," numbering about 5000 in all. After the long and dangerous four-month journey across the desert to Jerusalem, the people went to their native towns in Judah to claim their inheritances (under the protection of the king as given in the letter) and Ezra began to prepare Jerusalem for the return and restoration of the old tradition of the law. He and his people were not empty-handed as they arrived, for they brought with them gifts of considerable proportions provided by the colony of the faithful in Babylonia, and a draft on the king's treasury. Thus, it seems that they were, on the whole, well received.

When work on the Temple was done to Ezra's satisfaction and when he was otherwise ready, he responded to the request of the people for a reading of the law. Ezra issued a call, though he was in no apparent hurry to do so, and with great joy and enthusiasm he read from his precious book. On hearing the requirements of the law which Ezra read, no doubt with an eye to the laxities of the practices he had seen all around him, the people wept and lamented their condition. But Ezra told them it was a day of Feast, one of joy and gladness; and the Feast of Booths was observed by all the people summoned for the occasion. During the days of feasting more of the law was read.

At last the time came to deal with the sins of the people. A fast was called and the people again summoned for it. There was much to be done in the way of reform. There had been much mixing of the Jews with the local peoples and a thorough confusion of customs. The people stood before Yahweh and confessed their sins. Ezra was forced to insist that men leave the wives they had taken from among the local people and promise to forsake the local "abominations."

At last he secured the necessary words of promise in these matters, the law was read before the people, separation as promised occurred in accord with a plan hastily worked out "because of the heavy rain," and the covenant with the Lord was renewed, signed and sealed. The temple services were properly ordered and provided for by self-imposed taxation. Ezra's mission was accomplished, and a new era in Jerusalem and in Judaism was begun. Ezra who "had set his heart to study the law of the Lord, and to do it, and to teach his statutes and ordinances in Israel" had now set the stage for the religious community envisioned by Ezekiel. See NEHEMIAH, ZERUBBABEL.

F

FELIX – *Happy, Fortunate.*
Acts 23:24.

Procurator of Judaea by Roman appointment who, though interested in Paul's preaching, kept him in prison hoping to receive a bribe for his release. Felix was removed from his position after Paul had been in prison for two years. In general, Felix was kind to the Apostle, giving him considerable freedom and more privileges than the ordinary prisoner received. Often during the two years he talked with Paul and knew him to be innocent. Yet when he left, he kept Paul in the prison simply to do the Jews a favor. The fact that Drusilla, his wife, was a Jewess might have had some influence on his decision. He was not highly regarded in Rome.

FESTUS (Porcius) – *Joyful, Happy, Prosperous.*
Acts 24:27; 25:13ff.; 26:24-32.

Festus was Felix's successor as governor of Judaea, appointed by Nero. At first he seemed to want to favor Paul as against his Jewish enemies, but pressure on him was very great; and Paul, expecting sooner or later to be turned over to the Jews, appealed to Rome. Festus arranged a hearing for him before King Agrippa II, who had come down with his sister Bernice to greet Festus, the new governor. Agrippa thought Paul might have been set free except for the fact that he had already appealed his case to Rome. Festus, a worthy governor, did not ask for money or hint at a bribe, seeming to want to be a responsible procurator. He died while in office.

FORTUNATUS – *Prosperous, Happy, Fortunate.*
I Corinthians 16:17f.
A Christian of Corinth in whom Paul seemed to take especial pleasure. When he visited Paul in Ephesus, he and his companions, Achaicus and Stephanas, "refreshed" Paul's spirit. The three brought a message from Corinth, and in writing to the Church Paul told the Corinthians that they should be happy to have such men in their congregation.

G

GAAL – *Rejection, Rejected as Foul or Loathsome.*
Judges 9:26-41.
A son of Ebed who "moved into Shechem with his kinsmen" after Abimelech had made himself king over the people. The citizens of Shechem hated Abimelech and were glad to allow Gaal to become their leader against him. The king had a good lieutenant in the city in the person of Zebul, however, and by following Zebul's advice to attack the Shechemites from ambush, he drove Gaal from the city.

GABRIEL – *Man of God, God Has Shown Himself Mighty.*
Daniel 8:15ff.; 9:21ff.; St. Luke 1:5-19; 26-38.
The archangel who acted as messenger from God to announce events to come, Gabriel is listed as one of seven archangels in Hebrew literature. He appeared twice to Daniel: once to interpret a vision, and again, coming in swift flight at the time of the "evening sacrifice," he spoke of desolation to come. Here he is described as "a man."

Gabriel appeared to Zacharias and Elizabeth, speaking of himself as "Gabriel who stands in the presence of God," sent to bring good news of the gift to them of a son, John, who was to become John Baptist.

He appeared also to Mary, saying, "Hail, thou highly favored one." Then he announced the coming of the Lord Jesus as Incarnate Son of God.

GAD – *Good Fortune, A Troop.*
1. Genesis 30:11; 35:26; 49:
19; Numbers 1:24f.; Joshua
18-22.

The son of Jacob by Leah's
maid, Zilpah, and founder of
the tribe of his name which became a large and war-like clan.
The tribe roamed Gilead beyond Jordan, to which territory
it was assigned in the conquest
of Canaan. The Ammonites
were a constant threat to the
Gadites, and they were delivered from Ammonite pressure
by Jephthah, who became leader
of the Gadites, or Gileadites as
they were often called, in exchange for his services. The
tribe of Gad gave David good
support, and when Solomon
died they gave their assistance
to Jeroboam, son of Nebat, allowing him to establish his
headquarters at Penuel in their
land. The Gadites succumbed
to the Syrian-Israelite-Edomite
alliance which defeated Ahaz,
king of Judah, c. 715 B.C.
2. I Samuel 22:5; II Samuel
24:11; I Chronicles 21:9ff.

Gad was a prophet in David's
reign and known as "David's
seer." It was he who, after the
"numbering of the people" by
David and his repentance for
that act, offered the king three
choices of penance: (a) three

years of famine in the land; (b)
three months of flight before his
enemies; or (c) three days of
pestilence in the land. David
chose to "fall into the hand of
the Lord" rather than into "the
hand of man." In three days of
pestilence 70,000 of his people
died!

GAIUS – *Glad, Happy.* A Common Roman name, as Gaius
Julius Caesar.
1. Acts 19:29.

A companion of Paul who was a
native of Macedonia and involved with him in a near riot in
Ephesus which was stimulated
by the commercial jealousy of
Demetrius the silversmith.
2. Acts 20:4.

Another companion of Paul
from Derbe in Lycaonia.
3. Romans 16:23;
I Corinthians 1:14.

A man baptized by Paul in
Corinth, and his host there.
4. III John 1.

The unknown man, Gaius, to
whom III John was written. An
"elder" in the Church.

GALLIO (Lucius Junius) – The
name probably was derived
from the Latin word Gallia,
signifying Gaul; but as in this
case the name was adopted
rather than given, it would

almost certainly have no significance.
Acts 18:12-27.
Gallio was a Roman proconsul in Achaia before whom St. Paul was brought on a false charge. When he learned the nature of the situation, he ran the accusers out of the tribunal on the ground that they were wasting his time over a "matter of questions about words and names." Gallio was the younger brother of Seneca. Pliny wrote that Gallio went to Egypt after his term at Corinth, suffering from a lung hemorrhage, and tradition states that both he and Seneca were forced by Nero to commit suicide.

GAMALIEL – *God is Rewarder, Reward of God.*
1. Numbers 1:10; 2:20; 7:54, 59; 10:23.
A son of Pedahzur and a chief in the tribe of Manasseh who was chosen to assist in the "numbering of the people" in the wilderness.
2. Acts 5:34; 22:3.
Gamaliel was the great teacher of the Pharisees who advised the Jews to let the apostles be; for, he said, if the movement be of men it will fail of itself—but if it is of God, nothing can be done to stop its progress.

St. Paul claimed that he had been brought up at the feet of Gamaliel, and so could be counted as a "Pharisee of the Pharisees." Gamaliel represented the very best in Pharisaism.

GEDALIAH – *Yahweh is Great.*
1. II Kings 25:22-25; Jeremiah 39:14; 40:5-41:18.
Gedaliah was a grandson of Shaphan, the secretary to King Josiah of Judah. Like Jeremiah, Gedaliah thought Nebuchadrezzar of Babylon represented the hand of the Lord in judgment on Jerusalem and so, like Jeremiah, opposed the revolt of Zedekiah which produced the destruction of the Temple and Jerusalem, in 586 B.C. The king of Babylon appointed Gedaliah governor "of the cities of Judah," and the captain of the Chaldean guard released Jeremiah into his custody.

Friends tried to warn Gedaliah of a plot to murder him, but he refused to hear the warning and was murdered just two months after taking office. The rebel band also killed all the Jews with Gedaliah at Mizpah, and the Chaldean guard as well. This revolt and fear of its consequences led the Jews, whom Gedaliah had persuaded to return to Jerusalem from such places as Moab and Ammon, to flee now to Egypt—with Jeremiah and Baruch among the fugitives.

2. Jeremiah 38:1-4.

Gedaliah the son of Pashur was one of the several who, on hearing Jeremiah say that Jerusalem would fall to Babylon, advised King Zedekiah that the prophet should be put to death. Jeremiah was then thrown into a miry cistern where he would have died but for the appeal made to the king by Ebedmelech, a eunuch of Ethiopia.

3. I Chronicles 25:3, 9.

One of the sons of Jeduthun who, directed by their father, "prophesied with the lyre in thanksgiving and praise of the Lord."

4. Ezra 10:18.

One of the sons of the priests who, having married foreign women, promised after the reading of the law to put his wife away.

5. Zephaniah 1:1.

The grandfather of the prophet Zephaniah.

GEHAZI – *Valley of Vision?*

II Kings 4:12-36; 5:20-8:5.

"The servant of Elisha the man of God." Perhaps he should have received Elisha's mantle as Elisha received that of Elijah, but Gehazi was not the man for it. Yet it was he who suggested to Elisha that the Shunammite woman who had refused other means of payment for her kindness might accept a son.

When the child was given and then died, Gehazi, using Elisha's staff at the prophet's bidding, tried to restore its life, but his efforts failed.

After the healing of Naaman's leprosy Elisha refused any reward; but Gehazi asked a small gift for Elisha and his "guests." He hid Naaman's gifts from Elisha, but the prophet was not to be deceived. He cursed Gehazi with Naaman's leprosy, and nothing more is said directly about the poor, greedy man. There is, however, a story about the "servant of the man of God," possibly Gehazi. This man, seeing in the early morning an army of Syrians surrounding the city and being frightened, cried out to his master. Elisha prayed the Lord to open the servant's eyes; when opened, the eyes beheld the mountain "full of horses and chariots of fire round about Elisha." The Syrians were then stricken blind through Elisha's prayer, and he led them into Samaria and into the hands of the king of Israel.

GENTILES – *The Nations.*
References are too numerous to be listed. The Gentiles are simply the "nations" not included in the covenant between God and the children of Israel.

GERSHOM – From a word meaning *"a Thing Thrust or Put Forth." A "Stranger?"*
  1. Exodus 2:22; 18:3;
     I Chronicles 23:15f.;
     Joshua 21:6.
A son of Moses given this name as a symbol of Moses' sojourn "in a foreign land." Zipporah, the daughter of Ruel (Jethro, Hobeb) the Midianite priest, was Gershom's mother. One of Gershom's descendants was thought to be Jonathan, a priest of the shrine at Dan; and in I Chronicles 26:24 one of his sons, Shebuel, was described as "chief officer in charge of the treasuries."

  2. Judges 18:30.
Gershom was father of Jonathan, whose sons "were priests to the tribe of the Danites . . . ," where the graven image taken from Micah during the Danite migration was set up.

GERSHON (Another form of Gershom)
  Genesis 46:11; Exodus 6:16f.;

Numbers 3:17; 4:21-28, 38-41.
Gershon was the first of the sons of Levi whose name was given as a tribal name to his descendants, the Gershonites. In the accounting of Numbers the Gershonites were to be "encamped" behind the tabernacle on the west, and they were in charge of the tent of the tabernacle, "the screen for the door of the tent of meeting, the hangings of the court . . . and its cords . . . and all the service pertaining to these."

GESHEM – *Corporealness, Substantial.*
Nehemiah 2:19; 6:1f.
Geshem was one of the Arabians who opposed the work of Nehemiah in his efforts to rebuild Jerusalem.

GIDEON, JERUBBAAL –
  Hewer, a Great Warrior.
Judges 6:11-8:35.
Gideon was a farmer who became a warrior when Israel was threatened by idolatry on the one hand and the Midianites on the other. While threshing wheat in a wine press in order to hide it from the Midianites, who would have taken it from him had they seen it, Gideon received a call from "the angel of the Lord" to "Go in this might

of yours and deliver Israel." Suspicious, Gideon asked for a sign, which was given in a divine fire which consumed both his offering of kid-flesh and moistened cakes and the rock on which it was offered.

The divine word directed him also to use his father's bull to pull down his father's altar to Baal and the Asherah beside it. Out of fear of his family Gideon did this at night; but his father defended Gideon instead of Baal, saying "Let him (Baal) contend for himself." Gideon then was called "Jerubbaal," that is, "Let Baal contend against him"; and his father, Joash, apparently turned with Gideon to worship Yahweh.

Gideon's attention was turned thereafter to the Midianites. The army he raised was too unwieldy, too filled with the "fearful and trembling." Of 33,000 only 10,000 survived his first test; only 300 remained after the water-lapping test. With this small number, carrying trumpets, empty jars, and torches, he attacked the Midianite camp by night. Trumpets were blown, jars were broken and torches were lighted on every side of the camp. To add to the confusion shouts and cries were uttered. The Midianites were frightened, confused, and began to fight each other.

Gideon's company pursued the defeated Midianites "across Jordan," and being "faint" he asked for help in the towns of Succoth and Penuel. In each case the townsmen scorned him. To the men of Succoth he promised, on his return, a flailing of them with thorns and briers; to Penuel he promised the destruction of their tower fortress. In each case he made good his promise. He killed the elders of the latter city and two kings of the Midianites, as well.

For his success Gideon was asked to be king over Israel. He replied: "I will not rule over you, and my son will not rule over you; the Lord will rule over you." Although he went back to his farm, Gideon was remembered as a mighty man of valor, as perhaps the best of the warrior-judges.

GILEAD – *Strong, Firm, Rocky.* Although best remembered as a place name, Gilead was also the name of several individuals.

1. Numbers 26:29f.; Joshua 17:1.

A son of Machir and grandson of Manasseh. It was in this clan of the tribe of Manasseh that a pair of women, granddaughters of Gilead, was given an inheritance.

2. Judges 11:1f.

Gilead was the father of Jephthah. Because Jephthah was the son of a harlot, he was not recognized by the rest of Gilead's sons.

3. I Chronicles 5:14.

A Son of Michael, who was a descendant of Gad. This Gilead lived in Bashan.

GOG, MAGOG – *High, Mountain.*

1. Genesis 10:2; I Chronicles 5:4.

Here Gog is used to denote a tribe associated with the name of Reuben.

2. Ezekiel 38-39.

In the Book of Ezekiel Gog, the "chief prince of Meshech and Tubal," of the "land of Magog," would come with his people from the "uttermost parts of the north" like a "cloud covering the land" to accomplish a "great shaking in the land of Israel." But God's real purpose in being summoned as a potential destroyer would be to show God's greatness and to "make myself known in the eyes of the nations"; for, "says the Lord God . . . I am against you, O Gog . . ." Thus Gog was to be used as an instrument to show forth the glory of God among the nations.

3. Revelation 20:8.

Gog and Magog are here spoken of as leaders of the hosts of Satan which will be consumed in the final holocaust at the end of the thousand years of Satan's imprisonment.

GOLIATH – *An Exile, A Soothsayer.*

I Samuel 17:4, 23; 21:9; 22:10; II Samuel 21:19.

The famous giant of Gath, champion of the Philistines, before whom the champions of Saul's army trembled daily until David, the young shepherd boy, wandered into camp with provisions for his older brothers. Although Goliath is said to have been about nine feet tall, David, who had fought bears as tall as Goliath, had no fear of him. A smooth stone from David's sling killed the giant, whose sword and armour were placed as trophies in the shrine at Nob.

With Goliath gone, the Philistine army broke camp and departed.

GOMER – *Completion, Heat.*

1. Genesis 10:2f.; I Chronicles 1:5; Ezekiel 38:6.

A grandson of Noah, who was

father of an ancient people. Some have thought that these might have been progenitors of the tribes of the "north countries," possibly of the Celts.

2. Hosea 1:3.
The wife whom the prophet Hosea took in response to the command, "Go, take to yourself a wife of harlotry." See HOSEA.

H

HABAKKUK – *Embrace*.

The Book of Habakkuk.

"O Lord, how long shall I cry for help," and see violence and wrong, destruction and strife, wrongs and justice perverted? This was the cry of despair which the prophet Habakkuk raised probably during the reign of the cruel King Jehoiakim of Judah (c. 608-597 B.C.).

The answer to the question, "How Long?" was given in a vision of the Chaldeans, "that bitter and hasty nation," as "doing a work . . . that you would not believe if told." Scoffing at kings, laughing at fortresses, men "whose own might is their god," the Chaldeans had been "ordained" of God as a judgment" on the people. Judah fell to them in 597 B.C.

In the answer to the first question a new question is raised. If the Chaldeans are the instrument of God to "chastise" the wicked what about the Chaldeans themselves? Are not they quite as wicked as those they have been appointed to humble? The prophet asks this question as earnestly as he had asked the former one. In listening for an answer he went to his "stand to watch . . . and look forth to see what he will say to me . . ." From his prophetic watchtower Habakkuk saw a vision saying, plainly: "Wait." Let the righteous continue to live by their faith and they will see that the Chaldeans, like him "who builds a town with blood," will in their turn be destroyed. The vision urged the righteous to remember that "The Lord is in his holy Temple," and that in due time "the earth will be filled with the knowledge of the glory of the Lord as the waters cover the sea."

The time of waiting was a long one, for the Babylonians did not fall from power until Cyrus the Persian rose to the occasion in 539 B.C.

Meanwhile, Israel in exile learned well the lesson of Habakkuk that "the righteous shall live by his faith," a truth built into the core of the teaching of St. Paul. See Romans 1:17, Galatians 3:11, and see also Hebrews 10:38.

Nothing is known about the prophet Habakkuk as a person, and there is considerable debate about his little book.

HADAD – *Mighty.*
1. Genesis 36:35f.;
   I Chronicles 1:46f.

A king of the Edomites who defeated the Midianites "in the country of Moab." It is said that his "city" was named Avith.

2. I Kings 11:14ff.

In David's time Joab destroyed "every male in Edom" but Hadad, who was yet a child, and a few servants who fled to Egypt. Here young Hadad was raised in Pharaoh's house, mar-

ried to Pharaoh's daughter, and given an allowance of food and land. When David died, Hadad became restive in Egypt and returned to Edom as ruler and soon was an adversary of Solomon.

3. I Chronicles 1:30; Genesis 25:15; 36:35, 39.

The Chronicler lists Hadad as a son of Ishmael; the Book of Genesis lists probably the same person as Hadar, in one place, as Hadad in another.

HAGAR – *Flight.*
Genesis 16:1ff.; 21:9ff.; 25:12; Galatians 4:24f.

Hagar was Sarai's (later Sarah) Egyptian maid who was given by her to Abram (later Abraham) when Sarai had no children of her own. Realizing herself to be "with child" Hagar made the mistake of "looking with contempt on her mistress," who drove her away. Hagar was found in the wilderness by an angel who told her she would bear a son, Ishmael, a "wild ass of a man, his hand against every man and every man's hand against him." Obeying the angel, she returned to Abram's tent until Isaac was born to Sarai (now Sarah), who again turned jealously on Hagar and had her driven out again.

She and Ishmael settled in Paran.

St. Paul uses the story of Hagar (spelled Agar in KJ New Testament) and Sarah to illustrate the two covenants and the conditions of mankind under the terms of each. See ABRAHAM, SARAH.

HAGGAI – *Festive, Festal.*
The Book of Haggai; Ezra 5:1; 6:14.

The writings of this prophet, who probably was born during the exile in Babylon, are carefully dated in the second year of Darius Hystaspes, 520 B.C. Haggai had one purpose in mind—to encourage the people under Zerubbabel to rebuild the Temple in Jerusalem. Many fine private houses had been erected to the neglect, in the prophet's sight, of the Temple, which alone could provide for the people that which they most needed. As an encouragement he said that "The latter splendor of this house shall be greater than the former," and that the Lord would himself shake the nations and add their treasures to the wealth of Israel. So enthusiastic was Haggai about Zerubbabel that he spoke of him as the Lord's "signet ring," his "chosen one."

Haggai and Zechariah were contemporaries. See ZECHARIAH.

HAM – *Swarthy, Hot?*
Genesis 5:32; 9:18, 22; 10:6; I Chronicles 1:8; 4:40.

One of the sons of Noah. The father of Canaan. Genesis declares that from Ham, Shem, and Japheth, the three sons of Noah, "the whole earth was peopled." Thus the name Ham was also applied to his descendants who were thought to be, in general, the African peoples. I Chronicles (4:40) states that the "former inhabitants" of Gedor (Gerar, in the Septuagint) "belonged to Ham." Gedor was a "native" area from which the Simeonites drove the Hamites, according to the chronicler. Psalm 105 suggests that Jacob "sojourned in the land of Ham."

Genesis states, moreover, that Ham's son, Cush, was ancestor of the Ethiopians; that Cush's son, Nimrod, was ancestor of the Assyrians; that Ham's son, Egypt, was father of the Egyptians; and that his son, Canaan, was father of the early inhabitants of Palestine, the Canaanites. It was Ham's son Canaan who was cursed by Noah because Ham had seen his father lying naked in a drunken stupor.

HAMAN – *Well Disposed.*
Esther 3:1-9:24.
Minister to King Ahasuerus who was promoted to a "seat above all the princes who were with him," but who fell from power when a plot he laid to eliminate all the Jews failed. He was hanged on the gallows he had had prepared especially for Mordecai the Jew, a cousin of Esther whom he adopted and brought up as his own daughter. It was Esther who, being made queen, brought about Haman's downfall. See ESTHER, MORDECAI.

HAMOR – *Large Jackass.*
Genesis 34; Joshua 24:32; Judges 9:28.
A Chief of Shechem from whom Jacob purchased land.
It was Hamor's son, Shechem, who raped Dinah, the daughter of Jacob and Leah, and who then wanted to marry her. Simon and Levi, her brothers, felt themselves insulted; and having tricked Hamor and his men into circumcision as a condition for the marriage, they attacked the "Shechemites" while they were "still sore," and killed them, taking all their property as they went. Jacob was displeased at their action, for he envisioned reprisals from the Canaanites and Perizzites who who more numerous than Jacob's people.

HANAN – *Gracious, Merciful.*
1. I Chronicles 8:23.
A son of Shashak who was a descendant of Benjamin.
2. I Chronicles 11:43.
One of the mighty men in David's armies.
3. Ezra 2:46; Nehemiah 7:49; 8:7; 10:10, 22, 26; 13:13.
Several men of this name are listed in these references as having part in the work of Ezra-Nehemiah.
4. Jeremiah 35:4.
A man associated with the Temple whose "sons" were entitled to a chamber in the Temple "near the chamber of the princes." It was into this chamber that Jeremiah was instructed to take the Rechabites and to "offer them wine to drink." See RECHAB.

HANANEL, HANANEEL – *God is Gracious.*
Jeremiah 31:38; Nehemiah 3:1; 12:39; Zechariah 14:10.
The builder of a tower at some point in the north wall of Jerusalem. The location is not known, nor is anything known of the man who built it.

HANANI – *Gracious.*
  1. I Kings 16:1, 7.
The father of Jehu, a prophet
who was instructed by the word
of the Lord to speak against Baasha, king of Israel by way of
the murder of Nadab the son
of Jeroboam I. See JEHU, BA-
ASHA, NADAB.
  2. Nehemiah 1:2; 7:2.
One of the "brethen" of Nehemiah who brought to him the
news of the "great trouble and
shame" of the survivors in Jerusalem of the exile and of the condition of the city's walls and
gates. Later Hanani was appointed a gatekeeper in the city.
  3. Nehemiah 12:36.
The "son of a priest" who was a
musician appointed to serve in
the ceremony of the purifying of
the walls of Jerusalem.
  4. I Chronicles 25:4, 25.
One of the sons of Heman, a musician who was trained by his
father in the use of cymbals,
harps, and lyres in the music as
employed in the Temple.

HANANIAH – *Yahweh is Gracious.*
  1. Jeremiah 28.
Hananiah was a prophet who
spoke of peace and of the fall of
Nebuchadnezzar when Jeremiah
was speaking of the yoke of captivity still to be endured. Hana-

niah broke the symbolic yoke
worn by Jeremiah to emphasize
the meaning of his words and to
discredit the latter prophet.
Later, Jeremiah returned to his
rival with a yoke of iron, saying
that the Lord had replaced
wood with iron, and that Babylon's end was not yet to come.
He called Hananiah a liar, a
false prophet, and foretold his
death, "because you have uttered rebellion against the Lord."
  2. Nehemiah 7:2.
The "governor of the castle" at
Jerusalem who, with Hanani the
brother of Nehemiah, was appointed co-ruler of the city. Hananiah was described in the text
as "a more faithful and God-
fearing man than many."

HANNAH – *Grace, Gracious is
  Yahweh.*
I Samuel 1-2:21.
A wife of Elkanah, an Ephraimite, and the mother of Samuel.
A childless woman, she poured
out her troubles and her heart
before the Lord at the sanctuary at Shiloh, where Eli was
priest in charge. Her barren-
ness was intolerable, even
though she was much loved by
her husband. Eli heard her mut-
terings and accused her at first
of drunkenness. Later, however,
he prophesied the birth of a son.

She in turn promised to devote her son to the Lord. This she did; and as soon as Samuel was weaned at the age of three, he was brought to serve Eli at Shiloh. Five other children were later born to her.

Hannah's song of thanksgiving, strikingly similar to that of Mary the Mother of the Lord, is a late insertion into the story. It is really a song of thanksgiving for the deliverance of Israel taken from some collection of such poems. It seemed to the editor a fitting expression of Hannah's feelings. Note the Messianic allusion in 2:5. Compare this song with St. Luke 1:46-55; compare also with Psalm 116.

HANUN – *Gracious.*
II Samuel 10:1ff.; I Chronicles 19:2ff.

In this case the meaning of the name is quite contrary to the action in which the individual was involved. Hanun was a king of the Ammonites to whom David sent messengers of sympathy on the death of Hanun's father, who had "dealt loyally with David." But Hanun's advisors called the "comforters" spies, and on their advice Hanun shaved off half the beard of each one, "cut off their garments in the middle, up to their hips, and sent them away." This discourtesy aroused David's anger, with the result that his generals, Joab and Abishai, defeated an army of Ammonites and Syrians.

HATHATH – *Bruised.*
I Chronicles 4:13.

A Kenazite who was the son of Othniel and a craftsman.

HATTUSH – *Contender.*
1. I Chronicles 3:22.

A descendant of the kings of Judah, through Shecaniah.

2. Ezra 8:2; Nehemiah 3:10; 10:4.

One who went from Babylon to Jerusalem with Ezra, or with Zerubbabel. Allegedly he was a descendant of David.

3. Nehemiah 12:2.

A priest who returned to Jerusalem with Zerubbabel.

HAVILAH – *Circle, District.*
Genesis 10:7; I Chronicles 1:9.

A descendant of Ham, the son of Cush.

This name refers also to a district said to be rich in gold, onyx, and aromatic gums. In I Samuel 15:7 Saul "defeated the Amalekites, from Havilah as far as Shur, which is east of Egypt."

HAZAEL – *God Sees.*
I Kings 19:15; II Kings 8:7ff.;
9:14f.; 10:32; 12:17f.; 13:3, 22,
24f.; II Chronicles 22:5f.;
Amos 1:4.

A courtier of the king of Damascus who, having been anointed to be king of Syria by Elisha, actually became king by murdering Ben-hadad II. Hazael was said to be the instrument of the Lord in punishing the sins of Ahab. Having become king of Syria, he took lands from Israel and carried everything of value from both the Temple and the city of Jerusalem. Amos spoke of the destruction of the "House of Hazael" by "fire."

HEBER – *Shoot, Associate, Companion.*
1. I Chronicles 5:13; 8:22.

Two men are listed in these references: first, the head of a clan in the tribe of Gad, and second, a son of Sheshak, of the tribe of Benjamin. In both instances the spelling is given as "Eber." See EBER.

2. Genesis 46:17; Numbers 26:
   45; I Chronicles 7:31f.; St.
   Luke 3:35.

The son of Beriah, of the tribe of Asher, who is listed in the geneology of Joseph, the husband of Mary.

3. Judges 4:11, 17, 21; 5:24.

Heber the Kenite was the husband of Jael, the woman who killed Sisera, the general of the armies of Jabin, king of Canaan. Heber was technically an ally of Jabin and Sisera, and it might have been supposed that Jael should give Sisera refuge. It seems that such was the thought in Sisera's mind when he fled from the defeat of his armies at Kishon in the direction of Heber's tent; for Judges 4:11 reports that Heber had pitched his tent apart from the clan. The Kenites were smiths, craftsmen, some of whom might well have had a part in the fabricating of Sisera's "chariots of iron." Heber might have been a smith following the army to repair armor and weapons. See JAEL, DEBORAH, SISERA, BARAK.

HEBREW, HEBREWS – *One* (or the people) *from Across* (the river), *From "Over There."*
Genesis 14:13; 39:14; 40:15;
43:32; Exodus 1:15f., 19; 2:6f.;
Deuteronomy 15:12; I Samuel
4:6, 9; etc.

The history of the Hebrew tribes is in itself a special study and cannot be treated in detail here. Suffice it to say that the Hebrews were a group of Arabic tribes who, from the biblical point of view at any rate, traced their descent to Abraham and to his forebears. It is a vast oversimplification to state that the people of the Hebrews were descended from the twelve sons of Jacob, or that they are to be accounted for by the term Israelites. Indeed the history of the tribes of the Hebrews is not fully known, and one of the books given in the bibliography should be consulted for information on the several theories about their origin and development.

HEMAN – *Faithful.*
   1. I Kings 4:31; I Chronicles 2:6.
A wise man, son of Mahol, with whom Solomon was compared. Solomon was "wiser than all other men, wiser than Ethan . . . and Heman. . . ."
   2. I Chronicles 6:33; 15:17, 19; 16:41; 25:1ff.; II Chronicles 5:12; 29:14; 35:15; Psalm 88.
This Heman was a musician called "the singer," and was tallied by the Chronicler as the grandson of Samuel the prophet and judge. He was one of the first three Levites in David's reign and made responsible for music in the service of the sanctuary.

HERMAS – *Hermes,* *Interpreter.* Greek name for the Messenger among the gods. Latin, *Mercury.*
Romans 16:14.
This man might have been the author of *Pastor,* or *The Shepherd,* a first century book of devotion. In the same verse greetings are sent to one "Hermes." The *Apostolic Constitutions* attribute the work to him and refer to his brother, "Bishop Pius," as Bishop of Rome.

HERMOGENES – *Begotten of Hermes,* or *Mercury.*
II Timothy 1:15.
One with whom Paul had been associated in Asia, but who "turned away from me."

HEROD THE GREAT – *Son of Hero; Glory of the Flesh?*
St. Matthew 2:1.
The king of Judaea who was "sorely troubled" at the news of the birth of Jesus. It was he who, taking no chances, ordered the slaughter of all males under the age of two years. Although he was cruel, passionate, and murderous, he did work hard and with some success to preserve the rights of the Jews against an increasing pressure from the Roman conqueror. In Herod's time (37 B.C.—4 A.D.)

the Jews were almost independent, enjoying relative self-government. When he died, the Jews—perhaps to avoid government by other cruel Herods—petitioned for direct Roman government.

Herod the Great is remembered, in spite of his strong qualities as ruler, for his fear of the Christ and his terrible reaction to the news of the birth of Jesus, designated the "Messiah."

Herod is the name of a dynasty of seven rulers, all of whom appear in the New Testament. Space does not permit an account of all of them in this place; but see ANTIPAS, HEROD ANTIPAS, HERODIAS. The Herods were in power, more or less from 55 B.C.—93 A.D.

HEROD ANTIPAS
St. Matthew 14:1.
The tetrarch of Galilee whom Jesus referred to as "that fox." Craftiness and cunning served to keep him in position for years, until he was deposed in A.D. 39-40.

He married first Aretas, then set her aside for Herodias, the wife of his brother. This lustful act earned for him the anger of many strict Jews and made him the target of the indignant preaching of John Baptist. Herodias had the head of John Baptist served up on a platter, but her avarice eventually caused the deposition of her husband. She suggested that he ask Caesar for the title "King." The Emperor smashed his ambitions, instead, by taking from him the title "Tetrarch," and banished him to Gaul where he died in exile.

HERODIAS
St. Matthew 14:3; St. Mark 6:17, 24.
Herodias, daughter of Aristobulus, son of Herod the Great, was married first to her uncle Philip, then to Philip's brother, Herod, tetrarch of Galilee. John Baptist criticized Herod for taking his brother's wife. Herodias, smarting under the criticism, "had a grudge against" John, and Herod put him in prison. Herodias found opportunity to kill him when the king, pleased with her daughter's dancing, offered the girl "Whatever you ask me . . ." Herodias told her daughter to ask for the "head of John the baptizer." Thus did she dispose of the prophet whom she regarded as her greatest enemy.

HETH – Etymology and meaning unknown, but *Terrible* has been suggested.

Genesis 10:15; 23; 27:46; 49:32.
A son of Canaan and ancestor of the Hittites. The Hittites, according to Genesis, the "sons of Heth," sold Abraham a cave, the cave at Macpelah, in which Sarah was buried. Rebekah complained to Isaac at the prospect of Jacob's marriage to a Hittite woman, and used that as an excuse to get her favorite son away from the wrath of Esau. Isaac agreed with Rebekah, and Jacob was sent to Paddan-aram for a wife. Esau, however, out of spite, married a Hittite. See HITTITES.

HEZEKIAH – *The Might of Yahweh, Yahweh is Strength.* II Kings 16:20; 18:1-20:21; 21:3; I Chronicles 3:13; 4:41; II Chronicles 28:27-33:3; Isaiah 1:1; 36:1-39:8; Jeremiah 15:4; 26:18f.; Hosea 1:1; Micah 1:1.
Certainly one of the greatest kings of Judah, though not a military success. Hezekiah was son and successor of Ahaz, who had become a puppet to Assyria. As Hezekiah came to the throne (c. 715-687 B.C.) the Egyptians, Babylonians, and Israelites began to put pressure on Assyria. Hezekiah joined the alliance, though Isaiah opposed it, and on his own took Philistine territory which he was not able to hold when Sennacherib, king of Assyria, found time to give him full attention. He thus remained an Assyrian vassal after a valiant attempt to break free. He might have won had not Egypt failed to give the assistance promised. Tribute from Judah to Assyria was so heavy that gold from the temple doors was melted down for payment; and nearly 250,000 prisoners were taken into Assyrian captivity.

Later, Sennacherib made another invasion of Judah. This time he was turned back by pestilence and defeat in battle. Hezekiah was hailed as a deliverer, and the Lord was given credit for the victory.

Hezekiah, under the influence of the prophet Micah, was a religious reformer who had, on the whole, good relations also with Isaiah. The king did away with a bronze serpent which had been planted as an idol in the Temple and did his best to eliminate idolatry from the "high places" in Judah. It is said that he "held fast to the Lord" and that there was "none like him." before or after, among the kings of Judah.

As he was identified with important religious reforms, so was he associated with other signs of progress and prosperity in his kingdom. He encouraged agricultural and commercial advances, and strengthened the system of defense. Not the least of the improvements initiated by him was the building of "the pool and the conduit" which brought the flow from Gihon Spring into the city and so provided an adequate water supply —very important in case of attack or siege.

HEZRON – *Blooming*.
1. Genesis 46:12; Numbers 26:21; Ruth 4:18f.; I Chronicles 2:5, 9, 18, 21, 24f.; 4:1.

A Son of Pharez and grandson of Judah who was an important link in establishing the line of David.
2. Numbers 26:6; Genesis 46: 9; Exodus 6:14; I Chronicles 5:3.

A son of Reuben who was regarded as the founder of the "family of the Hezronites."

HIEL – *God is Living*.
I Kings 16:34; Joshua 6:26.
When Joshua destroyed Jericho, he laid a curse on the place, decreeing that it should never be rebuilt, except at the cost of the first born son of the man who

might lay new foundations and the youngest son of the man to set up new gates. Hiel, in the days of Ahab, built a new Jericho at the cost of his first and youngest sons. Probably the reference is to an ancient custom of offering human sacrifice on the foundations and the walls of a new city. Hiel is identified only as a citizen "of Bethel."

HILKIAH – *Yahweh is Protection*.
1. II Kings 18:18, 26, 37; Isaiah 22:20; 36:3, 22.
The father of Eliakim. The son, Eliakim, was head of King Hezekiah's household. The king of Assyria sent a commission to warn Hezekiah of his poor judgment in relying on an alliance with Egypt, or for that matter on the Lord God. The commission, headed by Rabsaris and Rabshakeh, and backed by an army, called for the king to come out to hear their words. It was Eliakim who came out and was instructed to carry the hard message to the king.
2. II Kings 22:4, 8, 10, 12, 14; 23:4, 24; I Chronicles 6:13; 9:11; II Chronicles 34:9, 14ff.; Ezra 7:1; Jeremiah 29:3.
The principal character bearing this name was the high priest in

the time of Josiah. Hilkiah was instructed by Josiah to give proper sums to craftsmen for repairs to the Temple. When the king's messenger arrived, Hilkiah told him of the discovery of "the book of the law," which had been found in the course of repairing the Temple. He brought the book, Deuteronomy, to the attention of the king through the king's secretary, Shaphan. When the book had been read, the king heard from Huldah, a prophetess, that it was genuine, and he authorized Hilkiah to begin immediately to institute the reforms the book required. Even a casual reading of II Kings 23:2-27 will show how extensive those reforms were.

3. Jeremiah 1:1.
Hilkiah, a priest of Anathoth, was the father of the prophet Jeremiah.

4. Nehemiah 8:4; 11:11; 12:7, 21.
Hilkiah was a priest who stood beside Ezra for the reading of the law to the people in Jerusalem.

5. I Chronicles 26:11.
A descendant of the legendary Merari, son of Hoash, this Hilkiah was listed as a keeper of the tabernacle gate in the time of David.

HILLEL – *Praised Greatly, He Has Praised.*
Judges 12:13, 15.
A Pirathonite, Hillel's son, Abdon, was a judge in Israel for eight years.

HIRAM – *Most Noble.*
II Samuel 5:11; I Kings 5:1ff.; 9:11ff.; II Chronicles 2:11ff.
Hiram was a king of Tyre who was a friend of David and Solomon. He gave David materials and loaned him craftsmen for the building of his palace; and he made an alliance with Solomon. An insight into the character and manners of the kings of the time is provided in the story of the exchange of gifts and courtesies between Hiram and Solomon. The latter presented Hiram with twenty cities in Galilee (I Chronicles says *Hiram* presented the cities to *Solomon*); whereupon Hiram, not to be outdone, sent Solomon sixscore talents of gold, a prodigious sum. Hiram cooperated with Solomon in commercial ventures at sea. It is probable that the gifts of cities and gold were in fact payments for services.

Another Hiram, also fromTyre but whose mother was a woman of Naphtali, was an artisan sent by King Hiram to supervise preparation of the furnishings for Solomon's Temple. His name might well have been Huramabi rather than Hiram. See I KINGS 7:13ff.

HITTITES – In the Old Testament the name is equated with Heth, whose sons the Hittites were said to be. *Terrible?*
Genesis 23:10; 25:9f.; 26:34; Judges 1:26; 3:5.

The Hittites were a non-Semitic people whom the patriarchs met in Canaan, and who were met again as the Israelites forced their way into Canaan after the deliverance from Egypt. Abraham bought the famous cave at Macpelah from Ephron the Hittite; Esau married two Hittite women, Judith and Basemath; it was from Uriah the Hittite that David took Bathsheba, the mother of Solomon. In the days of Moses the Hittites defeated an army of Rameses II, but failed to follow up the victory. Some think that the Egyptians learned the use of iron-tipped weapons, chariots, and laminated bows from their experiences with the Hittites, who were also known in later times as expert breeders of horses.

The Hittites produced two ascendant kingdoms: the first c. 1900-1650 B.C., in the time of the patriarchs; the second, c. 1500-1200 B.C. It was the Hittites who destroyed the Babylonian kingdom of Hammurabi —c. 1550 B.C.—and whose capital, Carchemish, was in turn taken by Sargon II in the eighth century B.C. After that calamity the Hittites ceased to be an active power in the affairs of the world.

HOBAB – *Beloved.*
Numbers 10:29; Judges 4:11.

There is considerable confusion between Hobab and Jethro; and when Reuel is mentioned in connection with either of these names, the confusion is in no way diminished. Hobab might be the son of Reuel; Jethro might be the son of Reuel. Hobab-Jethro might be the father-in-law or the brother-in-law of Moses. Hobab and Jethro are called the father-in-law of Moses.

At any rate Hobab was invited by Moses to go with the Israelites into Canaan. He had helped Moses lead the people thus far, and Moses referred to him as having served "as eyes for us." Hobab knew the country and acted as guide. He declined the invitation, saying that he would return to his own land, to Midian. Notice, however, that Judges 4:11 suggests that

Hobab was a Kenite rather than a Midianite. See JETHRO.

HOPHNI – *Strong.*

I Samuel 1:3; 2:34; 4:4, 11, 17. One of the sons of Eli the priest of Shiloh: the other son was Phinehas. Hophni and Phinehas were also priests who served the sanctuary in the old age of Eli, and who because of their arrogance and selfishness were appointed, in Eli's vision, to die on the same day and be replaced by a "faithful priest." They were called to take the ark of God to the camp of Israel in the hope that the sacred box might bring Israel, very hard pressed, victory over the Philistines. As the ark arrived, the Philistines put on a great surge of power, defeated Israel, took the ark and killed Hophni and Phinehas. News of the capture of the ark caused Eli to fall "over backward from his seat" and break his neck. Thus Eli the faithful priest and his two sons, blasphemous priests, according to one strand woven into the story, died on the same day. See PHINEHAS, ELI, ICHABOD.

HOSEA – *Yahweh is Help, Salvation.*

The Book of Hosea.

A prophet native to the northern Kingdom of Israel, Hosea was born in a time of trouble for his people. He spoke prophetically toward the end of the reign of Jeroboam II (c. 786-746 B.C.) and his successors whose reigns were very short. King Jeroboam in his early days had strengthened his kingdom, but now it had begun to crumble. Hosea, and Amos shortly before him, pointed to apostasy as the cause of unhealth in the kingdom. As faithlessness is disastrous to a home, so is apostasy the seed of ruin to a kingdom. Hosea used his raw experiences with Gomer, his "wife of harlotry," to illustrate the condition of the kingdom and the results of that condition. But, he said, as he could not allow Gomer to leave his house for love of her, so did God love his people; and after pointing out the rottenness in Israel "who has forgotten his maker," Hosea warned the nations that God will yet "heal their faithfulness" and "be as the dew to Israel."

Hosea presented a remarkable teaching of the willingness, the eagerness, of God to forgive his wayward people. Few books have made so lasting and deep an impression on the minds of later thinkers. Significant is the fact that the Book of Hosea is quoted more than thirty times in the New Testament.

HOSHEA – *Jahweh is Help.*
1. Numbers 13:8; Deuteronomy 32:44.

Hoshea, or Oshea, was the original name of Joshua the son of Nun.
2. II Kings 15:30; 17:1ff.

The last of the kings of Israel whose unsavory reign came to an end (c. 732-724 B.C.) when Shalmaneser IV, king of Assyria, laid siege to Samaria for three years and starved the city into submission. Since many of the Israelites were deported, it is presumed that Hoshea was taken captive. His reign began with his assassination of Pekah and ended with the loss of a kingdom.

HULDAH – *Weasel.*
II Kings 22:14; II Chronicles 34:22.

Huldah was the wife of Shallum the keeper of the wardrobes for King Josiah; but she was better known as a prophetess. It was Huldah to whom Josiah turned for guidance when Hilkiah the priest produced from the Temple a book purporting to be the Book of the Law. Huldah told the king it was genuine, and he authorized the reforms made necessary by the new book.

HUR – *Noble.*
1. Exodus 17:10, 12; 24:14.

During the Exodus when Israel was in battle with the Amalekites, the battle went Israel's way as long as Moses held his hands up with his staff aloft. Aaron and Hur stood by to assist Moses when his arms became tired. This Hur helped also with oversight of the people while Moses was on Mount Sinai; and he might have been the husband of Miriam, Moses' sister.
2. I Kings 4:8.

Hur was an officer of Solomon's household. Here he is called "Ben-hur," the son of Hur.
3. Exodus 31:2; 35:30; 38:22.

Hur was a son of Caleb, the son of Hezron.
4. Numbers 31:8; Joshua 13:21.

Hur was one of the five kings killed with Balaam, kings who had tried to pay Balaam to pronounce a curse on Israel.

There are several others, but they need not be listed.

HUSHAI – *Quick.*
II Samuel 15:32; 16:16ff.; 17:5-15; I Kings 4:16; I Chronicles 27:33.

Hushai was an Archite, the friend of David, who helped in "defeating" the counsel of Ahithophel to Absalom to attack David immediately after driving him out of Jerusalem. Hushai wanted to go with the king as he fled the city, but David persuaded him to go back and infiltrate Absalom's company of rebels, pretending to be a traitor to the king. Hushai accomplished his mission, and it was his success in doing so that led to Absalom's defeat; for had Absalom attacked David immediately, following up his advantage, he almost certainly would have taken the throne from his father.

HYMENAEUS – *Nuptial*, a title of Bacchus.
I Timothy 1:20; II Timothy 2:17.
Hymenaeus was one who, by "rejecting conscience" had made "shipwreck" of his faith. St. Paul, in writing to Timothy, "delivered" Hymenaeus and Alexander to "Satan that they may learn not to blaspheme." It is possible that these two were moving toward Gnosticism.

I

ICHABOD – *No Glory, Inglorious.*

I Samuel 4:17-22.

Ichabod was the son of Phinehas and was born just after receipt of the news of his father's death. He was named "No Glory" to commemorate the loss of the ark of God to the Philistines. Phinehas had been captured with the ark, along with his brother Hophni, and had been killed by the enemy.

IDDO – *Festal, Favorite, Opportune, Honorable.*

Of the seven men bearing this name we shall list only two.

1. II Chronicles 9:29; 12:15; 13:22.

Iddo was a "seer" in whose visions the Chronicler said the reader would find the acts of Jeroboam, Solomon, Rehoboam and Abijah. Nothing more is said about his visions and prophecies, but the references suggest that they were readily available in written form to the Chronicler's readers.

2. Ezra 5:1; 6:14; Zechariah 1:1, 7.

Iddo was an ancestor of Zechariah the prophet, reputed in these references to be his father.

IRA – *Watcher.*

1. II Samuel 20:26.

Ira was a priest in David's reign who must have been counted among his most able advisers, for he is listed in company with Zadok, Abiathar, Joab, and Benaiah.

2. II Samuel 23:38; I Chronicles 11:28; 27:9.
An Ithrite member of David's guard of thirty captains.
3. II Samuel 23:26; I Chronicles 11:40.
Another member of David's guard, a Tekoite.

IRIJAH – *Yahweh Sees.*
Jeremiah 37:13f.
At the approach of an Egyptian army to Jerusalem, the army of the Chaldeans withdrew. As they did so Jeremiah left the city to go to the "land of Benjamin to receive his portion there among the people." At the Benjamin gate a sentry named Irijah blocked his way and accused the prophet of deserting to the Chaldeans. Jeremiah's protests availed him nothing and Irijah took him before the princes who beat him and put him in prison.

ISAAC – *Laughter, One Laughs.*
Genesis 17:19, 21; 21:3-22:13; 24:1-28:13; 31:18; 32:9; 35:12-29; 46:1; 48:15f.; 49:31; 50:24; Exodus 2:24; 3:15f.; 4:5; St. Matthew 8:11; 22:32 (e.g.); Romans 9:7; Galatians 4:28; Hebrews 11:9-20.
Isaac, the son of promise, born to Abraham and Sarah "out of due season." The stories about him suggest that he was all a son could be. Without murmur or protest he obeyed when his father seemed about to offer him in sacrifice.

Without protest, too, he accepted Rebekah as his wife, although—according to the priestly editor of Genesis—he had to wait for her until he was forty years old.

After the birth of Jacob and Esau, a famine drove Isaac and his family to Gerar where, under the protection of Abimelech he became very wealthy and the envy of the Philistines. That envy and fear of his growing strength prompted another move to Beersheba, where he settled and grew even stronger.

The story of Jacob and Esau is a familiar one. It does reveal the unusual fact that Isaac was engaged in both agriculture and grazing. Jacob's "appropriation" of Esau's birthright, with the help of Rebekah, created a schism between the descendants of Isaac which was healed only when the two brothers were brought together briefly by their father's death.

Isaac was buried, so the story states, in the Cave of Machpelah at Hebron. See ABRAHAM, ISAAC, ESAU, ISRAEL.

ISAIAH – *Yahweh is Helper,*
Yahweh is Salvation.
Isaiah 1-39; II Kings 19:2-
20:19; II Chronicles 26:22;
32:20, 32.
In the minds of most Bible students Isaiah was the greatest of
the prophets. His work is dated
approximately 742-700 B.C., during the reigns of Uzziah (Azariah), Jotham, Ahaz (Jehoahaz),
and Hezekiah.

Isaiah was the son of Amoz,
probably a man of considerable
stature in Judah, for the prophet
seemed at ease in his association
with nobility and kings. At any
rate, he spent most of his life in
Jerusalem, was often consulted
by the royalty on matters of
state, and seemed to have the
right of free access to the kings.
His use of symbolic language in
his prophecies is a characteristic
he shares with all the prophets,
and he was forced by the circumstances of his times to speak
in much the same vein as all the
others. Like Hosea, he named
his children symbolically. Although he warned that Tiglath-
Pileser would bring the judgment of God on the people of
Israel, he yet spoke of a "remnant" which would return and
re-build, "when the Lord shall
have washed away the filth of
the daughters of Zion."

Although like the other
prophets, Isaiah was distinctive
in asserting more than any other
the universality of the power
and purpose of God. Further,
he affirmed in a remarkable way
for his times the holiness of the
Lord and his character as
uniquely and idealistically ethi-
cal. Distinctive also was his doctrine of the "remnant"; and his
teaching about the coming of
"Immanuel," "God is with us,"
as the Messiah, left an indelible
mark on the future of Israel.

Since the early days of the
Christian era, many of the words
and passages in the Book of Isaiah have seemed to apply more
to God's great gift in Christ than
to the situations to which the
writer or writers directed their
remarks.

It must be observed, also, that
many of the passages most loved
by readers in our times were not
produced by the prophet Isaiah himself. Most readers know
that the Book of Isaiah does not
represent one man or one period
of time. Chapters 1-39 comprise
a collection of prophecies belonging to the time of the
prophet; but just how many of
them are precisely from Isaiah it
is not possible to determine.
Chapters 36-39, for example, are
the equivalent of II Kings 18-20.

Chapter 6 contains the prophet's glorious account of his call and the germ of Isaiah's entire message to his people. Many passages in chapters 1-39 are not from the prophet himself, although it is in these pages that his message is given.

Chapters 40-55, containing many of the most beautiful and memorable passages, belong to the "Deutero-Isaiah," or "Second Isaiah." They come to us from a writer of the period of Cyrus the Persian, c. 540-522 B.C., and are directed to the strengthening of the captives in Babylon. Herein appears the note that God will deliver his people and make them "a light to the Gentiles," carriers of the truth that there is only *one* God who through Israel will reveal himself to all nations. One writer refers to the Second Isaiah as a "rhapsody," a "spiritual epic," produced by a poet and a theologian "rather than a prophet," whose purpose was to encourage through song and imagination, through passion and enthusiasm.

Chapters 56-66 seem to be post-exilic and form still a third or "Trito Isaiah," produced perhaps about 450 B.C.

The reader is referred to an adequate commentary for a full discussion of the problems in the Book of Isaiah, and to the work itself, for enjoyment of some of the finest passages in Holy Scripture. Every Bible student should know well the book which has exercised a "unique influence" on Judaism and Christianity alike.

ISH-BOSHETH – *Man of Shame.*

II Samuel 2:8; 3:1-20; 4:4ff. In I Chronicles 8 Ish-bosheth is called Eshbaal, the "man of Baal," or Ishbaal. Probably this was the original and correct name of the fourth son of Saul, and was changed by later writers who could not tolerate the name "baal" in a son of Saul and who, therefore, changed it to "bosheth," meaning "the shameful thing."

After the death of Saul, Ish-bosheth, supported by Abner, his father's great general, opposed David for a period of some seven years. As leader of the Israelites his headquarters were in Mahanaim. Had he managed to keep the loyalty of Abner, he might have held out longer in spite of increasing pressure brought to bear on him by David. His fall was hastened by a quarrel with Abner over one of Saul's concubines, and by the need of the tribes to unite for protection against the Philistines. With Abner's defection, Ish-bosheth's forces would not remain loyal to him. Two of Saul's former captains, of the tribe of Benjamin, slipped into the house of Ish-bosheth and beheaded him. They took his head to David and were hanged for their trouble. The head of Ish-bosheth was buried in Abner's tomb.

"Then all the tribes of Israel came to David at Hebron . . . and they anointed David king over Israel." With Ish-bosheth's death the rule of the house of Saul in Israel was finished.

ISHMAEL – *May God Hear, God is Hearing.*
1. Genesis 16:11-17:20; 25:9ff.; 28:9; 36:3; I Chronicles 1:28f.

The son of Abraham by Hagar, who with his mother was driven into the wilderness after the birth of Isaac, the son of God's promise. His hand thereafter was against the hand of every man. He is regarded as founder of a small tribe which wandered over poor lands, constantly fighting for a place in the sun. He was called "an expert with a bow." The only contact between him and Isaac was at the burial of their father Abraham.

2. II Kings 25:23, 25; Jeremiah 40:8ff.; 41:1-18.

This Ishmael was a member of the royal family of David; he objected to the appointment by Nebuchadnezzar of Gedeliah as governor of Judah. He and ten men attacked and killed Gedeliah, and the Jews and Chaldeans with him.

Ishmael and his sympathizers then fled to Egypt.

Four other men named Ishmael need not be presented here. See ABRAHAM, HAGAR, SARAH.

ISRAEL, JACOB – Israel, *God Persists, Perseveres; He Who Strives with God;* Jacob, From a word meaning "heel," *Closely Following, Supplanter.* Genesis 25:26-34; 27:6-35:29; 37:1ff.; 42:1-50:25; etc.

Israel and Jacob were one and the same. References to both Jacob and Israel are too numerous to be listed in full, and the reader is referred to a concordance for greater detail. *Young's Concordance,* for example, gives nearly seven pages of references for Israel, nearly a full page for Jacob. The difference in number of references indicates the importance of Israel as the patronymic for the people of the Hebrews who were better known as the "people of Israel."

Jacob, the son of Isaac and Rebekah and twin brother of Esau, in apparent contrast to Esau, was a "quiet man," a "tent dweller." Esau was especially beloved of Isaac, and Jacob was the favorite of Rebekah. Esau was "first-born" of the twins, but Jacob "had taken hold of his heel" as he was born. The text intimates that the delivery was not an easy one for Rebekah and that the boys were marked from birth as vastly different.

Esau, coming famished from the field, asked his brother for "some of that red pottage" and was given it—in exchange for his birthright. Jacob was clever as well as quiet; for not only did he take his brother's birthright, but with Rebekah's help he took Esau's blessing from the aged and almost blind Isaac, as well, by allowing himself to be passed off as Esau while hiding under skins to be "hairy" to the touch, as was Esau.

Esau had not expected final loss of his right of birth, and he vowed to kill Jacob once he realized the nature of his loss. Again Rebekah intervened with the result that Isaac's mistake in blessing Jacob was made to stand, and Jacob was hustled off to Haran, as Rebekah put it, to

find a proper wife. Actually he was sent away to escape the wrath of Esau.

On the way to Haran Jacob lay down to sleep, using a stone for a pillow. As he slept he dreamed of the since famous "Jacob's ladder," and heard the voice of the Lord grant him the land on which he lay, together with divine protection. On arising at daylight, he used the stone pillow as a pillar to mark the awesome spot and named the place Bethel—the "house of God."

In Haran, shepherds of his uncle Laban took Jacob to their master's house where first he met Rachel (whom he loved at once), then to Laban. After a month Laban offered Jacob wages for his work and Jacob asked for Rachel. Here began a contest of wits between two of the finest rascals in history. Laban promised Rachel, but after seven years gave Leah— the elder and less attractive daughter. Jacob, discovering the trick too late, worked another seven years for Rachel, although she was given to him within the week. After fourteen years with Laban, and an attempt to gain his release from Laban's service by persuasion, Jacob took his wives, seven sons and a daughter, half or more of Laban's flocks, and began to make his way toward Canaan. Laban, of course, followed with the idea of forcing Jacob back to his own "house." At a meeting between them each accused the other of cheating, and rightly. Since neither could find further advantage from the other, the two men agreed to stay each on his own side of an agreed landmark, which was duly placed and dedicated. The text admits that Jacob had outdone his uncle, and that Rachel had stolen her father's "household gods," which in fact guaranteed to Jacob, by right of possession, title to all he had taken from Laban.

Jacob also made an uneasy truce with Esau, though not an especially honorable one; and after a sordid and bloody adventure at Shechem (see Hamor), he moved on, slowly, to Bethel. There he was told in a vision that his name henceforth would be not Jacob but Israel. Finally, according to one of the stories, he arrived at Hebron in time to join Esau at the burial of Isaac. After the burial rites Jacob and Esau parted never to meet again.

Another form of the story, a much more dramatic one, states that Jacob's name was changed to Israel after a mysterious wrestling match with an unknown opponent who put his thigh out of joint but could not subdue him. At dawn the stranger asked to be released. Jacob demanded a blessing before the release and received the new name "Israel," because he had "striven with God and with men," and had "prevailed." Some might say he had wrestled with his conscience.

Whatever or whoever the strange opponent, Jacob's status in life was now regarded as secure. No longer a fugitive from Esau or Laban, he and his many sons began to grow into a strong family unit, and, the story suggests, he was wealthy and comfortable until a widespread famine changed the whole course of his latter years.

Rachel died giving birth to Benjamin, the last of Jacob's twelve sons. At this point Jacob's (Israel's) story fades into that of his sons who sold Joseph into Egypt, an event which ultimately led the father and his family into the Egyptian province of Goshen, where they were driven by the famine and drawn by the invitation of Joseph, the son sold into slavery by his brothers.

For all his trickery and cleverness, Jacob, who became Israel, is gladly acknowledged by later writers as the true founder of the people who bore his latter name. See ISAAC, ESAU, JOSEPH, RACHEL, LABAN.

J

JABAL, JUBAL – Jabal – *Moving;* Jubal – *Playing, Nomad.* Genesis 4:20f.

Jabal and Jubal were sons of Lamech by Adah. Jabal was legendary father of "those who dwell in tents and have cattle," of the nomadic people; Jubal was said to be father of "all those who play the lyre and pipe," of musicians. It is likely from one of the suggested meanings of his name that he, too, was a "tent-dweller."

JABIN – *Intelligent, Discerning.* Joshua 11:1; Judges 4:2ff.; Psalm 83:9.

Jabin was the name of two kings of "Hazor." The first, the story of whom is in Joshua, sent out a call to the tribes to make an alliance against the Hebrews. He was defeated by Joshua "at the waters of Merom."

The second was that king in Canaan whose general, Sisera, was defeated by Barak. See DEBORAH, BARAK, JAEL, SISERA.

JACOB

See ISRAEL

JAEL – *Chamois* (a wild goat). Judges 4:17ff.; 5:24-27.

The wife of Heber the Kenite who killed the Canaanite commander, Sisera, after he had escaped death in battle with the armies of Barak and Deborah. Jael invited the exhausted Sisera into her tent, fed him with milk and lulled him to sleep. While he was sleeping—according to one form of the story—she drove a tent pin through his head.

Hailed by the Israelites in the Song of Deborah as an act of courage, Jael's disposition of Sisera was certainly treacherous: not only had she invited him into her tent, but between the Kenites and the Canaanites there was a state of peace. In theory Sisera should have been safe in the tent of Heber the Kenite.

JAIR – *Yahweh Enlightens.*
1. Numbers 32:41; Deuteronomy 3:14; I Kings 4:13; I Chronicles 2:22; Joshua 13:30.

There is some confusion about the stated ancestry of Jair. Probably he was descended from Manasseh. He was the conqueror of several cities, "tent villages," in Bashan which he called Havvoth-jair. There is also uncertainty as to the location of the Havvoth-jair.

2. Judges 10:3, 5.

This Jair is possibly the same as the one listed above. He was a "judge" in Israel for twenty-two years. He had "thirty sons who rode on thirty asses; and they had thirty cities, called Havvoth-jair to this day, which are in the land of Gilead."

3. Esther 2:5.

The father of Mordecai, the Jew, the cousin and protector of Esther.

JAIRUS – *Yahweh Will Enlighten.*

St. Mark 5:22; St. Luke 8:41ff. Jairus was a ruler of the synagogue whose twelve year old daughter Jesus healed. People in Jairus' house said she was dead; but Jesus said, "She is not dead but sleeping." At Jesus' command she responded—to the amazement of her parents.

JAMBRES – *Opposer.*

II Timothy 3:8.

A magician in Pharaoh's court who, with a companion named Jannes, was said to have opposed Moses before Pharaoh.

JAMES – The Greek form of the name *Jacob; Supplanter, Follower.*

Although there is debate on the matter, the New Testament refers to five men named James. Three will be considered.

1. St. Matthew 4:21; 10:2; 17:1; St. Mark 1:19, 29; 3:17; 5:37; 9:2; 10:35, 41; 13:3; 14:33.

James the son of Zebedee, brother of John. Zebedee was a fisherman of Galilee and his wife, Salome, was probably a sister of Mary the mother of Jesus. James and John would then be cousins of Jesus. The Zebedees were fishing partners of Simon and Andrew. They were called from their nets to become followers of Jesus.

James and John, energetic and zealous in their work, high spirited and probably hot-tempered too, were known as "Boanerges," as "sons of thunder." The Zebedees asked the Lord for high position in his kingdom. This displeased the rest of the disciples and elicited from Jesus something of his knowledge of the suffering in store for him. James, with Peter and John, was present at the Transfiguration as one of the "inner circle of three" disciples.

This James was martyred under the violent hands of Herod the king.

2. St. Matthew 10:3; St. Mark 3:18; St. Luke 6:15; Acts 1:13.

James the son of Alphaeus, called "the Little" or "the Less," perhaps because he was small in stature or because he was young, was another disciple of Jesus. It is said that his mother was "the other Mary" who was at the Crucifixion and who later, with Mary Magdalene and Sa-

lome, took spices to the sepulchre to anoint the Lord. He was in the upper room after the Ascension with those who "devoted themselves to prayer," and was counted one of the Twelve. This James had a brother, Joses, also mentioned in the New Testament.

3. St. Matthew 13:55; St. Mark 6:3; Acts 12:17; I Corinthians 15:7; Galatians 1:19; 2:9, 12; James 1:1.

James was called the brother of the Lord. St. Matthew's Gospel mentions James and Joses and Simon as "His brethren," as does St. Mark; and St. Paul speaks of "James, the Lord's brother."

Some argue that "James the Lord's brother" and "James the son of Alphaeus" are one and the same person. This argument which has a strong position in the tradition of the Western Church, seems to have had its origin in Jerome's writings, in which he states that as St. Paul refers to James as an Apostle he must have had reference to James of Alphaeus, since James of Zebedee was dead. Jerome in later writings, however, did not press the point. Against this point of view is the fact that "James, the brother" is carefully distinguished from the Twelve in John 2:12, Matthew 12:47-50, Acts 1:14.

The James who was called "brother" was not at first a follower of Jesus; probably with others of the family he thought Jesus mad. Nevertheless, he is known as one to whom the Risen Lord made a special appearance (which probably effected his conversion), and quickly he became head of the Church in Jerusalem, although he was *not* one of the Twelve. If, as some believe, he was the writer of the Epistle of St. James, he shows remarkable understanding of the Lord's teaching and its relation to the law.

JARED – *Descending, Descendant.*

Genesis 5:15f., 18ff.

Jared was a descendant of Seth and the father of Enoch. As such he appears in the Lukan genealogy of Jesus. St. Luke 3:37.

JASON – *Healing* (in Greek Mythology the hero of the *Argo* and the *Golden Fleece*).

Acts 17:5-9; Romans 16:21.

It was from the house of Jason in Thessalonika that he himself and several others of the "brethren" were dragged before the city authorities and accused of being associates of Paul and Silas (for whom the excited mob was really searching), men "who have turned the world upside down," and who "are acting against the decrees of Caesar." The city fathers put Jason and the "brethren" under bond and let them go.

JEHOAHAZ

See AHAZ.

JEHOASH

See JOASH.

JEHOIACHIN – *Yahweh Appoints.*

II Kings 24:6-17; 25:27; II Chronicles 36:8ff.; Jeremiah 52:31; Ezra 1:2.

An eighteen year old king of Judah, son of Jehoiakim, whose reign (c. 598 B.C.) lasted only three months. At eighteen he was the father of seven sons. Nebuchadnezzar carried him off captive to Babylon where he lived thirty years. In spite of the defeat and disgrace of captivity, Jehoiachin was well regarded—perhaps because of his youth—and he became a sort of popular king in exile. His uncle, Zedekiah, was left as governor in charge at Jerusalem.

JEHOIADA – *Yahweh Knows.*
1. II Samuel 8:18; 20:23;
23:20, 22; I Kings 1:8, 26,
32, 38, 44; 2:25ff.; 4:4; I
Chronicles 11:22, 24.
Jehoiada was the father of
Benaiah, one of David's great
generals. The Chronicler states
that his home was in Kabzeel,
and that he was himself a "valiant man."
2. II Kings 11:4, 9, 15, 17;
12:2, 7, 9; II Chronicles
22:11; 23:1-24:25.
The high priest at Jerusalem
who helped save Joash from his
murderous grandmother, Athaliah, and who later set in motion
the program to make him king.
It was Jehoiada, also, who gave
the order for the assassination
of Athaliah after Joash had been
crowned. He then became ad-
viser to Joash.
3. Jeremiah 29:26.
A priest in Jerusalem before the
exile, who by an oracle of Jeremiah was replaced by Zephaniah, another priest.
Three others named Jehoiada
are Bible characters, but more
minor even than these.

JEHOIAKIM (ELIAKIM) –
Yahweh Sets Up.
II Kings 23:34-24:7, 19; I
Chronicles 3:15f.; II Chroni-
cles 36:4-8; Jeremiah 1:3;

22:18, 24; 24:1; 25:1; 26:1,
21ff.; 27:1, 20, etc; Daniel
1:1f.
A king of Judah of the puppet
variety who, in reverting to the
religious practices prior to the
reforms of Josiah, made himself
the butt of Jeremiah's prophecies. He paid tribute to Egypt
and contributed forced labor
crews in addition to money payments. Jeremiah told Baruch,
his secretary, to read in public
his prophecies in protest of the
king's policies. The king had
the writings of Jeremiah burned
and began to persecute the
prophets, killing one and forcing Jeremiah to take flight.
Then came the Babylonians
who were worse masters than
the Egyptians. Jehoiakim led a
revolt which finally brought up
a Persian army of regulars to in-
vade the country. Jehoiakim
died (c. 598 B.C.) just before
the army arrived, and was succeeded by his son Jehoiachin.
So much a vassal of Egypt
was Jehoiakim that when
Pharaoh-Necho changed his
name from Eliakim to Jehoiakim, the latter name was the one
preserved for posterity.

JEHONADAB – *Yahweh is Lib-
eral, Bounteous.*
II Kings 10:15, 23.

When Jehu (c. 842-815 B.C.) killed King Jehoram of Israel and Ahaziah of Judah, and himself became king of Israel, he needed to secure his place on the throne by getting rid of every possible association with the house of Ahab. Having killed the sons of Ahab, Jehu was riding in his famous chariot and met Jehonadab, a Rechabite, whom he took into the chariot and made his assistant in religious reform. Jehu was not much interested in religion, as was Jehonadab, but he used the Rechabite to gather up all the priests of Baal left over from Ahab's days and had them killed by his guard. He "demolished the house of Baal, and made it a latrine to this day."

JEHORAM, JORAM – *Yahweh is Exalted.*
These are coincident kings of Israel and Judah. Joram is a shortened form of Jehoram, and the two spellings are used interchangeably.
   1. II Kings 3:1, 6; 9:24; II Chronicles 22:5ff.
The son of Ahab, Jehoram was king of Israel after his unfortunate brother, Ahaziah, who fell through the lattice of his upper chamber. Jehoram persuaded Jehosaphat of Judah to join him

in putting down a Moabite rebellion. Elisha, with some reluctance, prophesied a victory for the coalition of Israel, Judah, and Edom, out of "regard for the king of Judah." After the victory in the field, the combined armies pursued Moab into their cities and besieged them. The king of Moab sacrificed his own son as a burnt offering upon the wall of the city, hoping thereby to receive divine help. Israel, disgusted and angry, retired without full victory.

Later Jehoram was wounded in a battle against Syria and retired to Jezreel to recuperate. In Jehoram's absence Jehu allowed himself to be anointed—at the suggestion of Elisha—and pretending to visit the wounded king he shot Jehoram "at the property of Naboth" which Ahab had taken years before. In Jehoram the house of Ahab came to an end; for as Ahaziah, king of Judah, was shot down at the same time at Jehu's command, and Jezebel, Jehoram's mother, was thrown to the dogs, the old prophecy of Elijah was fulfilled. Jehoram reigned in Israel c. 849-842 B.C.
   2. I Kings 22:50; II Kings 1:17; 8:16, 25, 29; 12:18; II Chronicles 21:1-20.
Jehoram of Judah (c. 849-842

B.C.) was the son of Jehoshaphat. When he found himself established on the throne he killed all his brothers to be sure of keeping himself there. He was married to Athaliah, daughter of Ahab and Jezebel, and was said to have walked in the ways of Ahab, encouraging the worship of Baal. In his time Edom revolted successfully, and the Philistines and Arabians captured his wives and sons, except Ahaziah. When he contracted an incurable bowel disease and died in "great agony," there was no one in the city of David to regret his death.

JEHOSHAPHAT – *Yahweh is Judge.*
   1. I Kings 15:24; 22:4-51;
      II Chronicles 17:1-12;
      18:1-31; 19:1-8; 20:1-37;
      21:1f., 12; 22:9.

The son of Asa and king of Judah whose reign coincided in part with those of Omri, Ahab, and Jehoram of Israel (c. 873-849 B.C.). He was king, in effect, during the last five years of his father's life, for Asa "in his old age . . . was diseased in his feet" and turned over to his son much of the responsibility of the kingdom.

Under Jehoshaphat Judah and Israel became allies against the Syrians and the Moabites. His son Jehoram was married to Athaliah, daughter of Ahab, in the hope that the alliance might be a strong and permanent one.

In his time the Edomites gave trouble which led to Edomite independence in the reign of Jehoram. Yet he was respected by the smaller nations, many of which sent him presents. He worked at the defenses of the kingdom and enjoyed a certain prosperity. He organized an expedition of ships to be sent to Ophir, probably for gold (Ahaziah of Israel was eager to be a part of this), but the ships were wrecked at Ezion-geber before they could accomplish the king's purpose.

Jehoshaphat tried to "do what was right in the sight of the Lord." The remnant of a cult of male prostitutes was exterminated, and an attempt was made to effect other religious improvements. He sent priests and Levites to the cities of Judah to teach the law, and he made some worthwhile changes in the judicial system. The Chronicler suggests that he organized the Sanhedrin! He was "a good king"; but the prophet Jehu accused him of helping the wicked and of hating those who love the Lord.

2. II Samuel 8:16; 20:24;
I Kings 4:3; I Chronicles
18:15.
". . . Jehoshaphat the son of
Ahilud was recorder" in the administrative and judicial system of David.

3. II Kings 9:2, 14.
Jehoshaphat was the father of
Jehu, the "usurper," who became king of Israel by the
anointing of Elijah and by killing Joram.

4. I Kings 4:17.
One of Solomon's "twelve officers over all Israel, who provided food for the king and his
household . . ."

5. I Chronicles 15:24.
A priest who was appointed,
with others, to "blow the trumpets" when the ark was brought
from Obed-edom to Jerusalem.

JEHU – *Yahweh is He.*
1. I Kings 16:1, 7, 12;
II Chronicles 19:2; 20:34.
A seer or prophet, the son of
Hanani, who pronounced the
wrath of the Lord on Baasha,
king of Israel and who criticised
the attitudes of Jehoshaphat,
king of Judah.

2. I Kings 19:16f.; II Kings
9:2-10:36; 12:1; 13:1;
14:8; 15:12; II Chronicles
22:7f.; 25:17; Hosea 1:4.

A commander in the army of
Jehoram (Joram) of Israel who
murdered his master and Ahaziah, king of Judah, as well, and
took the throne of Israel for
himself. The book of II Kings
states that one of Elisha's young
prophets started the whole thing
by obeying the great prophet's
command to "anoint" Jehu and
give him, as upstart king, the "er-
rand of destroying Jehoram and
Jezebel and all seventy of Ahab's
sons," and so to bring an end to
the house of Ahab, in accord
with the prophecy of Elijah.
Jehu is thus presented as God's
agent.

Once anointed, Jehu let it be
known in Ramoth-Gilead; he
heard the trumpets and the
proclamation, "Jehu is King!"
Then he "sealed" the city so that
news could not get to king Jehoram at Jezreel, and then he
"mounted his chariot" to go to
Jezreel where Jehoram, recovering from battle wounds was re-
ceiving a visit from Ahaziah,
king of Judah. The two kings,
in the tower at Jezreel, were told
of Jehu's approach and sent out
messengers to identify him.
When the messengers, obeying
Jehu, did not return, the tower
watchman reported that the oncoming chariot was manned by
someone "driving like Jehu the

son of Nimshi; for he drives furiously."

Hearing this, Jehoram and Ahaziah, "each in his chariot," went to meet Jehu, asking, "Is it peace, Jehu?" The answer, referring to the "harlotries and sorceries of Jezebel," was enough to make Jehoram turn and flee. Jehu had him shot as he fled. When Ahaziah tried to escape, Jehu said, "Shoot him also." Thus both kings died with two bowshots.

Jehu then went to Jezreel, now in full control. Here, as Jezebel taunted him from an upper window, he asked, "Who is on *my* side? Who?" The result was that Jezebel was thrown from the window and trampled by the horses.

Jehu "the son of Nimshi" was king, reigning c. 842-815 B.C. But his reign was not at all a success, for though things went well for Israel under him at first, soon allies began to fall away; and his own ruthlessness in killing off all of Ahab's kin and all the priests and worshippers of Baal made the people suspicious and afraid. Moreover, while he destroyed the followers of Baal, he kept the golden calves set up by Jeroboam at Bethel and Dan. He appears to have used the alleged prophecy of Elijah for his own purposes, and "in those days the Lord began to cut Israel short." Hazael of Syria was a veritable thorn in his flesh. See JEHORAM.

3. I Chronicles 12:3.

Jehu was a Benjamite from Anathoth who joined David's outlaw forces at Ziklag.

JEHUDI – *A Jew.*

Jeremiah 36:14, 21, 23.

Jehudi was an officer of King Jehoiakim of Judah who was sent by the princes to ask Baruch, Jeremiah's secretary, to read for them the prophet's writings of warning and doom. When the king heard of the content of the scroll, he sent Jehudi for it and had him read it. As Jehudi read "three or four columns" the king "would cut them off . . . and throw them into the fire," in a gesture of contempt. See BARUCH.

JEPHTHAH – *God Opens, the Opposer.*

Judges 11:1-12:7; I Samuel 12:11; Hebrews 11:32.

A mighty warrior, son of Gilead (a man important enough to give his name to the area in which he lived), whose childhood was tragic because he was a harlot's son, and whose greatest victory was also a tragedy because it cost the life of his only daughter.

As an outcast, Jephthah gathered a powerful band of ruffians and became a noted raider. When the Ammonites troubled Israel, the "elders of Gilead" begged Jephthah to lead their armies. He reminded them that they had made him an outcast and warned that if he led them, he would be their head both during the fighting and afterwards. An agreement was made and Jephthah took over as leader.

Warrior that he was, he yet tried to reason with the Ammonites, asking why they fought Israel so fiercely. The answer was given that Israel had taken lands from Ammon as the people came out of Egypt. Jephthah tried still to reason with the king of Ammon, saying Israel had asked for free passage through the lands and being denied it, took the lands out of necessity—with the help of the Lord, who, in fact, simply dispossessed Ammon.

When finally he went to war against Ammon, Jephthah vowed that if the Lord would give victory then "whoever comes forth from the doors of my house to meet me . . . shall be the Lord's." The first one out,

coming "with timbrels and dances," was his daughter. He "rent his clothes"—but he kept his vow. He offered his lovely daughter for a burnt offering.

It is well to notice how seriously ancient and primitive peoples regarded a promise to the Lord. Yet, and strangely, this is the only case recorded of a human burnt offering made by the Hebrews to their God, Yahweh. Hebrews offered such sacrifices to other Gods, but the story of Abraham's willingness to offer Isaac, and the Lord's refusal to have him offered, was a powerful influence in the religious life of Israel.

JEREMIAH – *Whom Yahweh has Appointed.*

The Book of Jeremiah; II Chronicles 35:25; 36:12, 21f.; Ezra 1:1; Daniel 9:2; St. Matthew 2:17; 16:14; 27:9.

From the words of this great prophet, gloomy and dour for the most part, has come the phrase, "to utter a Jeremiad," to speak in a tone of lament and complaint. He saw clearly the decline of his people, and he understood well that their downfall came as much as the result of interior decay as from the superiority of the invader. He spoke his mind, using his own personal situation again and again to illustrate his meaning; and in so doing he gained the reputation of being a chronic pessimist with perhaps a taint of treason about him.

Born at Anathoth near Jerusalem, he was a man of some means. From his garden he was able to look out on the city. As one from a priestly family he was keenly aware of the fact that in Jerusalem one could see every sort of religious practice, and he was disturbed in seeing a false attitude prevalent toward even the poorest varieties of pagan worship. Men put their faith in external things, in outward observances, rather than in inner meanings. Worship, of whatever god, might be punctilious, but it was empty. People offered sacrifice in due form and felt that in having done so they had performed all their religious duty. The people, he saw, had forsaken Yahweh and had "hewed out for themselves broken cisterns that can hold no water." They were wont to cry, "The temple of the Lord! The temple of the Lord! The temple of the Lord!"—and to put their trust in the Temple itself rather than the Lord. "Deceptive words are these," cried Jeremiah; but the people did not hear.

Jeremiah resisted the call to prophecy strenuously. To the call he responded, "Ah, Lord God! Behold, I do not know how to speak, for I am only a youth." He did not want to say, as instructed, "I see a pot boiling, facing away from the North"; nor did he want to be "an iron pillar, and bronze walls against the whole land." The Lord's promise of personal deliverance from the irate people to whom he must say these things was small comfort to him; for it hurt to tell his own people that the Assyrians, then the Egyptians, then the Chaldeans would overrun the land.

Jeremiah's prophecies were delivered over a long period (he lived c. 640-587 B.C.), covering part of the reigns of Josiah, Jehoiakim, and Zedekiah. He saw the promise of genuine religious reform under Josiah stop with mere externals and Josiah's demise in battle with the Egyptian. He saw Jehoahaz, the son and successor, carried away in bonds to Egypt, and Jehoiakim made king of Judah by Pharaoh Necho—for a price. He saw Jehoiakim become vassal also of Babylon and his utter rout, after a short rebellion, by successive bands of Chaldeans, Syrians, Moabites, and Ammonites. Jehoiachin, on the throne three months, gave himself up to Babylon, and Nebuchadnezzar laid seige to Jerusalem, took the city after two years and burned it thoroughly. Only "some of the poorest of the land" were left there as vine-dressers and plowers.

During all this Jeremiah lamented, because while other prophets told the people, "You shall not see the sword, nor shall you have famine," he, Jeremiah, was called to say that the prophets and "the people to whom they prophesy shall be cast out in the streets of Jerusalem, victims of famine and sword, with none to bury them." In saying such things Jeremiah was hated by friends and neighbors so that he cried out, "Woe is me, my mother, that you bore me, a man of strife and contention . . . I have not lent, nor have I borrowed, yet all of them curse me." He was ordered beaten by Pashur the priest and put in stocks as a public spectacle, but he was not silenced. Not even the threat of death or imprisonment was effective in preventing the utterance of his oracles, once he was resigned to his unpleasant task. He made good use of his secretary Baruch, both as a writer and a public reader of the things he had to say.

When disaster fell at last on Jerusalem in c. 587 B.C., the prophet was carried away captive with the others of rank and position. By Jehoiakim and Zedekiah he had been regarded as a possible traitor, but Nebuchadnezzar treated him with kindness. In Babylon he tried to encourage the people with words of comfort. It seems that he was allowed to go freely to Mizpah, the seat of the governor, Gedaliah, appointed by the Chaldeans. After Gedaliah's assassination Jeremiah and Baruch fled to Egypt, where again he spoke the word of the Lord to the Jews who had taken on the religious practices of the Egyptians. Probably he died there.

This great prophet should be remembered, not for his complaints, laments, personal sufferings, and difficult words; but rather for the clarity of his judgment; for the constant appeal he made to the people to turn from their errors and become again God's own; for his clear teaching that inward health is not produced by outward conformity alone; for the striking symbolic terms in which he stated what he had to say. Perhaps the most memorable verse in the book is found at 31:33, "This is the covenant which I will make with the house of Israel after those days, says the Lord; I will put my law within them, and I will write it upon their hearts . . ." Thus Jeremiah is, after all, a prophet of hope. See BARUCH, JEHOIAKIM, JOSIAH, GEDALIAH, ZEDEKIAH.

JEROBOAM – *The People Increase,* thus, *Enlarger, Increaser of the People.*
Two kings, both of the Northern Kingdom of Israel, were named Jeroboam.
1. I Kings 11:26-40; 12:3, 12-20, 25-14:20; II Chronicles 9:29; 10:2-13:20.

Jeroboam I, son of Nebat, was a "servant of Solomon," very able and industrious. Solomon, seeing these qualities in him, put him in charge of the forced labor crews at work on the repair of the city walls. In a meeting with the prophet Ahijah outside Jerusalem, Jeroboam was given the idea that ten of the twelve tribes would follow him in a revolt against Solomon, and that because of Solomon's apostasy such a revolt would be supported by Yahweh. Solomon, hearing of the conspiracy against him, tried to have Jeroboam killed, but he took refuge in

Egypt until the king's death.

When Rehoboam succeeded Solomon, Jeroboam returned from Egypt and, as a representative of a large group of the northern tribes, asked the king for a lightening of "the hard service of your father." Rehoboam stupidly accepted the counsel of his own group of irresponsible hot-heads instead of the wise advice of the old men and answered: "I will add to your yoke. My father chastized you with whips, but I will chastize you with scorpions." Jeroboam's group then "departed to their tents" in rebellion against the heavy hand of the king, and established the Kingdom of Israel with "Shechem in the hill country of Ephraim" as headquarters.

Jeroboam wanted a complete break with Jerusalem, and he therefore reverted to the old northern tribal religious practices, which involved bull worship. He set up calves of gold at Bethel and Dan as a means of breaking the custom of the people of going to Jerusalem for worship. He appointed priests to serve at these shrines and at other "high places," and thereby broke the line of the Levitical priesthood. The enmity between Israel and Judah, always lurking beneath the surface, had now begun openly, started by a "man of the people" who wanted to be loyal—but not at any cost. The situation was made all the more difficult by the creation of religious differences which were still a matter of contention in our Lord's time.

Jeroboam I ruled for twenty-two years, c. 922-901 B.C.

2. II Kings 13:13; 14:16; 14:23-15:1; I Chronicles 5:17; Hosea 1:1; Amos 1:1; 7:9-11. Jeroboam II was a strong king of Israel (c. 786-746 B.C.) who gave good military leadership under which territory formerly lost to Syria was recovered. His was a time of material prosperity and relative security from attack and invasion by either Syrians or Assyrians.

His reign was marked, however, by the spiritual weaknesses which so often plague a prosperous people. Amos said that the people "sold the needy for a pair of shoes," that they were irreverent in "the house of their God." Hosea said that in the land there was "no faithfulness or kindness, and no knowledge of God," but "swearing, lying, killing, stealing, and committing adultery." Isaiah observed that the "prophet who teaches lies" had led the people astray, and warned that the Syrians and the Philistines would "devour Israel." The prosperity in Jeroboam II's time was not a sound one, and the people had not really profited from it.

JERUBBABEL – *Contender with Baal.*
See GIDEON.

JESSE – *Yahweh Exists.*
Ruth 4:17, 22; I Samuel 16:1-22; 17:12-18, 58; Isaiah 11:1, 10; St. Matthew 1:5f., etc.

Although Jesse was the father of eight sons, only David, the youngest, lingers in the mind. Of his sons three were in Saul's army when—according to one of the two accounts of his appearance—David took provisions for them and killed Goliath. Both stories of the discovery of David suggest that Jesse's sons were splendid specimens of manhood, so much so that without divine guidance and counsel Samuel would not have been able to make a choice from among them. The stories speak of Jesse as a man of some wealth and stature among his fellows. Perhaps it is appropriate, even so, to say that his greatest assets were invested in his sons, for his name is forever revered because of David's rise to fame as king of a united Israel. And more, Jesse is renowned because the ancestry of Jesus was traced through David to him as "the stem."

JESUS (JOSHUA) – *Yahweh Saves, Yahweh is Saviour, Saviour.*
A book of this sort is not the place to write of Jesus who is called the Christ, the Anointed One, the Lord. Let it be said of him here only that by Jews he is regarded as a great prophet; that by Christians he is known as the difference between the Old and the New Testaments; that by the latter, indeed, he is understood as the fulfillment of the promises of God to the Israelites.

Many excellent books are available for the study of the life of Jesus. Suggested first, of course, are the four Gospels, which, while not biographies, give the essential facts forming the basis for all other studies of Jesus. W. R. Bowie's *The Master* is helpful. For local color *The Nazarene*, by Sholem Asch, is very good. *The Story of Jesus*, by Theodore P. Ferris, and *Jesus in His Homeland*, by Sherman E. Johnson, and *The Life and Ministry of Jesus*, by Vincent Taylor, are quite worth reading, as is

Jesus of Nazareth, by Bornkamm. Other titles are listed in the bibliography.

JETHRO (REUEL, HOBAB) – Jethro, *Abundance, Excellence;* Reuel, *God is Friend;* Hobab, *Beloved, Circumciser?* Exodus 2:18ff.; 3:1; 4:18-20; 18:1ff.; Judges 4:11; Numbers 10:29-32.
These three names are used to identify the father-in-law of Moses in the several strands of the Pentateuch, although Hobab is also called Moses' brother-in-law in one of the sources. The names Reuel and Jethro seem to point to the same person in the Moses stories. The name Raguel is also used, however, in Numbers 2:14, apparently referring to Jethro-Reuel.

Using either or any of the three or four names, the person meant was a priest of Midian who was friend, father-in-law, and counselor of Moses. It is also thought that Jethro was a Kenite.

When Moses fled from Egypt he went into the "land of Midian," somewhere in the vicinity of Mount Sinai, or Horeb. There he met and gave courteous assistance to the daughters of Jethro, an interesting though far from clear figure in the development of Moses' character and, indeed, of Israel's religion. Moses married Zipporah, one of Jethro's seven daughters, and lived as his son and chief herdsman for a number of years.

It was as he cared for Jethro's flocks that Moses encountered the "burning bush," and it was with Jethro's blessing that he returned to Egypt in response to his "vision" of Yahweh. After the deliverance from Egypt, it was to Mount Sinai and to the country of Jethro that Moses led the people.

News of the deliverance preceded Moses and when they arrived in the area of Midian, Jethro—with Zipporah and Moses' two sons who had returned to Jethro—went to the camp and led in a sacrifice of thanksgiving for the deliverance. It appears that Jethro was here not only priest but instructor-priest to the Israelites. Thus scholars ask: What influence did Jethro have on Moses' religious beliefs and practices? Was it from him that Moses learned the Name, Yahweh, and the principles of worship? Was the God whom Jethro worshipped the God also of Abraham, Isaac and Jacob?

After the sacrifice, Jethro watched Moses as he sat in the judge's seat, trying to deal with the myriad problems brought to him by the people. He called Moses aside and advised him to "choose able men" to judge the people in "small matters," leaving only the hard cases for his own consideration. This wise counsel Moses accepted, and he set up a system of judicial administration which served Israel well.

Jethro observed the fruits of his suggestions and, refusing Moses' earnest invitation to remain, "went his way into his own country." See MOSES, ZIPPORAH.

JEZEBEL – *Un-exalted, Un-husbanded?* Probably *Baal Exalts.*
I Kings 16:31f.; 18:4, 13, 19; 19:1-8; 21; II Kings 9:7, 10, 22, 30ff.

The infamous and determined wife of Ahab, king of Israel, mortal enemy of Elijah the Tishbite, unyielding exponent of the worship of Astarte and the Baal of Tyre, Jezebel became the symbol of all that was considered evil in pagan worship as it plagued the spiritual leaders of the people of Israel. She seemed in her own way, however, to have been a good wife to Ahab; for she tried to be loyal to him and to please him.

As a bride she brought with her to Samaria a religious tradition to which she was unalterably committed, together with a battery of priests to support it. The more she was told to abandon her gods of Tyre, the more determined she became to be loyal to them and to spread their influence in her new home. Ahab was preoccupied and indifferent to the whole matter, which he regarded as a nuisance; and Jezebel was thus free to do as she pleased. Her personal charm and beauty—buttressed by intelligence, shrewdness, and courage—made her a formidable and almost invincible opponent for Elijah.

Jezebel's influence was not much checked even after the slaughter of the prophets and priests of Baal at Mount Carmel. When she heard the news of Elijah's victory, she dared to send him a threat which drove him into the wilderness. She said: "As surely as you are Elijah and I am Jezebel, so may God requite me and worse, if I do not make your life as the life of one of them by tomorrow about this time." Her position was strengthened by the marriage of her daughter into the royal house of Judah, as well as by Ahab's hearty dislike of Elijah.

Two great stories are built around Jezebel. First is the contest between Elijah and the prophets of Baal, referred to above; the other is the story of Naboth's vineyard which Jezebel acquired for her husband by treachery. Learning of Ahab's desire for the property which Naboth would not sell, she arranged to have Naboth accused of having "cursed God and the king." Naboth was stoned to death and Ahab took the vineyard by confiscation.

No doubt the righteous in Israel had great satisfaction in the story of Jezebel's death; for she was thrown out the window of her palace to be trampled by the horses of the "usurper" Jehu, and left for the hungry dogs to mangle—thus bringing to reality the terrible prophecy of Elijah about her death. See AHAB, ELIJAH, JEHU.

JOAB – *Yahweh is Father* (My Father).
I Samuel 26:6; II Samuel 2:13ff.; 3:22-34; 8:16; 10:7ff.; 11:1, 6f., 11-25; 12:26f.; 14:1ff.; 18:2-19:13; 20:23; 23:18, 24; 24:4, 9; I Kings 1:7, 19, 41; 2:5, 28, 35.
One of David's mighty men and a brilliant field general who, in the early years of David's career,

was loyal almost to a fault, but who at the end of the reign turned to Adonijah, the rightful heir, instead of to Solomon as David's successor.

Joab led the armies of David against Ish-bosheth and Abner to put David securely on the throne. He arranged for the murder of Abner because he saw him as a threat to David, as well as for personal vengeance. When age and administrative duty kept the king from personal leadership in battle, Joab was in charge and readily gave David credit for his victories. In the intrigues of Absalom Joab was loyal to the king; although in killing Absalom when he found him caught in a tree, he disobeyed the king. In the revolt of Adonijah Joab took part because he thought, and rightly, that Adonijah had the right of succession over Solomon. Joab apparently became disgusted with David's lack of capacity for administration, with his vacillating policies and his hesitation in naming his successor. When Solomon came to power he immediately put Joab on the list of those to be "liquidated," and ruthlessly had him struck down as he clung to the horns of the altar, a place of refuge. Joab died there as bravely as he had

lived. Of David's "three mighty men," Joab stood in first place. See DAVID, ABISHAI, ASASHEL, ABNER, ABSALOM.

JOANNA – Feminine of John: *Yahweh is Gracious.*
  1. St. Luke 8:3; 24:10.
Joanna was the wife of Chuza, Herod's steward, listed with Mary Magdalene as one of the "women who had been healed of evil spirits" and who "provided for" Jesus and the twelve "out of their means." Joanna was also with the two Marys at the Sepulchre on the morning of the Resurrection.
  2. St. Luke 3:27.
Here the name is spelled Joanan and refers to a man, the son of Rhesa, in the ancestry of Jesus.

JOASH – *Yahweh Supports, Yahweh has Given.*
Eight men named Joash may be found in the Old Testament. We shall list only six.
  1. I Chronicles 27:28.
Joash—no father's name is given —was appointed over the "stores of oil" in David's administration, according to the chronicler.
  2. Judges 6:11-31; 7:14; 8:13-32.
The father of Gideon (Jerubbabel). He was a worshipper of Baal; but when his son pulled

down the altar of Baal and "the Asherah that is beside it," Joash did not complain as expected. Instead, to Gideon's surprise, his father took his part against the angry men of the town, saying in effect that Baal would have to contend for himself, "because his altar has been pulled down." Thus encouraged by his father and the word of the Lord delivered by an angelic messenger, Gideon went on a rampage against the Midianites.

3. I Kings 22:26; II Chronicles 18:25.

A son of Ahab about whom little is known except that Ahab instructed him to keep the prophet Micaiah in prison because he prophesied the king's death in battle at Ramoth-gilead.

4. II Kings 11:2; 12:19f.; 13:1, 10; 14:1, 3, 17, 23; I Chronicles 3:11; II Chronicles 22:11; 24-25.

This Joash, also called Jehoash, was son of Ahaziah, king of Judah. Ahaziah was shot by Jehu the "usurper" to the throne of Israel; and his mother, Athaliah, destroyed all the royal family except Joash who, a small child, was hidden by his aunt in the temple for six years. When Joash was seven, Jehoiada the priest arranged to have the palace guard put the young king on the throne and do away with his murderous grandmother. Joash reigned for forty years (c. 839-800 B.C.). He ordered the repair of the Temple and, after twenty-three years of mismanagement by the priests, he finally saw his objective accomplished.

When Hazael, king of Syria, threatened Jerusalem, Joash bought him off with the treasures of the Temple.

He was assassinated by his own "servants."

5. II Kings 13:9-14:27; II Chronicles 25; Hosea 1:1; Amos 1:1.

Joash was a grandson of Jehu, son of Jehoahaz. He reigned as king in Israel for sixteen years (c. 801-786 B.C.). He fought against Amaziah, king of Judah; he fought also against Hazael of Syria, recovering from Syria cities taken by Hazael in the reign of his father.

As Elisha was ill on his deathbed, Joash wept before him, crying "My father, my father! The chariots of Israel and its horsemen!" Elisha bade him take a bow to shoot an arrow "eastward" in the direction of Syria, as a sign of victory; then he told Joash to strike the ground with arrows. Joash struck three times and when he stopped Elisha cried angrily, "You should have struck five or six times," indicating the number of victories he might have won over Syria, a complete triumph, instead of recapturing only a few cities. Joash failed to follow through on his victories.

In battle against Amaziah of Judah Joash was more successful, for he captured Amaziah, broke down the walls of Jerusalem and carried to Samaria the treasures of the Temple and of the king's house.

6. I Chronicles 12:3.

In David's outlaw days at Ziklag a group of Benjamites, bowmen and slingers, kinsmen of Saul, joined the outlaw band. One of them was Joash, son of Shemaah, who could shoot or sling stones with either hand.

JOB – *Hated, Persecuted, Afflicted, Object of Enmity?*
Meaning Unknown.
The Book of Job; Ezekiel 14:14, 20; St. James 5:11.

Was there such a person as Job, the man who was made to suffer so much for no apparent reason? Or is he only a literary or legendary character? Except for the Book of Job, which has many of the elements of a dramatic poem dealing with a bewildering human problem, the only other references to Job are two verses in Ezekiel and one in James which refer to him as a righteous and patient man who stood firm under affliction. Scholars are of the opinion that he is a legendary figure from the dim past whom the writer of the poem used to make a point about the righteousness and justice of God and the problem of human suffering.

The Book of Job is opened with an ancient folk story about a righteous man whose incredible sufferings were borne with unyielding devotion to God in spite of many temptations to "curse God and die." So "blameless and upright" was he that he offered sacrifice not only for himself but for his sons and daughters who might have "sinned and cursed God in their hearts" without being aware of it. In all this he prospered, and in his times it was thought that so righteous a man as he should prosper; for it was granted that God favors the righteous and strikes down the sinner.

But to Job "there was a day" when all his good life turned sour and he was beset by every sort of calamity. He patiently endured loss of properties, of sons and daughters. Satan, at the root of all this, observed that he did not "sin or charge God with wrong." Then Satan suggested,

"Skin for skin . . . touch his bone and his flesh . . ." In Satan's power, Job became so vile with sores that he "scraped himself" with a potsherd and "sat among the ashes." Still he did not "sin with his lips."

His condition now, however, was such as to make friends and neighbors think that God had repudiated him. Therefore, they thought, he *must have sinned;* for does not God bless the righteous with all that had been taken away from Job? Even Job, protesting innocence, thought he must have sinned in some, hidden, grievous way of which he was not aware; but he stoutly maintained that he had not done anything to account for this visitation from God. Three friends came to visit and to "comfort" him in his misery. For seven days they sat with him, "and no one spoke a word . . ."

It is here that the poem begins. Job, the first to speak, "cursed the day he was born," asking "Why . . . why . . . why?" Eliphaz the Temanite, very cautiously and politely, raised the question: "Who that was innocent ever perished? Or where were the upright cut off?" "Can mortal man be righteous before God? can a man be pure before his maker?" Then, slyly

it seems, he intimated that Job had been caught in his own "craftiness," saying that "the schemes of the wily are brought to a quick end." Job's response was to wish for a quick end to his miseries, to recount some of his good deeds, to ask, "If I sin, what do I do to thee, thou watcher of men," and to say, "Teach me . . . make me understand how I have erred." He assumes that there must have been some transgression, some iniquity which, if he could understand, he would confess; but as it was, all he could do was to ask to be "cut off."

Then Bildad the Shuhite entered the dialogue. He was not so gentle in his remarks. Said he: "If you are pure and upright, surely then he will rouse himself for you and reward you." "God," he said, "will not reject a blameless man, nor take the hand of evil doers." He intimated that only a word of proper penitence from Job would be sufficient to put all things right again. Job only insisted the more emphatically that he was innocent. "I am blameless; I am innocent," he declared; and he mused as to how he, only a man, could argue with the almighty God. Should he try to do so, the only result possible was that his own mouth would condemn him. "There is no umpire" between God and man who can lay his hand on both and issue a judgment. God is in control. But Job felt that he could ask of God, "Why?" For "Thou knowest that I am not guilty, and there is none to deliver out of thy hand." Here Job stated that it would be better that he had not been born at all than for him now to be in his present condition for no reason but that God chooses to "hunt me like a lion." He asked only that God would "let me alone, that I may find a little comfort before I go whence I shall not return, to the land of gloom and darkness."

At this point Zophar the Naamathite stated very bluntly that in his opinion God had been "manifold in his understanding," for he had "exacted" of Job, as he said, "less than your guilt deserves."

Thus all of Job's friends, seeing his condition, were certain of his guilt and equally sure that God was punishing him in accord with his deserts, though they could not detect his sins. Job was adjudged guilty if for no other reason than that he had cried out so in defiant questioning of God's treatment of him. All the speeches of the friends contained the wisdom of the times and expressed the attitude of the wise men toward sin, righteousness, and the divine judgment.

The attitude is directly expressed in Zophar's words. "If you will set your heart aright . . . if iniquity is in your hand, put it far away, and let not wickedness dwell in your tents. Surely then you will lift up your face without blemish; you will be secure . . . you will forget your misery . . . and your life will be brighter than the noonday . . ."

Job was irritated and weary of all this sort of talk. He was quite aware of such notions as these. "I have understanding as well as you; I am not inferior to you," he said. "What you know I know also." He was tired of hearing all the platitudes, and said to his friends, "Will you speak falsely for God?" The force of the question was that in Job's mind all ancient sayings about these deep matters are merely nonsense. Then he put a disquieting question to the friends: "Will it be well with you when he searches you out?" Then Job gives his answer to their observations. "Your maxims are proverbs of ashes, your defences are defences of clay."

In a second round of speeches the friends berated Job even more severely, and Job was led on to speak of his innocence in its several and manifold particulars. Rejecting the wisdom of the times he began to ask that God himself would stand forth and answer the question, "Why do the wicked live, reach old age, and grow mighty in power?" And why is the wicked man "spared in the day of calamity" and "rescued in the day of wrath?" *This*, said Job, not the other, is the truth—and you know it! In view of this, which you can see for yourself anywhere you look, "There is nothing left of your answers but falsehood." The answer of Eliphaz to this was little more than a reiteration of what had been said before; namely, "He delivers the innocent man; you will be delivered through the cleanness of your hands."

Job then began to say that if only he could find God, if only there were "times of judgment kept by the Almighty," he would appear before God and present his arguments before him with assurance, not only of a hearing, but of vindication. He began to be reminded of the old days "when the friendship of God was in my tent," and of the good

deeds he had done, the good reputation he had enjoyed. Of these things he would speak if only God would disclose himself and grant a hearing. Yet, as he spoke of these things, becoming more and more a man "justified in his own eyes," the reader can detect little by little a change in Job's attitude, a diminishing assurance about both his good arguments and the meaning of his righteousness. From the discussions with the friends Job emerged a man still miserable, still proclaiming his innocence, but ready now, as he was not before, to turn his attention from himself and his sad state to God —if only he could find God. At this point Job had become more anxious to hear from, than to declare himself to, "the Almighty."

(Scholars are at one in their judgment that chapter 28 is an insertion and that chapters 31-37, which contain the angry speech of the younger Elihu, are not part of the original poem. We note these facts here and go on, although it might be well to say that scholars are agreed that several of the speeches of Job and his friends are out of place in the present form of the book.)

With the subtle skill of the artist, the author of the poem leads the reader to the moment of high drama, to the moment when, at last, the Lord, God, the Almighty —the principal character in the story—appears, shrouded mysteriously in a whirlwind.

The first words of the Lord were shattering. "Who is this that darkens counsel by words without knowledge?" Then with terrifying clarity Job's wish was granted, his challenge met; for the voice of the Lord demanded of Job, "Gird up thy loins like a man. I will question you, and you shall declare unto me." Then the questions, the unanswerable questions, were poured forth; and Job, bidden to answer, could say only, "I am of small account . . ." The Job who so wanted to declare himself to God discovered that all his words, his cries of lament, his protestations of righteousness and innocence, were in the presence of God irrelevant. But the Lord pursued a matter Job was now quite willing to forget. The Lord asked: "Will you even put me in the wrong? Will you condemn me that you may be justified?" Having poured forth questions about the nature of the universe, the Lord now spoke of man and of his place in it and of the sovereignty of the Lord over all.

In the Lord's words, however, there was no vindication of the arguments of the three friends; rather was there vindication for Job; for although Job's question about the meaning of human suffering was not answered directly, he found himself in the presence of God and in a new relationship with him. Said he: "I had heard of thee by the hearing of the ear, but not my eye sees thee; therefore I despise myself, and repent in dust and ashes."

The poem ended, the writer picked up the folk-tale ending for an epilogue in which, in the new relationship with God, Job was said to have been given "twice as much as he had before," and in which the three friends were rebuked for having spoken falsely of the Lord.

The book of Job deserves careful and thoughtful study. The reader who gives the book the time it deserves will return to it again and again with pleasure.

JOBAB – *Howling.*

1. Genesis 10:29; I Chronicles 1:23.

One of the sons of Joktan, a descendant of Shem, leader of a tribe whose territory "extended from Mesha in the direction of Sephar to the hill country of the east," that is, in Arabia.

2. Genesis 36:33f.; I Chronicles 1:44f.

Jobab was said to be the second king of Edom.

3. Joshua 11:1.

Jobab was a king of Madon who allied himself with Jabin, king of Hazor and others, to form a large army to oppose Joshua "at the waters of Merom." Joshua "came suddenly on them" and "fell upon them," putting all the kings and their people to death.

4. and 5. Two Benjamites listed in I Chronicles 8.

JOCHEBED – *Yahweh is Honour.*

Exodus 6:20; Numbers 26:59.

Jochebed was the daughter of Kohath and the aunt as well as the wife of Amram. She was the mother of Moses and Aaron.

JOEL – *Jahweh is God.*

The Book of Joel; Joel 1:1; Acts 2:16.

Fourteen men named Joel may be found in the Old Testament, but we shall be concerned only with Joel the son of Pethuel who wrote the second of the books of the Minor Prophets.

Little is known about Joel. References to the Temple suggest that he lived in Jerusalem, and a number of factors lead modern scholars to feel that his work could not have been written before c. 400-350 B.C.

The small book begins with a vivid description of a plague of locusts followed by a drought.

"What the cutting locust left,
    the swarming locust has eaten.
What the swarming locust left,
    the hopping locust has eaten,
and what the hopping locust left,
    the destroying locust has
        eaten . . .
The fields are laid waste,
    the ground mourns . . ."

The prophet envisions a nation "powerful and without number" coming against the land; and he calls for the gathering of a solemn assembly of the people in the house of the Lord to "cry to the Lord." That which is to come upon the land is the terrible "Day of the Lord." "Who can endure it?"

But the prophet hears the Lord say: "Return to me with all your heart . . . return to the Lord your God . . ." Perhaps he will himself turn and leave a blessing behind him. When the people cry, "Spare thy people, O Lord," the Lord will answer in pity and the land will be restored. Moreover, there will be outpourings of his spirit on all flesh; and with signs in the heavens and the earth before the final Day of the Lord, the nations which have spitefully treated the Lord's people will be gathered in a great "valley of decision." There the voice of the Lord will roar from Zion, and the nations will see that the Lord is a refuge, a "stronghold" for his people Israel. Thus the book ends with tranquility and peace after locusts, drought, darkness, and terror for Israel.

Verses 2:12-13 and 2:28 have been often quoted by Christians. They are:

". . . rend your hearts and not your garments. Return to the Lord, your God, for he is gracious and merciful, slow to anger, and abounding in steadfast love, and repents of evil."

"And it shall come to pass afterward, that I will pour out my spirit on all flesh; your sons and your daughters shall prophesy, your old men shall dream dreams, and your young men shall see visions."

The message is thus relieved by a note of hope. The prophet's language is so sharp and clear, and the book so short, that it should require not more than ten minutes to read. It makes exciting reading.

JOHN – *Yahweh is Gracious.*
1. St. Matthew 3:1, 4, 13f.; 4:12; 9:14; 11:2-18; 14:2-10; 16:14; 17:13; 21:25, 26, 32; St. Mark 1:4, 11, 14; 2:18-22; 6:14-29; 8:25; 11:30-33; St. Luke 1:13ff.; 3:2-20; 5:33; 7:18-35; 9:7-9, 19; 20:4-8; St. John 1:6, 15, 19-42; 5:33-41; 10:40-42; Acts 1:5, 22f.; 10:37; 11:16; 13:24f.; 18:25; 19:3f.

A prophet, often called the last and greatest of the prophets, John "the Baptizer" was a child of promise, a cousin and the "fore-runner" of Jesus of Nazareth.

John was the only son of Zechariah, the priest, and Elizabeth, both of whom were advanced in years and childless until the belated birth. As he performed his usual duties in the Temple, Zechariah was informed by an angel of the coming birth of a son who should be named "John." With the vision he was left dumb until John was born and brought to the Temple to be presented and named. Because he could not speak, he wrote the name "John" to confirm the name given by Elizabeth. In writing the name his "tongue was loosed, and he spoke, blessing God."

In maturity, John became known as a great preacher of repentance and of baptism as a sign of newness of life. He spoke of the coming of God's Holy One who was expected in the near future. Of that One he preached with certainty and enthusiasm, saying that he would be "mightier than I," that he would give a baptism not of water but of the Holy Spirit and of fire. Throngs followed this powerful man who was simply clad in "camels' hair and a leather girdle," who ate locusts and wild honey and who preached forcefully, but as "one crying in the wilderness: Prepare the way of the Lord." From the throngs he gathered a band of loyal supporters, some of whom surely thought of him as "the one to come," or if not, then surely at least Elijah returned as herald for the Messiah and the kingdom. There was enough talk of him as the Messiah to elicit from John a denial.

Jesus appeared before John, was baptized by him in the river Jordan, and was then acknowledged as "the One."

In his preaching John was particularly hard on Herod, who had married his brother's wife. Herod put John in prison, and Herodias, his wife, persuaded her daughter, Salome, to ask John's head as gratuity for an exhibition of dancing.

A story in conflict with that which states that John recognized Jesus as Messiah immediately at the baptism is told in St. Matthew and St. Luke. These accounts state that John, in prison, sent his disciples to Jesus to inquire whether he was the One to come or whether they should look for another. After John's death at least some of his followers became disciples of Jesus. John's movement must have been widespread, for St. Paul found his disciples in Ephesus. Acts (18:24; 19:1) gives testimony to indicate that many of John's disciples were absorbed by the Church.

2. St. Matthew 4:21; 10:2; 17:1; St. Mark 1:19, 29; 3:17; 5:37; 9:2, 38; 10:35, 41; 13:3; 14:33; St. Luke 5:10; 6:14; 8:51; 9:49, 54; 22:8; Acts 1:13; 3:1, 3, 4, 11; 4:13, 19; 12:2; Galatians 2:9.

John the Apostle was the brother of James the son of Zebedee. Their mother, Salome, is said to have been the sister of the Virgin Mary. Like James, he was a fisherman and was asked to leave the nets to become a "fisher of men" in the cause of the Lord. Before he was called to be with Jesus, he had been a disciple of John the Baptist.

As the ministry of the Lord

developed, John, with Peter and James, became one of the "inner core" of the Twelve. John and James were sent on special missions and served well in spite of the title, "Boanerges," or sons of thunder, earned for them by their explosive tempers and heavy-handed ways. They were not above seeking special privileges for themselves in the kingdom and their efforts in that direction did not help in their relations with the rest of the Twelve. Yet the Scriptures leave the clear impression that there was in John a soundness of spirit and a loyalty which drew him into a very close association with his Master. Indeed he was called "the disciple whom he loved," and in tradition has been given the title, "the Beloved Disciple." He was with Jesus at the Transfiguration and in the Garden of Gethsemane. To John the Lord from the Cross committed his mother; he and Peter were first to go to the tomb and John was first to recognize the Risen Lord at the Lake of Tiberias.

John is seen also as a partner in Christ's work of healing after Pentecost. He and Peter were together when the lame man was healed at the Beautiful Gate of the Temple; they appeared before the Sanhedrin and went to Samaria to bestow the Holy Spirit, by the laying on of hands, on those who had been baptized there.

The tradition persists, in spite of much scholarly opinion to the contrary, that John wrote the Fourth Gospel which bears his name, and that he is somehow responsible for all the so-called Johannine literature in the New Testament. Many of the faithful prefer to ignore the writings of the learned scholars and to keep the pious thought that the Beloved Disciple did actually write these books.

The historian Eusebius wrote that John was banished from Ephesus, where tradition says John became patriarchal bishop, and went to Patmos; and that later he returned to Ephesus to consecrate Polycarp as Bishop of Smyrna. Evidence of John's residence in Ephesus is too weighty to be cast lightly aside. He is said to have died quietly in that city, "In his sleep," the only one of the Twelve to die a natural death.

Whether or not the literature bearing his name was produced by him, the influence of that literature on the thinking of the Christian Church is incalculable. From it, and the tradition surrounding it, John has been presented as a kindly man in his later years, one who left for posterity the benefit of a long experience with the Lord, both in the flesh and Risen, and with the Church. Although not a martyr, he is remembered nevertheless as one who gave his life for Christ and his Church. See JAMES, ZEBEDEE, MARK.

JONAH (JONAS, JONA) –
Meaning unknown, but possibly *A Dove*, from word meaning "mourn," the mournful note of the dove.
The Book of Jonah; II Kings 14:25; St. Matthew 12:39ff.; 16:4; St. Luke 11:29f.; St. John 1:42; 21:15.
The prophet Jonah referred to in II Kings lived in the Eighth Century B.C. at Gath-hepher. He is called the son of Amittai, and is said to have foretold the victories of Jeroboam II in restoring to the borders of Israel territories extending "from the entrance of Hamath as far as the Sea of Arabah."

But this prophet was not the author of the Book of Jonah. Rather, the anonymous writer of the book tells a story about Jonah with the purpose of calling Israel again to the task of bringing all the peoples to the salvation God desires for them. As, however, the Jews of this period (c. 400 B.C.) had no desire to see other nations enjoy the blessings they believed God had promised to Israel, or anything even remotely resembling those blessings, Jonah was presented as one who disobeyed the divine command to warn the Ninevites of imminent disaster so that they might repent and be saved. Jonah frankly did not want to see the Ninevites saved; he thought they deserved destruction, not the mercy of "a gracious God . . . slow to anger, and abounding in stedfast love." He therefore took ship from Joppa to Tarshish, "going away from the presence of the Lord," away from Nineveh. A great storm arose and all aboard, except Jonah who was asleep in the hold of the ship, began to pray to their gods. Discovered by the captain, Jonah was interrogated and confessed that since he was fleeing from his God, "Who made the sea and the dry land," the storm was no doubt "because of me." He suggested that he be thrown overboard to save the ship. At first the company hesitated, but after prayer they did throw Jonah into the sea. Then it was that he was "swallowed up" by the "great fish" which kept him for three days and deposited him "upon the dry land."

After this strange series of events in his effort to flee from the word of the Lord, Jonah heard the Lord a second time, saying as at first, "Go to Nineveh." This time he went and said what he had been told to say, but with poor spirit and great reluctance; for even yet he was not convinced that the city really ought to be allowed to repent and so to avoid destruction. Having spoken his warning he sat outside the city to see what would become of it. As he sat God caused a plant to grow up to shade him, then sent a worm to destroy the plant and a "sultry east wind" to plague him. As Jonah complained, the Lord used the plant and the worm—neither of which Jonah could control—to point out to him that as he had pitied the plant in its destruction so did the Lord pity Nineveh. Thus the story about Jonah is intended to convey to Israel the difference between God's love for all people, his great mercy extending to all, and the selfish attitude of the Israelites who would keep God's rich gifts for themselves alone.

JONATHAN – *Whom Yahweh Gave.*
Of the long list of men named Jonathan only four stand out from the crowd.

1. Judges 18:30.
Jonathan the son of Gershom was a priest in the city of Dan where the Danites set up a graven image taken from Micah. See MICAH, DAN.

2. II Samuel 15:27, 36; 7:17, 20; I Kings 1:42f.
Jonathan was the son of Abiathar the priest who was long in the service of David. Abiathar joined the attempt of Adonijah to take the throne. While Adonijah and his guests were assembled for what was to have been a joyous occasion, the sound of trumpets was heard. Jonathan rushed in to give the news, sad news indeed to the group, that Solomon had been named king. Jonathan's news caused the guests of Adonijah to tremble, and they "rose, and each went his own way." See ADONIJAH, JOAB, DAVID, SOLOMON.

3. Jeremiah 37:15, 20; 38:26.
As an army of Chaldeans withdrew from Jerusalem at the approach of an army of Egyptians, Jeremiah intended to go from the city to "the land of Benjamin to receive his portion." He was accused of "deserting to the

Chaldeans." He was beaten and imprisoned in the house of "Jonathan the secretary," which had been made into a prison.

4. I Samuel 13:2ff.; 14:1ff.; 18:1ff.; 19:1-7; 20:1ff.; 23:16, 18; 31:2; II Samuel 1:4f., 22ff.; 4:4; 9:1, 3, 6f.; 21:7, 12ff.

Jonathan, better known as friend of David than as son of Saul, was a splendid warrior, brave and resourceful. As eldest son of Saul he should have been king; but the rising prowess of David overshadowed him and it seemed obvious that he would become king in Jonathan's place. Saul was clearheaded enough to see this. Furthermore, the story of Samuel's anointing of David might have come to Saul's ears and aroused his fears and jealousy. Saul was even more infuriated when he discovered that Jonathan was wholly in sympathy with the idea and satisfied to have David take the throne. Jonathan's friendship with David was an unusually close one, and in frank talk with him about the throne Jonathan asked only that he be made second to David. Modestly, David at this time hesitated to hear himself spoken of as king-to-be, but he agreed to make Jonathan next in power

to himself should he become king. Saul, in anger over the situation, tried to kill David and, in a burst of fury at Jonathan's friendship with David, tried to kill his own son, too.

When Jonathan was victorious over the Philistines, both with an army of a thousand men and a single armour-bearer, he was an inspiration to the Hebrews who, under Philistine oppression, had taken refuge in holes and caves. When they heard of Jonathan's victories, they took courage and began to come out of the hills to join Saul and his son. Jonathan was convicted of eating, though innocently, in violation of Saul's vow that he and his people should fast until he was "avenged on" his enemies, and was automatically condemned to death when his act was determined by lot. But because of his success and popularity he was ransomed by the people. Jonathan was thus well respected, even if not as exciting to the popular eye as the more spectacular David.

When Jonathan was killed in the battle which brought an end to Saul as well, David declared a time of public mourning in which he appeared as chief mourner. His eulogy included

Saul, but spoke tenderly and personally of Jonathan. "How are the mighty fallen," he lamented. Then, "I am distressed for you, my brother Jonathan." The friendship between these two has been idealized and compared to that of Damon and Pythias in the stories of the Greeks. See SAUL, DAVID.

JORAM
See JEHORAM.

JOSEPH – *May He Add, He Shall Add, Increaser.*
Four men named Joseph need attention, although eleven Josephs are named.
1. Genesis 30:24f.; 33:2, 7; 35:24; 37:39-50.

The son of Jacob and Rachel, the last to be born while Jacob was with Laban. As the first son to be born to Rachel whom he loved, Jacob loved Joseph more than his other children. Joseph probably made the most of the situation, and on at least one occasion gave his father a poor report on his brothers' care of the sheep. The brothers hated him, and all the more when Jacob gave him a splendid coat "of many colors" to wear. Joseph's dream in which it seemed that his sheaf stood upright and

those of the brothers bowed down before it, indicating Joseph's pre-eminence, did not make matters better.

Thus, when opportunity came, they intended to kill him; but at Reuben's plea they sold him instead to a band of Ishmaelites (or Midianites) who took him to Egypt as a slave. The brothers took the fine coat, shredded and bloody, to Jacob with the story that Joseph had been killed by beasts.

Joseph became a slave in the household of an official of Pharaoh's army and quickly showed his abilities as an administrator of his master's estates. After an unfortunate experience with his master's wife, who tried to seduce him, Joseph landed in prison. There he met Pharaoh's chief butler and baker, imprisoned for some offense, who learned of Joseph's ability to interpret dreams.

Pharaoh dreamed strangely and there was no interpreter who could tell him the meaning of his dreams. The butler remembered Joseph and suggested that he be called to interpret the Pharaoh's dreams. Joseph's success led him to high position at court, where he had even greater success in preparing for the famine he had seen in the unraveling of Pharaoh's dream.

The famine was so widespread and severe that it caused suffering in Canaan and ultimately it brought Joseph's brothers to Egypt to buy food. When they came, Joseph recognized them and befriended them. His rather strange way of showing friendship seemed to be preparation for the time Joseph chose to reveal himself as the brother sold into slavery. He had his brothers bring the whole family into Egypt where they were settled in the land of Goshen as herdsmen in charge of Pharaoh's cattle.

Joseph is presented by both strands of the story as a man of noble character and great ability. His use of power indicates unusual high-mindedness, and his treatment of the brothers reveals not a trace of bitterness or of vindictiveness.

Joseph's name is used often to describe the combination of the tribes of Ephraim and Manasseh, or the whole of the Northern Kingdom of Israel.

2. St. Matthew 1:16, 18f., 20, 24; 2:13; St. Luke 1:27; 2:4, 16, 33, 43; 3:23; 4:22; St. John 1:45; 6:42.

The Gospels of St. Matthew and St. Luke trace Joseph's ancestry to Jesse, the father of David. The husband of Mary the mother of Jesus was a carpenter and a man of no wealth, but strict in his observance of the law and the customs of his people.

Bethlehem was his probable place of birth, but he moved to Nazareth where he was when espoused to Mary, Daughter of Joachim and Anna, who was "found to be with child."

Joseph was called a "just man" who, not willing to bring shame on Mary and her family, resolved to proceed with the marriage and quietly dispose of her afterward by divorce. A dream made him think he should accept both Mary and the child, whom he was instructed in the dream to name "Jesus."

There is uncertainty about it, but it seems that Joseph took Mary to Bethlehem either "to be taxed" or to avoid gossip. In any case Scripture tells us that Jesus was born in Bethlehem, the city of David, where Joseph and Mary had gone in obedience to "imperial decree" that every man should be taxed in his own city. The town was crowded by people such as they, and the child was born in a stable behind an inn. Here shepherds found them and worshipped the child.

On the eighth day after Jesus' birth Joseph saw that he was circumcised and given the name "above every Name." Later, when the Mother's time of purification was done, Joseph took her and the child to the Temple in Jerusalem, six miles from Bethlehem, to "present him to the Lord" and to offer customary sacrifice, "a pair of turtledoves and two young pigeons." This done, Joseph took his family back to Bethlehem, where the child was visited by "Wise Men from the East," and where Joseph was warned in a dream to flee the wrath of Herod. Obeying the dream, he quickly took Mary and Jesus to Egypt until news of Herod's death gave him freedom to return to Nazareth.

St. Luke's Gospel tells us that it was Joseph's custom every year to go to Jerusalem for the Passover. When Jesus was twelve years old he, too, made the trip and caused the family no little anxiety when he failed to leave the Temple in time for the return to Nazareth. There he was found after three days, perfectly content in the company of the doctors, "both hearing them and asking them questions."

Nothing more is said about Joseph, but tradition tells us that he died when Jesus was eighteen years of age; and that Jesus then became head of the household in Nazareth, as would be expected of a dutiful son, until his own ministry required his presence elsewhere. The question as to whether Mary and Joseph had children of their own is debated. It is sufficient to say here that the Gospels and Acts refer to Jesus' "brethren" and to "his mother and his brethren."

3. St. Matthew 27:57ff.; St. Mark 15:43; St. Luke 23:50.

A rich and "pious" secret disciple of Jesus was Joseph of Arimathea, who was also a "respected member of the council," the Sanhedrin. St. Luke states that he did not consent to the verdict of that body when Jesus was condemned. Some suggest that he was not present at the trial; others that he was present but lacking in courage to oppose the will of the group. St. Luke states simply that he did not consent "to their purpose and deed."

Nevertheless, after the Crucifixion, he had the courage to go to Pilate and request the right to bury the body of Jesus with proper care. A member of the family had that right, according to custom; but Joseph, not a relation, took a risk in approaching the governor to request the body of one crucified for treasonous activity. Joseph is remembered chiefly for the tenderness with which he cared for his Lord's body and for the fact that Jesus was laid in the tomb Joseph had made ready for himself.

The Fourth Gospel states, curiously, that Nicodemus, another disciple in secret, helped Joseph prepare Jesus for burial.

    4. St. Matthew 13:55; 27:56;
      St. Mark 6:3; 15:40, 47.

Joseph was the name of one of the brothers of Jesus, given in the Greek form, "Joses," in the King James Version.

JOSHUA (HOSHEA, JESHUA, JESUS) – *Yahweh is Salvation, Yahweh Saves.*

The Book of Joshua; Exodus 17:9ff.; 24:13; 32; 17; 33:11; Numbers 11:28; 14:6ff.; Deuteromony 1:38; 3:28; 31:3ff.;

Judges 1:1; 2:6ff.; 21, 23; I Kings 16:34.

Moses—leader, lawgiver, deliverer and judge of the People of Israel. Aaron—spokesman, priest. Joshua—mighty man, assistant and successor to Moses, with the duties of general of the straggling tribal armies, of winning a place for Israel in the new lands and of making Israel strong and united enough to hold what could be taken. This is the position which tradition gave to Joshua.

Once out of Egypt, there was a natural tendency for the recently enslaved people to break off into "splinter" groups and to merge with the surrounding peoples, or to be wiped out by them. Moses knew, therefore, the need to appoint a man strong enough and sufficiently respected to be able by force or persuasion to keep the clans in motion toward a common objective. As Moses' experience grew, so said the tradition, he would "recite it in the ears of Joshua," who in later times made such use as he could of Moses' wisdom. In this, however, Joshua was only partially successful.

Joshua—in one version of the story—stood with Caleb when

the returning spies reported to Moses that the land of Canaan could not be taken; but these two insisted that the land was conquerable and worth the effort. They, of all the spies, escaped the plague.

Under his leadership the Amalekites were defeated and the towns of Jericho, Bethel, and Ai were taken. It is well to remember that the Books of Joshua, Judges and, to some extent, Numbers, deal with the same events in different ways and from different points of view. Even without reference to the stories in the late materials in the Book of Joshua, Numbers, Exodus, and Deuteronomy, in which he and the events in which he was involved were idealized and taken out of proper focus, Joshua the son of Nun, minister and successor to Moses, emerges as a man of stature and character.

So does the main stream of the biblical story draw the picture of Joshua; but scholars remind us that the Bible as we have it represents the prevailing Judaean point of view with regard to Israel's history, and that there is another story of Joshua which might be seen from study of incidental references in the Old Testament and from other ancient documents and recent archaeological discoveries.

This story suggests that Joshua was the leader of a northern group of the tribes of the Hebrews active in Palestine about a hundred years before the Exodus of the Joseph tribes and/or Levi from Egypt. It tells of a law given and a covenant established under the leadership of Joshua, of battles fought and victories won at places and times which do not fit into the scheme of things as presented in the Moses story. Thus archaeologists find that Ai was, and had long been, uninhabited at the time of the Exodus; and scholars point out a number of references in the Bible itself which indicate very clearly a grouping of northern tribes which were active well before the Exodus could possibly have taken place, and which seem to have had little contact with the southern grouping of tribes under the leadership of Moses. Not only was there a grouping of northern and southern tribes, but also there was such tension between the groups on religious and political levels alike, that the two groups were never able quite to overcome it, except when in the time of Saul and David they were drawn together by the need to face a common enemy in the Philistines. When that crisis was passed the uneasy alliance was readily dissolved. Meanwhile, however, the influence of the tribe of Judah marked powerfully the literature of the Israelites, with the result that formerly sharp distinctions in tradition were so blended and blurred that it is difficult to show in precise terms just what the story of Joshua, for example, might once have been.

JOSIAH – *Whom Yahweh Supports.*

II Kings 21:24-23:34; II Chronicles 33:25-36:1; Jeremiah 1:2; 22:11-26:1.

Josiah, son of Amon, was only eight when he was made king of Judah. Amon had been killed by a clique within the court, but the people in turn killed the members of the intrigue and put the young Josiah on the throne. His reign was a long one, c. 640-609 B.C.

During his youth certain moneys which should have been used for Temple repairs were misused by the priests, and the old, alien religious practices continued unabated. When he had been king ten years, however, he asked for an accounting of the Temple funds or for direct delivery of the funds to workmen who were supposed to keep the Temple in good repair. He sent his secretary to check on the situation.

Hilkiah the high priest informed the king's secretary that he had "found the book of the law in the house of the Lord." The book was read to the king who "rent his clothes" at the difference between common practice and the demands of the law as revealed in the new book— the Book of Deuteronomy, which might have been very carefully "planted" in the Temple. Convinced that the book was genuine, Josiah gave orders for reforms in accord with its provisions: he had it read publicly, first of all, and renewed the Covenant with the Lord; he deposed the idolatrous priests and closed all the "hinterland" high places with their shrines and altars, thus centralizing all public worship in the Temple at Jerusalem; he had all the vessels of Baal and Asherah burned; he destroyed the houses of religious prostitution and attempted to do away with the whole cult; he "defiled" Topheth, where human sacrifice to Molech was still practiced; he "put away" the mediums and wizards and the "teraphim and all the idols and abominations . . ."

All these reforms, extensive as they were, did not wholly accomplish the purposes of the priests of Yahweh who were Josiah's advisors; but Josiah's importance in the history of the Hebrew people lay in the attempt at religious reform rather than in any other aspect of his reign.

Josiah's counselors of state were not very capable. Taking their advice, the king joined battle with Pharaoh Necho at Megiddo and was killed. Josiah was remembered as a good king, just and well meaning, who was greatly loved. See HILKIAH, HULDAH, PHARAOH NECHO.

JOTHAM – *Yahweh is Upright, Perfect.*

1. Judges 9:5, 7, 21, 57.

Jotham, youngest son of Jerubbabel (or Gideon), was the only one of more than seventy brothers to escape the massacre perpetrated by Abimelech, who, having killed his brothers, declared himself leader, king indeed, of the clan. Jotham escaped by hiding himself well. Later he spoke vehemently against Abimelech, who by now had become robber king of Shechem. When his appeal for justice failed to get a hearing from Abimelech's followers, Jotham put a curse on them and hid himself again. The curse was realized on Abimelech—but only after he had cut a wide path of death and terror amongst surrounding peoples. It was Jotham's story about the trees which selected a bramble, a mere bush, for king that made the title "the bramble King" adhere to Abimelech. See ABIMELECH.

2. II Kings 15:5, 7, 32ff.; II Chronicles 26:21-27:9; Isaiah 1:1; Hosea 1:1; Micah 1:1.

The son of Azariah, leper king of Judah, Jotham appears first as keeper of the king's household, as governor, and finally as king. Only one act of his is recorded —that of rebuilding and decorating the gates of the Temple. Otherwise, he allowed sacrifice and the burning of incense on the high places to continue. If the years of his "regency" under Azariah are included (c. 750-742 B.C.) in his tenure (c. 742-735), he ruled in Judah for some sixteen years. The chronicler thought of him as one of the good kings and stated that he fought and prevailed against the

Ammonites, exacting tribute from them. Just before he died, the invasion of Judah by Syria and Israel began.

JUBAL
See JABAL.

JUDAH – *Praise, May Yahweh be Praised.*
Genesis 29:35; 35:23; 38; 43: 3-44:34; 49:10; Exodus 31:2; St. Matthew 1:2f.; St. Luke 3:33; etc.

The fourth son of Leah, and traditional founder of the tribe of Judah—spelled also "Juda" and "Judas," and in Anglicized form, "Jude." It was he—in one version of his story—who most hated Joseph and suggested, after Reuben's refusal to allow Joseph to be killed, that he be sold into slavery. Ironically, Judah also made the appeal to Joseph, when the brothers were in Egypt at the mercy of their unknown brother. This encounter, as presented by the writer, was intended not only to carry forward the story of Joseph, but also to show friendly relations between the two great divisions within the people of Israel, between the tribes of Judah and Joseph, more often

known as Ephraim. Judah offered himself as hostage instead of Benjamin, because he felt that his aged father could not survive news of the loss of his youngest and favorite son. He had also promised himself as surety for Benjamin when he urged Jacob to allow the boy to be taken to Egypt. In this situation both Joseph and Judah showed themselves to be men of dignity and stature, and—suggested the author—because of the attitude of each toward the other, a new unity within the greater family was made possible.

The tribe of Judah became a dominant one, largely by absorbing Simeon and by adding the Kenites and the Calebites and, eventually, Benjamin, which always stood with Judah. Thus it should be noted that when the kingdom was divided after the death of Solomon, the southern kingdom was known as Judah.

Although Judah was idealized in the Joseph stories by a writer who brought him to the fore, he is scandalously portrayed in Genesis 38 in a story probably circulated among the Edomites who had no love for the tribe of Judah. See JOSEPH, JACOB, BENJAMIN, REUBEN, EPHRAIM, MANASSEH.

JUDAS – Greek form of *Judah*.
St. Matthew 13:55; St. Mark 6:3.
Numbered with James, Joses (Joseph), and Simon as one of the brothers of the Lord; but little is known about him, other than that with his brothers he was skeptical about Jesus as Messiah until the Resurrection. After that event he was in company with the small group at prayer in the upper room when Jesus appeared.

That Judas is author of the Epistle of Jude is much disputed; it is very unlikely that he could have been the writer. See JUDE.

JUDAS ISCARIOT – *Judah, the Man of Kerioth.*
St. Matthew 10:4; 26:14, 47; 27:3ff.; St. Mark 3:19; 14:10, 43; St. Luke 6:16; 22:3, 47f.; St. John 6:71; 12:4; 13:2, 26, 29; 18:ff.; Acts 1:16, 25.
The meaning of the name given above is admittedly uncertain, since the location of the town of Kerioth, or Kiryoth, is unknown. It is even less likely that the designation "Iscariot" which was also applied to Judas' father, Simon, comes from the Latin word, *sicarius*, murderer or "dagger-man," or from Sycharite, the man of Sychar, both of which

meanings have been suggested as possibilities. In any case, Judas (Judah) was one of the Twelve, and became treasurer of the group, and betrayer of his Lord.

Some have thought of him as a weak character who yielded to disappointment and cupidity in selling out the Lord for thirty pieces of silver—the price of an ordinary slave. Others have felt that his act represented complete confidence in Jesus' supernatural power which could be brought into play if and when the time and circumstances were right, and that Judas was zealously, mistakenly, setting the stage for Jesus' triumphant self-delivery and final victory.

After he had made his agreement with the officers of the chief priests, he tried to back down. They refused to break the bargain and Judas, throwing away the money he had received, betrayed Jesus with a kiss.

As Judas saw the outcome of his betrayal he hanged himself; and the pieces of silver he had thrown away were used to buy a burial field for him and others.

JUDE (JUDAS).
The Epistle of St. Jude; St. Luke 6:16; Acts 1:13.

Several entries are needed under this name, and they follow; but we give special attention to the writer of the Epistle.

In the Epistle the writer is described as "Jude, a servant of Jesus Christ and the brother of James." This Jude is thought to be the one referred to in St. Luke 6:16 and Acts 1:13 as "the son of James."

The short Epistle makes an appeal to the "beloved" to "contend for the faith which was once for all delivered to the saints," against "some . . . ungodly persons who pervert the grace of our God into licentiousness and deny our only Master and Lord, Jesus Christ." The author intimates that some unnamed church had been infiltrated by immoral persons, by some who "reject authority and revile the glorious ones," by gamblers and malcontents, loud-mouthed boasters and "worldly people, devoid of the spirit." He reminded his readers that the apostles had predicted that "in the last times there will be scoffers, following their own ungodly passions."

The letter ends with a beautiful doxology which might well be memorized: "Now to him who is able to keep you from falling . . ."

JUDE.
1. St. John 14:22. See THAD-
DEUS.
2. Acts 5:37.
Jude, or Judas, the Galilean mentioned in the speech of caution made by Gamaliel, was said to be one who, having drawn some of the people after him "in the days of the census," perished with his followers. In the mind of Gamaliel his movement was obviously not, therefore, "of God." Gamaliel, thus suggested that a "wait and see" policy be adopted toward the movement associated with Jesus. Perhaps it would perish, as did that of Jude.
3. Acts 9:11.
When Saul arrived in Damascus after his great "vision" and conversion, he stayed in the "house of Judas," where he was found by Ananias.
4. Acts 15:22, 27.
Judas Barsabbas and Silas were chosen to go with Paul and Barnabas to Antioch as apostolic representatives and letter-bearers to the Gentile Church there.

JUDITH – *Jewess.*
1. Genesis 26:34.
A Hittite wife of Esau, beautiful, rich, and virtuous, who together with her husband "made life bit-

ter for Isaac and Rebekah."
Esau had two Hittite wives, of
whom Rebekah said (Genesis
27:46): "I am weary of my life
because of the Hittite women.
If Jacob marries one of the Hittite women such as these . . .
what good will my life be to
me?"

2. The Apocryphal Book of
Judith.

A widow favored by Holofernes,
the Assyrian; she charmed her
way into his tent, lured him into
excessive feasting and wine-
bibbing and cut off his head with
his own scimitar. She became
therefore a heroine, for the Assyrian armies without their leader were scattered from a siege
of the town of Bethulia. Holofernes (also spelled Holopher-
nes) was attacking the city, as
the story goes, because the Jews
had failed to send troops to support King Nebuchadnezzar's attack on the king of Media. He
also wanted the Jews to worship
King Nebuchadnezzar.

JULIA – Feminine of *Julius*.
Romans 16:15.
One of the "saints" in Rome to
whom special greetings were
sent with the letter from Paul to
the Church in Rome.

JULIUS – *Curly Headed*.
Acts 27:1, 3.
The centurion of the "Augustan
Cohort" who was made responsible for the group of prisoners
with which Paul was sent to
Rome. Julius was kind to St.
Paul, allowing him "to go to his
friends and be cared for" as they
made their way along the coast
to the town of Myra in Lycia.
At that place a change of ships
was made and Julius was relieved of his duty toward the
prisoners.

**JUSTUS – *Just, Righteous, the
Just One*.**
1. Acts 1:23.
Joseph Barsabbas, whose surname was Justus, was named
with Matthias as a possible
choice to replace Judas Iscariot
in the number of the Twelve.
When the lot was cast it "fell on
Matthias." See JOSEPH.
2. Acts 18:7.
Titius Justus was a Gentile be-
liever in Corinth to whose home
St. Paul went when the Jews
"opposed and reviled him." The
house of Justus was next door to
the synagogue. Verse 11 of this
chapter states that Paul "stayed
a year and six months" in Corinth possibly in the house of Justus.

3. Colossians 4:11.

"Jesus who is called Justus" was a disciple in Rome whose greetings were included in the letter to the Colossians. This man was referred to as a man "of the circumcision," a Jew, one of the few with the Apostle in Rome.

K

KEDAR – *Powerful.*

Genesis 25:13; Isaiah 21:16f.; Jeremiah 2:10; 49:28; Ezekiel 27:21; Psalm 120:5.

One of the sons of Ishmael, a grandson of Abraham by Hagar, who gave his name to a tribe which claimed territorial rights on an area "from Havilah to Shur . . . opposite Egypt in the direction of Assyria."

KETURAH – *Incense.*

Genesis 25:1-4.

The wife of Abraham after Sarah's death who gave him six sons, none of whom shared in the inheritance kept for Isaac. Abraham gave these sons handsome gifts and sent them away.

KISH – *Wall.*

I Samuel 9:1ff.; 10:2.

Although there are others named Kish, it was Kish the father of Saul who, by that very fact, made the largest contribution of any of them to Israel. It was as Saul was searching for his father's asses that he, as lost as the beasts, was led to the prophet Samuel, from whom he received an anointing as king-to-be. Kish was a man of wealth and prominence in Benjamin, and was spoken of as a thoughtful and kindly father, for Saul felt that after a reasonable time his father would be more concerned about his son than about the loss of the asses the son had been sent to find.

A Kish the son of Ner is by the Chronicler (I Chronicles 8:30; 9:36) called the father of Saul; whereas in I Samuel Kish is named as son of Abiel. The sequence seems to be this: Kish the son of Gibeon and brother of Ner; Ner, brother of Kish, had a son named Kish whom the Chronicler records as Saul's father.

KOHATH – *Assembly.*

Genesis 46:11; Exodus 6:16-18; Numbers 3:17-4:15; 26:57; Joshua 21:4f., 20-26; I Chronicles 6:1ff.; 15:5.

According to the late editors of the Pentateuch and the chronicler, Kohath was a son of Levi who gave his name to the Kohathites, from which family group came Amram, the father of Moses. Kohath was said to be a brother of Gershon and Merari.

The families of the sons of Kohath, in the accounting in Numbers, were to be stationed on the south side of the tabernacle. They were to be in charge of the ark, the table and lampstands, the altar and vessels of the sanctuary, the screen and "all the service pertaining to these." Numbers 1:47-10:10 details the manner in which these duties were to be performed.

Chronicles identified the Kohathites with Hebron and Shechem, and states that among the "sons of Kohath were noted singers." See GERSHON, MERARI.

KORAH – *Baldness.*

1. Genesis 36:5, 14, 18; I Chronicles 1:35.

One of the sons of Esau who also had a son named Korah.

2. Exodus 6:21; Numbers 16; 26:9-11; 27:3.

Korah is represented by one of the priestly editors of the Pentateuch as the leader of a rebellion against Mosaic authority and against the exclusive claims of the "sons of Levi" to the priestly offices. By another of the editors Korah is made to be a Levite protesting against the claims of the "sons of Aaron." By these editors Korah is made the leader, with Dathan and Abiram, of 250 "well known men" chosen from the congregation to rebel against Moses.

An earlier form of the story probably concerns Dathan and Abiram only, leaders of a group protesting against Moses' failure to produce the promised land, and against his heavy-handed authority.

The mixed story, however, links Korah, Dathan, and Abiram in protest and in refusal to comply with Moses' summons to appear before him. Moses separated them from the congregation and they were swallowed up by the earth which split open to receive them and all their households. The 250 "well known men" were consumed by fire.

L

LABAN – *White, Glorious.*

Genesis 24:29f.; 25:20; 27:43; 28:2, 5; 29:5, 10, 13ff.-32:4; 46:18, 25.

Laban, son of Bethuel, was brother of Rebekah, twice father-in-law of Jacob, for he was father of Leah and Rachel. He gave Rebekah to Isaac through the efforts of Abraham's nameless servant. Jacob fled to Laban after the theft of Esau's birthright and blessing, and he served Laban fourteen years and more for the two daughters. Laban was thoroughly a rascal, quickwitted, cunning, greedy and, at times, irresponsible; yet, on the other hand, he was hospitable and tended, in his own way, to be kindly and generous. Perhaps he really liked Jacob and wanted him to stay on with him; or perhaps he saw in Jacob the means of greater wealth and power. Or it might be that Jacob's cleverness stimulated Laban to the exercise of all his faculties.

Certainly the wily desert chieftain met his match in his equally tricky son-in-law who, when he departed at last from the control of his father-in-law, took two daughters, children, maids, servants, camels, sheep, and cattle—even Laban's household goods. Jacob had come to Laban empty-handed, a fugitive. He left a wealthy man. It appears that Laban profited from the relationship and had little reason to complain. See JACOB, LEAH, RACHEL.

172

LAMECH – *A Wild Man.*

1. Genesis 4:18-24.

Lamech, in one account of him a descendant of Cain, is remembered because his sons, Jabal, Jubal, and Tubal-cain, were known as the "fathers" of things important in the life of mankind. Jabal was "father of those who dwell in tents and have cattle"; Jubal was "father of all those who play the lyre and pipe"; Tubal-cain was the "forger of all instruments of bronze and iron."

Lamech, in a wild song, boasted to his wives, Adah and Zillah, that he had "slain a man for wounding me . . ." and that his vengeance therein might be considered as ten times that of Cain, his ancestor. This brief poem is regarded as a very ancient one and shows well the parallelism so characteristic of Hebrew poetry.

2. Genesis 5:25ff.; I Chronicles 1:3; St. Luke 3:36.

In this account Lamech is the son of Methuselah and father of Noah—all descendants of Seth.

LAPIDOTH – *Lamps, Lightnings, Torches.*

Judges 4:4.

Deborah the prophetess was wife of Lapidoth. See DEBORAH.

LAZARUS – Hellenized form of Eleazar – *Whom God Helps.*

1. St. Luke 16:19ff.

The name of the poor man in the Lord's parable of the rich man and a poor one whose circumstances were reversed in the after life. Graphically, he was pictured as being fed from scraps, in this life, and the dogs about the rich man's house and table licked his sores. But in the next life Lazarus was at ease while, Dives, the rich man, was in torment.

2. St. John 11:1ff.; 12:1ff.

The brother of Mary and Martha. At the news of his death "Jesus wept," for Lazarus was a friend.

Word came that Lazarus was sick at Bethany. Jesus went there, in a somewhat leisurely manner, and found that he had been dead four days. Jesus ordered the tomb opened and called, "Lazarus, come out!" Lazarus emerged, the grave clothes still around him. News of Jesus' power over life and death spread rapidly and the leaders of the Jews began to try to find a way to put him to death. Later Lazarus was at a dinner party served by Martha, at which Mary anointed Jesus' feet with a "costly ointment of pure nard."

LEAH – *Languid, Weary.*
Genesis 29:16ff.

The older daughter of Laban whom Jacob received for his wife after seven years of work, thinking the while that he had been given Rachel. Leah is described as having "weak eyes," as being less sparklingly attractive than Rachel. Leah bore six of Jacob's sons, and one daughter. She died before the great migration to Egypt and is said to have been buried in the Cave at Macpelah, with Abraham and Sarah, and where later Jacob was buried.

LEBBEUS (LEBBAEUS) –
Man of Heart.
St. Matthew 10:3.

One of the apostles supposedly surnamed Thaddeus, Lebbeus is also thought to be the same as Jude the brother of James. See THADDEUS.

LEMUEL – *Godward, Belonging to the Deity.*
Proverbs 31:1-9.

A king, not identified, but often alleged to be Solomon, and in the Revised Standard Version called king of Massa, whose mother's words warned against strong drink.

LEVI – *Joined, Attached* – to Aaron? To the Ark?
Genesis 29:34; 34:25, 30; 35: 23; 46:11; 49:5; Exodus 1:2; 6:16; Numbers 3:17; 16:1; 26:59; I Chronicles 2:1; 6:1, 38, 43, 47; Ezra 8:18.

Levi was Jacob's third son by Leah, who in naming him expressed the hope that now her husband would be "joined" to her. It is possible that the name Levi suggests also the dependence of Levi as a tribe on the association it had with the Temple, being landless.

Levi participated in the vicious murder of Shechem, who seduced Dinah and wanted to marry her.

Levi is titular head of the tribe bearing his name, which according to one of the stories was given no inheritance because of Levi's part in the murder of Shechem. The tribe was eventually absorbed by the tribe of Judah, but maintained partial identity through a traditional ministry in and around the "tent of meeting" and the Temple.

Levi's sons, Gershom, Kohath, and Merari were also regarded as tribal leaders, though hardly independent of the tribe of Levi itself. Moses, Aaron, and Mir-

iam were counted as descendants of Levi through Kohath.

LEVITES

Exodus 4:14; 6:25; 38:21;
Leviticus 25:32f.; Numbers 1:
46, 50ff.; 2:17, 33; 3:9, 12, 32,
41, 45; 7:5; 8:18; 35:2, 4, 8;
Deuteronomy 12:12, 18f.; 14:
29; 17:9; 18:7; Joshua 3:3; 14:
3; 21:3-41; Judges 17:7ff.; 18:
3, 15; 19:1ff.

Numerous references to the
Levites are found in I and
II Chronicles, Ezra, Nehemiah,
etc.

The story of the Levites is not
easy to unravel, for the functions
of the Levites as officers of the
Temple changed from time to
time, and while it might seem
that the priesthood came from
the Levites it is not true that all
priests were Levites. Yet the
priestly office is associated with
the tribe of Levi.

Moses and Aaron, sons of
Kohath, were "sons of Levi." In
the wilderness after escape from
Egypt, the people rebelled
against Moses who asked, "Who
is on the side of Yahweh?" The
Levites came to his side, killed
3,000 of the people and for their
loyalty were awarded the priesthood. This is a late story, not
quite in accord with the Levite

in Judges 17-18, an adventurer
who became a priest, not by
right but by choice and by con-
secration of Micah. When the
Danites came along, however,
they seemed to want the Levite
for their priest because he was a
Levite, and they "kidnapped"
him to make him their own
priest in their newly captured
city. Micah had been glad to
have him as priest because he
was a Levite.

In the late story in Exodus 32
there is the sound of truth, for it
is natural that the Levites would
take Moses' part, and the
priestly line in Israel goes back
to Moses and through him to
Aaron. Very early tradition in
Israel pointed to the displaced
tribe of Levi, or to a large number in it, as skilled in the giving
of oracles by lot and of perform-
ing other ministrations around
the "ark of God" and the altar.
In the later documents distinction was made between Aaron-
ites, who were to be priests, and
Levites, who could not approach the altar but served as
assistants to the priests and as
musicians, and so on. In Numbers the Levites were made responsible for the transportation,
setting up and preparing of the
"tent of meeting" for worship.

They were made custodians of all the appointments of the altar and for whatever menial services might be required by the priests in the conduct of worship.

The Levites were not awarded an inheritance in the divisions of the lands among the tribes, but they were given certain cities which became known as "cities of refuge" to which killers who perhaps would be guilty of "manslaughter" in our times might run for protection. The inheritance of the Levites was also said to be "from the altar," since a portion of the tithe given to the support of the priesthood was given to the Levites: their inheritance was also said to be "from Aaron," whose position and income were guaranteed to come "from the altar."

This brief sketch without mention here of the "Zadokite" priesthood cannot do justice to the complicated story of the "sons of Levi." One of the authorities listed in the bibliography should be consulted for further and more exact details.

LINUS – *Net? Song?* **The name of a mythological Minstrel?**
II Timothy 4:21.
Linus, a Christian of Rome, sent greetings to Timothy. This man could well be the Linus who became Bishop of Rome.

LOAMMI – *Not My People.*
Hosea 1:9; 2:23.
The son of Hosea, to whom this symbolic name was given as an illustrative warning to the people.

LOIS – *Good, Desirable.*
II Timothy 1:5.
In writing to Timothy the author of the Epistle remembered both Timothy's "sincere faith, a faith that dwelt first in your grandmother Lois, and your mother Eunice . . ."

LOT – *Concealed, Dark-Colored.*
Genesis 11:27-14:16; 19; St. Luke 17:28ff.
Abraham's nephew, the son of Haran, who left Ur in the Chaldees to go with his uncle to Canaan. Herdsmen of these two chieftains quarrelled and there was a parting of the ways. Abraham gave Lot a choice of the ways and he went to Sodom, was captured there and rescued by Abraham. For a time Lot remained at Zoar and then moved on into what was later called Moab.

Lot was not a man of noble

character, and probably is remembered better through his
nameless wife than in his own
right. As Lot with his wife and
daughters fled the destruction of
Sodom and Gomorrah, the wife
disobeyed the instructions of
the angelic warning not to look
back toward the burning cities.
Inquisitive, she glanced back
and "became a pillar of salt."

Moab and Ammon were ac-
counted Lot's sons by incestuous relationships with his
daughters, initiated by them,
when, as they lived in a cave, it
seemed there was no one else on
earth.

LUCIUS – *Of Light.*
1. Acts 13:1.
"Lucius of Cyrene" was one of a
group of prophets and teachers
in the Church at Antioch. While
the group was at worship, the
Holy Spirit directed them to
"set apart for me Barnabas and
Saul." After further fasting and
prayer the group "laid their
hands on them and sent them
off.
2. Romans 16:21.
Although this Lucius might be
the same as Lucius of Cyrene,
he is here said to be a kinsman
of Paul, who sent greetings from
Corinth to friends in the Church
at Rome.

LUKE (LUCAS) – *Light-giving.*
Colossians 4:14; II Timothy
4:11; Philemon 24.
"Luke the beloved physician"
who was with St. Paul on his
second missionary journey, author of the Gospel of Luke and
the Book of Acts. He was a
Gentile convert.

Luke was not an eye-witness
to the events of which he wrote
in the Gospel, but he claimed to
have obtained his facts from
those who were. He said he had
"followed all things closely for
some time past," and proposed
to write to his friend Theophilus
"an orderly account."

The Book of Acts at 16:10
changes from third person to
first person plural, "we," and it
is thought that at this point
St. Luke's narrative becomes an
eye-witness account of the
events that follow, with the exception of the section, Acts 17:1-
20:5. It is thought that Luke
ministered to Paul, not only as
one Christian brother to an
apostle but also as a physician.

In his Gospel Luke gave special attention to the stories of
the birth of John and Jesus; he
was interested in the healing
miracles and matters naturally
of concern to a physician. The
great story of the Good Samaritan was recorded by him and he

showed a particular interest in the poor and troubled.

Tradition places Luke in either Achaia, Alexandria, or Bithynia, and tells us that he lived to an advanced age, 74 years, dying peacefully, much beloved.

LYDIA – Probably refers simply to *a Native of Lydia.*
Acts 16:14ff.

A widow of Thyatira, in the district of Lydia, who lived in Philippi, a "seller of purple goods." She was probably first a convert to Judaism, then under the influence of Paul's preaching and teaching was converted to Christ. She and all her household were baptized; and she offered her house to Paul and Luke. As the writer of Acts says, "She prevailed upon us."

LYSIAS.
See CLAUDIUS LYSIAS.

M

THE MACCABEES – *The Hammers.*

The Apocryphal Books of Maccabees.

A family of Jewish patriots who stirred their people to revolt against Syria and became rulers of the new Jewish state. The ascendency of the family was during the years c. 165-138 B.C. After that, intrigues wrecked their high purposes and lesser men could not deal successfully with the rising power of Rome. The original name of the family was Hasmonaeus.

1. The first of the Hasmonaeans of influence was Mattathias, who led a revolt when, under Antiochus IV, an attempt was made to revive pagan worship in a town named Modin. He killed several officers and a Jew who was assisting at pagan sacrifices, and destroyed the altar. He then led a guerilla movement from the mountains until his death. The party of revolt led by Mattathias was known as the "chasidim," or "the pious."

2. Judas, son of Mattathias, became a skillful general whose nickname, because of his tactics, was "the Hammerer"—or "the Maccabee." He defeated Lysias, chancellor of Antiochus IV, and, having cleansed the Temple of pagan practices, he gathered and organized the Jews into something like a nation. Laxness on the part of the people, however, brought about defeat in a return battle with Lysias.

Despite defeat, and continued revolt as well, the religious

reforms were allowed to stand, except that Lysias appointed his own high priest.

Demetrius succeeded Antiochus IV and sent an army to stamp out the rebel Jews, but instead he and his army were defeated. Now Nicanor, the new Syrian commander, threatened to burn the Temple unless Judas were betrayed into his hands. This threat aroused the Jews to furious resistance and Nicanor was killed.

This left Judas precariously at the head of a state. Fearful of his position alone, he asked for Roman aid. A message from Rome to Demetrius, referring to the Jews as allies of Rome and warning Demetrius to act accordingly, was delayed so that the Jews once more lost heart and began to desert Judas. Shortly after his moment of greatest triumph he was killed in battle, at Eleasa, in 161 B.C.

3. Jonathan succeeded Judas. After a poor beginning his hard work and good leadership in time brought considerable success to the country. By giving support to Alexander, who succeeded to the throne of Syria, Jonathan's position was strengthened. He was made high priest and governor at home, and a prince of Syria in addition. Demetrius II then took the throne of Syria from Alexander and bought the support of Jonathan to hold it. Jonathan, however, was tricked by Tryphon into a situation which resulted in his assassination, 144 B.C.

4. Simon, brother of Jonathan, now succeeded, and managed in 141 B.C. to gain complete independence for Judaea. To maintain it he sought and secured active support from Rome. In 135 B.C. he was murdered at a feast given by Ptolemy, his son-in-law.

5. Simon's son, John Hyrcanus, now assumed leadership. He conquered the Idumaeans and the Samaritans, and he enjoyed greater prosperity and security than any of his predecessors. He died a natural death in 106 B.C.

6. Aristobulus, John's son, now came to power and was the first of the Hasmonaeans—or Maccabees—to take for himself a king's power. John's plan was that he should be high priest, his mother governor. Instead, the mother was thrown in prison to starve, and his brother, Antigonus, was also "liquidated," leaving Aristobulus with both the power and title "king." Aristobulus died naturally, 103 B.C.

7. He was succeeded by a brother, Alexander Jannaeus, who married his widow and assumed his titles. The Egyptians defeated Jannaeus and internal revolt followed. When he died, his widow, Alexandra, was governor until her death, 76 B.C.

8. Aristobulus II then took the powers and titles from Hyrcanus II, and he was thoroughly beaten by Pompey. The kingdom now became a vassal state under Rome. Hyrcanus II was soon involved in intrigues which got him in prison, minus his ears, and led him eventually to execution by Herod the Idumaean administrator, who ousted his master and took supreme power for himself.

The Maccabean kingdom was now in complete ruin. Herod killed off the heirs, including his own wife, Marianna, whose sons by him, however, were the later Herod the Great and the Herods Agrippa.

MACHIR – Sold.
Genesis 50:23; Numbers 26:29; 32:39f.; Deuteronomy 3:15; Joshua 13:31; 17:1, 3; Judges 5:14.
The son of Manasseh, whose children were said to have been "born on Joseph's knees" in Egypt. Machir's son was Gil-

ead, whose name came from the land assigned to Machir by Moses. The Song of Deborah (Judges 5:14) refers to "commanders" who "marched down from Machir," suggesting that the land was also known as the "land of Machir."

MAGDALENE
See MARY.

MAGOG
See GOG.

MAHLAH – Mild, Mildness.
Numbers 26:33; 27:1; 36:11; Joshua 17:3.
A woman descended from Manasseh, through a man named Zelophehad. Her father had no sons, and she and her sisters claimed an inheritance along with the sons of the tribe. Irregular though it was, their claim was acknowledged. Numbers 36:12, however, intimates that their claim did not matter since they were married to "sons of their father's brothers," thus keeping the inheritance within the tribe.

MAHLON – Mild.
Ruth 1:2, 5; 4:9f.
This was the elder son of Naomi and Elimelech. He was Ruth's first husband who died, along

with his father and brothers, in Moab. See RUTH, NAOMI.

MAHOL – *Dancer.*
I Kings 4:31.
The "sons of Mahol" were thought to be men of unusual wisdom. Solomon was said to be wiser than they.

MALACHI – *Messenger of the Lord. My Messenger.*
The Book of Malachi; St. Mark 1:1; St. Luke 2:4-6.
One of the "minor prophets" whose work is dated at c. 460-435 B.C., and whose book is the last in the canon of the Old Testament. Practically nothing is known about his personal history, or, indeed, whether there was such a person at all. It is thought by some that the prophecies of Malachi appeared in the days when, in the absence of Nehemiah from Jerusalem for a twelve year period, abuses he had tried to eliminate—mixed marriages, divorces and defection of the priests to paganism, and so on—became common again. Others think the words were written shortly before the arrival of Ezra in Jerusalem in 460 B.C. Indeed, some say he might have been Ezra himself. What the prophet had to say about conditions prevailing

would apply to either period.

In addition to his bewailing the conditions already mentioned, Malachi spoke of God's love for Judah and pointed toward the coming of the messenger of the Lord who would "prepare the way before me, and the Lord whom you seek will suddenly come to his Temple . . ." This herald of the "day of the Lord" would "purify the sons of Levi . . . till they present the right offerings to the Lord."

The Gospels of Mark and Luke quote, "Behold, I send my messenger . . ." as applying to John the Baptist, the "forerunner," who proclaimed the coming of the Messiah.

MANAEN – *Comforter.*
Acts 13:1.
One of the prophets and teachers in the Church at Antioch, who was said to be a member of the court of Herod the Tetrarch, and who obeyed the Holy Spirit in setting apart Saul and Barnabas for missionary work. Manaen was also said to be a foster brother of Herod Antipas.

MANASSEH – *Who Causes to Forget.*
1. Genesis 41:51; 48:1ff.; 50: 23; Numbers 26:28f; 27:1;

32:32ff.; Deuteronomy 3: 14; Joshua 13:31; 17:1ff; I Kings 4:13; I Chronicles 7:14, 17.

The son of Joseph who was commonly thought to be the founder of the tribe of Manasseh, which was closely associated with that of his brother, Ephraim. Joseph placed his sons in such wise before Jacob, his father, that Manasseh, the first-born, would receive the blessing of Israel's right hand; but the father crossed his hands and gave Ephraim the blessing, saying that the younger brother would be greater than Manasseh. In the numbering and allocation of lands Manasseh was referred to as the "half-tribe," with Ephraim regarded as the other half. It was in the tribe of Manasseh that a man's daughters were first said to be given lands as an inheritance because their father had no sons. See EPHRAIM, MAHLAH.

2. II Kings 20:21-21:20; 23: 12, 26; 24:3; I Chronicles 3:13; II Chronicles 32:33; 33:1ff.

The king of Judah who, coming to the throne at the age of twelve, deliberately revived heathen practices among his people which his father Hezekiah had tried to put away. Not only did he rebuild the altars of Baal and Asherah, but also he burned his own son as an offering, and "dealt with mediums and wizards." In consequence of these acts of his, the prophets of the Lord declared that God would "bring upon Jerusalem and Judah such evil that the ears of every one who hears of it will tingle . . . and I will wipe Jerusalem as one wipes a dish, wiping it and turning it upside down."

Judah in his time (687-642 B.C.) was under Assyrian pressure, and it is likely that some of the things done during his "fifty year reign" were acts of "appeasement." The prophets and religious "purists," however, made no allowances for external pressure. Even the house of Ahab would be used, they said, as a "plummet" to measure the uprightness—or lack of it—of Jerusalem.

In spite of the fulminations of the prophets against him, his was a prosperous as well as a long reign.

Manasseh was succeeded by his son Amon. See AMON, HEZEKIAH.

MANOAH – Rest.

Judges 13:2ff.; 16:31.

A Danite who was the father of

Samson. His wife had no children until an angel appeared to promise a son who would become a deliverer of Israel. The angel warned her against strong drink and unclean foods; told her also that her son was to be a Nazarite (see Numbers 6:1-21 for a description of the Nazarites), and so to be kept from wine, impure foods—and the razor. Manoah wanted to cooperate and asked that he, too, be instructed in the way the child should be raised so that no mistake would be unwittingly made. The angel then appeared again to both husband and wife to repeat the admonition about wine and unclean foods. When the child was born he was named Samson, and was reared strictly as a Nazarite. Manoah objected to Samson's marriage to a Philistine woman but made arrangements for the marriage, nevertheless, and went reluctantly to the wedding at Timnah. When the marriage came to an unfortunate end almost before it began, Samson "went back to his father's house." See SAMSON, DELILAH.

MARK (MARCUS) – *A Large Hammer? Polite?*
Acts 12:12, 25; 13:5, 13; 15:37;

II Timothy 4:11; St. Mark 14: 51.
John Mark may have been the lad mentioned in the Gospel who lost his clothes as Jesus was taken at the Garden of Gethsemane, who later, under the influence of St. Peter, wrote the Gospel which bears his name.
This Mark was the son of one Mary, a Jewess of Jerusalem, who believed in Jesus and offered her home to him and his disciples as a place of meeting and refuge. It is possible that hers was the "upper room" in which the Last Supper was held, and it almost certainly was the "upper room" in which the disciples were gathered for prayer when Jesus appeared after the Resurrection. The disciples were again in that room for prayer when Peter was miraculously released from prison. He knew where to find his brethren. Thus, through his family, Mark was close to the events of Jesus' life and old enough to remember some of them. No mention is made of his father.
It is probable (tradition insists) that John Mark came to know Peter well in the early days of the Church in Jerusalem; and that later in Rome, he heard from the great apostle himself

the account of things written in the Gospel. It has strongly been stated, indeed, by several of the early Church fathers that he wrote the Gospel with the direct assistance of Peter, if not at his dictation. Peter referred to Mark as "his son"—if the apostle wrote the first Epistle of Peter. If he did not, still the close relationship must have been well known.

But Mark was companion of others beside Peter. He was sent with Barnabas, a cousin, and Paul on the first missionary journey, perhaps as secretary, with the title "minister." At Cyprus Mark left them. Barnabas wanted to take Mark on the second journey, but Paul thought best not to take Mark, "one who had withdrawn from them . . ." This caused conflict which was resolved when Barnabas and Mark went in one direction, Paul and Silas in another.

Yet, later, Paul wrote well of Mark and Barnabas as two of the few of the "circumcision," the Judaising party, among his fellow workers to give him any comfort. Mark was with Paul in Rome and was well spoken of, so that eventually the break between them was healed.

Mark's special contribution

seems to have been in his ability to use Hebrew, Greek, and Latin, and in his further ability to understand the manner in which the Gospel story needed to be phrased for Roman readers —for Gentile readers at Rome were the audience to whom his Gospel was addressed. For modern Christians, his Gospel as first of the four is of incalculable value; for in it are to be found elements of fact, drama, and interpretation much needed in the telling of the story in our own times.

MARTHA – *Lady.*

St. Luke 10:38-42; St. John 11:1, 5, 19ff.

The sister of Mary and Lazarus, friends of Jesus, who often made their home available to him. Martha seemed to be in charge of the household, and on one occasion realized that her duties prevented her participation in the dinner table conversation and in the Lord's teaching. She complained, asking Jesus to tell her sister Mary to help with the chores. The Lord's answer was: "Martha, Martha . . ."

It was Martha who met Jesus as he came to her family on the death of Lazarus, and who spoke in assurance that had he been there her brother would not have died. It was to Martha that Jesus said: "I am the resurrection and the life . . ."

MARY (MIRIAM) – Bitter.

Although the name Mary seems to have been written as Miriam in the Greek, the derivations are not the same, and they will be treated separately.

Four women in the New Testament named Mary are important.

1. S. Matthew 1:16, 18-24; 2:11; 13:55; St. Mark 6:3; St. Luke 1:26-2:34; St. John 2:1-12; Acts 1:14.

Mary the mother of Jesus. For one about whom legend and tradition have clustered so brilliantly, there is little definite information in Holy Scripture. She is introduced as a troubled young woman of Nazareth to whom the angel Gabriel had appeared with the message that she would be favored of the Lord as the mother of the one to be called Jesus, the Son of God. She was troubled because at the time she was betrothed to Joseph and did not wish to bring him shame. The child was born in Bethlehem where, tradition said, the Messiah should be born. Truly, Mary and Joseph were

called to bear exceptional responsibilities.

Tradition states, further, that Mary was the daughter of Joachim and Anna; and that Mary was herself a child of miracle, since her parents were old and childless until she was born. That she and Elizabeth—the mother of John the Baptist and Mary's cousin—were both bearers of children announced by angels makes the story even more remarkable. Mary and Elizabeth and Joseph were, all three, "of the house and lineage of David."

It was Mary's lot in life to deal with many unusual situations. The visit of the angel; the curious beginning of her relationship with Joseph; the visit of the shepherds and wise men to the birthplace of her child; the lowly place of his birth and all the strange events having to do with his coming; the flight into Egypt to save him from the crazy wrath of a mad king; the need to understand that the boy Jesus "must be about his father's business"; the sight of the mature Jesus as he became before her eyes first as teacher, then as prophet, then Messiah, who would reject her plea that he give up the work leading to certain death; the knowledge of his power to do signs and wonders; the Cross; the Resurrection; the Ascension—all these experiences were unique, not to be shared with or understood by anyone but the God to whom she prayed as the initiator of them all.

Thought about the sort of life that was hers, of the quiet way in which she bore it and the gifts which came to all mankind through her, is liable to produce the kinds of stories that indeed have been produced in legend and tradition about Mary, the Mother of the Lord. There is little to wonder at, humanity being as it is, that in playing on such a theme the traditions about her have grown to almost unmanageable proportions. The believing world is prone to say with Elizabeth: "Blessed is she who believed that there would be a fulfillment of what was spoken to her from the Lord."

2. St. Matthew 27:56, 61; 28:1; St. Mark 15:40, 47; 16:1; St. Luke 24:10.
"The other Mary," the mother of James the Less (or the "little" or the "younger") and of Joses. This Mary was a follower of Jesus from Galilee, and probably was in Jerusalem at the time of the Crucifixion, because she be-

lieved the Messiah would declare himself and bring his kingdom into being during the season of the Passover. She was probably the wife of Clopas. As she was one of the women at the foot of the Cross, so was she at the tomb on the Day of the Resurrection.

3. St. Matthew 27:56, 61; 28:1; St. Mark 15:40, 47; 16:1, 9; St. Luke 8:2; 24:10; St. John 19:25; 20:1, 11, 16, 18.
As Jesus and the Twelve went through the cities and villages there were with them also "some women who had been healed of evil spirits and infirmities; Mary, called Magdalene, from whom seven demons had gone out, and Joanna . . . and Suzanna and many others . . ." These women apparently "provided for them out of their means" as Jesus and his entourage made their second preaching journey through Galilee.

In Jewish thought, to be possessed of seven devils was to be lost, abandoned. Mary, for that reason, is said to have been the harlot whom the Lord rescued. Probably he was criticized for having her in his company. Having been healed, she was grateful beyond measure. She was at the Cross and at the tomb where she wept to find it empty. It was this Mary who first saw the Risen Lord.

4. St. Luke 10:38-42; St. John 11:1-46; 12:1-11.

By collating passages from the Gospels of Luke and John the picture of "Mary of Bethany" can be made to appear clearly. She was a member of a warm, friendly, and pious family who must have known Jesus well; for he was in their home for dinner at a time when it seemed to Martha that Mary should have helped with household duties rather than to be "at the Lord's feet." In the exchange Jesus seemed to take the part of Mary, though the rebuke to Martha was more a sigh than an expression of opinion. He also responded to their call when Lazarus, their brother, died, and raised him to life again.

When, later, Jesus was at the home of Simon the leper, Mary entered during the feast and anointed his feet with "pure nard," wiping them with her hair. Mary was a warm-hearted, generous and devoted woman. See MARTHA, LAZARUS.

For Mary, the mother of John Mark, see MARK.

MATTHAT – *A Gift.*
St. Luke 3:24, 29.

In the Lukan genealogy, Matthew was the name of two ancestors of Joseph, husband of Mary.

MATTHEW – *A Gift of God,* probably from an earlier form meaning *A Gift of Yahweh.*
St. Matthew 9:9; 10:3; St. Mark 3:18; St. Luke 6:15; Acts 1:3.

Matthew was a tax collector who was sitting at the tax office when Jesus called him to be a disciple. He became one of the Twelve, listed seventh in St. Mark and St. Luke, eighth in St. Matthew and in Acts.

When he became a disciple, he drew into the company of Jesus other "tax collectors and sinners," people who were generally scorned and despised as cheats and frauds.

Matthew is known in the New Testament also as Levi. Luke and Mark list him under that name. While scholars agree that he was not himself the author of the First Gospel as it stands, it is thought by some that he might have been responsible for its special features through a collection of "sayings" which he kept and from which excerpts were taken by the compiler of the Gospel. It is believed that

Matthew might have been the collector of that body of "sayings" known as "Q" or "Quelle," meaning "a source," which lies behind the first three Gospels.

MATTHIAS – *A Gift of Yahweh.*
Acts 1:23-26.

The Apostles agreed that the vacancy in the number Twelve created by Judas' treachery and suicide should be filled. They decided, further, that one of those who had been with Jesus from the beginning of his ministry should be chosen. Two men were nominated, Joseph Barrabas, and Matthias. After prayers for guidance, lots were cast and the lot fell to Matthias who was then "enrolled with the eleven Apostles." Nothing else is recorded about him; he is not mentioned again in the New Testament.

MEDAD
See ELDAD.

MEDAN – *Judgment.*
Genesis 25:2; I Chronicles 1:32.

A son of Abraham who was born to him through his second wife, Keturah.

MELCHIZEDEK (MELCHISEDEC) – *King of Righteousness.*
Genesis 14:18; Psalm 110:4; Hebrews 5:6; 6:20; 7:1ff.

The priest-king of Salem (the ancient name of Jerusalem) who met and entertained Abraham as he returned from his foray to rescue Lot from the captivity of Chedorlaomer. The priest gave Abraham a blessing in return for which he gave Melchizedek a tenth of the spoils he had taken during the expedition in behalf of Lot.

Because Melchizedek is mentioned as the first priest in Salem he is always regarded in Scripture as an archetype of the priesthood. Psalm 110 refers to his ideal kingship-priesthood in the words concerning Israel's king: "You are a priest forever after the order of Melchizedek." The Epistle to the Hebrews follows the same thought in referring to a priesthood in the ideal, one above the priestly line of Aaron. Christ is that ideal priest, the one true priest. Melchizedek caught the imagination of the author of Hebrews, because in the story of Abraham he merely appears, without antecedents, having "neither beginning of days nor end of life, but resembling the Son of God he continues a priest forever." As Melchizedek in priest's orders antedated the Levitical priesthood, the argument goes, so does that of Christ antedate and transcend the priesthood of Melchizedek.

MENAHEM – Comforter.
II Kings 15:14ff.

An upstart king of Israel who took the throne from Shallum, who took it from Zechariah, but could not hold his place against Assyrian power. He "ruled" ten years, but as a vassal to Pul, the king of Assyria, at the cost of a thousand talents of silver; and his vassalage led ultimately to the complete "annexation" of Israel. Although II Kings states that he ruled ten years, modern scholars give him the years c. 745-738 B.C.

MENELAUS – Abiding or Withstanding People.
II Maccabees 4-7.

A high priest who bought the office from Antiochus Epiphanes and in doing so displaced the "vile Jason" who previously had been appointed to the position. Jason sent Menelaus with tribute money to the king in order to secure his place; but while there Menelaus offered a higher price by "300 talents," and took over

the job. Menelaus, however, did not have the money to pay, and gave a promissory note with the idea that he would rob the Temple of the necessary funds. He stole and sold some vessels from the Temple, used others to pay his henchmen, and managed by deceit, murder, and treachery to retain his job until finally he was executed by the order of Antiochus Eupator. So little did he think of the Temple and the tradition of the people, that he acted as guide when Antiochus walked into the "holy of holies" and handled the sacred vessels.

MEPHIBOSHETH (MERIB-BAAL) – Mephibosheth – meaning uncertain, but perhaps "Water of Shame"; Meribbaal – Baal is (My) Advocate.
II Samuel 4:4; 9:1ff; 16:1ff; 19:24ff; 21:7ff. I Chronicles 8:34; 9:40.

The son of Jonathan who was made a cripple when Saul's family became refugees after his father's defeat and death. The child was injured permanently when his nurse, in haste to escape, fell on him. Although David, smartly, seemed reluctant to have it so, Saul's family was killed off, one by one. David's apparent distaste for killing in these cases had to do with the fact that they were of "the Lord's anointed." Why, except good politics, should David have been concerned for them as such if, as the story carefully states, he was himself anointed to replace Saul?

As a political expedient, therefore, David was glad to be especially kind to Mephibosheth. He was harmless; he was Jonathan's son; he was also the only surviving member of Saul's house. And, incidentally, he could use his kind treatment of Saul's grandson as proof of his official attitude toward Saul's descendants and of his magnanimity, as well. Mephibosheth understood his position. As he did obeisance to David he said: "What is your servant, that you should look upon a dead dog such as I?" He bore himself well under the circumstances, and barely managed to avoid implication in the revolt of Absalom. See ZIBA.

MERAB – *Increase.*

I Samuel 14:49; 18:17ff.
Saul's eldest daughter who was promised to David as a reward for his success against the Philistines. Saul had no intention of making David his son-in-law; hoped actually that with Merab as bait he could encourage

David to get himself killed by the Philistines. Saul gave Merab to Adriel instead of to David —an insult. Years later, David gave the five sons of Merab and Adriel to the Gibeonites to be hanged in vengeance for Saul's "zealous" slaughter of this branch of the Ammonites whom the Israelites had agreed not to kill off. Thus did King David pay his debts.

MERARI – *Bitter, Excited.*

Genesis 46:11; Exodus 6:16-19; Numbers 3:20, 33-37; 4:29-33; Joshua 21:7; I Chronicles 6:1, 16, 19; 15:6, 17; 23:6; Ezra 8:19.
The third son of Levi and head of the families known as the Merarites, the Mahlites, and the Mushites. In the listings of Numbers the Merarites were to encamp on the north side of the tabernacle and be responsible for the frames of the Tent of Meeting, the bars, pillars, bases, and other accessories, such as pegs and cords. Thus they were expected to set up, take down, and transport these essential items.

The "sons of Merari" were identified in Chronicles with the cities of Tabor and Rimmon; they were also said to have had some duties in connection with temple music.

MESHA – *Freedom.*
II Kings 3:4ff.
A King of Moab who, on the death of Ahab of Israel to whom he paid tribute, rebelled against Jehoram. The latter appealed to Jehoshaphat of Judah who, with the king of Edom, joined Jehoram against Mesha. It was in the campaign against Mesha that Elisha, as an assistance to the kings, prophesied that water would come "from Edom" to make this dry stream-bed full of pools." The kings of Israel and Judah defeated Mesha and the coalition of princes he had mustered for the battle. Seeing the early morning sun shining blood red on the water in the formerly dry pools, Mesha thought that Jehoram and Jehoshaphat had been at war with each other and he threw caution to the winds. When the battle went against him, Mesha offered his own son as a sacrifice, as "burnt offering upon the wall." At the sight of this Israel "withdrew" from the battle in anger and disgust.

MESHACH – *Agile?*
Daniel 1:7; 2:49; 3:12ff.
One of Nebuchadnezzar's eu-

nuchs gave this name to Michael, one of Daniel's friends.

METHUSELAH – *Man of the Javelin?*
Genesis 5:21ff.
Son of Enoch, father of Lamech, grandfather of Noah, this man was accorded a life spanning nine hundred sixty-nine years by the reckoning of the priestly genealogist! Methuselah is remembered therefore as having been called the oldest man who ever lived.

MICAH – *Who is Like Yahweh.*
1. The Book of Micah; Jeremiah 26:18.
Memory of the prophecy of Micah "Who prophesied in the days of Hezekiah king of Judah" helped save the life of Jeremiah, who had been seized by the mob for saying the same thing nearly a hundred years later. Micah's prophecy, given c. 725-700 B.C. in the reign of Jotham, Ahaz, and Hezekiah, was: "Zion shall be plowed as a field: Jerusalem shall become a heap of ruins."

Micah did so speak of the fate of Jerusalem; but also he gave promise of the restoration of Zion, saying that God would destroy because a false people with false prophets made destruction necessary. Judgment and destruction, however, would be tempered with mercy and followed by renewal.

Micah 5:2 was quoted to Herod to indicate the place of birth for the Messiah. "But you, O Bethlehem Ephrathah, who are little to be among the clans of Judah, from you shall come forth for me one who is to be ruler in Israel." Another oft-quoted verse is 6:8: "He has showed you, O man, what is good; and what does the Lord require of you but to do justice, and to love kindness, and to walk humbly with your God?"

2. Judges 17:1-18:27.

An Ephraimite named Micah stole 1100 pieces of silver from his mother, confessed, and returned them to her. Grateful, she had the silver melted down and made into a graven image. She gave it to Micah who made a household shrine and installed one of his sons as priest. A Levite passed by looking for a "place in the sun" for himself (the Levites had no "inheritance" and had to make their own way), and was installed as priest in Micah's house, replacing the son. Subsequently, the Danites, also looking for a place for themselves, passed by and observed both the shrine and the Levite in attendance. When

they had established themselves at Laish, renaming it Dan, they sent back to the House of Micah to take from him both his graven image and his Levite. The story is used thus to support the idea of the antiquity and propriety of the Levitical priesthood.

Five other men named Micah are not prominent enough to be given space.

MICAIAH – Who is Like Yahweh?

I Kings 22:8ff.; II Chronicles 18:7ff.

Ahab and Jehoshaphat intended to go to war against Syria and sought the prophets to "inquire of the Lord" as to the chances of victory. Some four hundred prophets agreed that victory would attend their efforts, and Ahab was pleased. Jehoshaphat, however, was suspicious of such unanimity of opinion. "Is there not another prophet of the Lord of whom we may inquire?" he asked. "Yes," replied Ahab, "there is one man . . . Micaiah the son of Imlah; but I hate him, for he never prophecies good concerning me, but evil."

Micaiah, knowing the king wanted him to say, "go up, and prosper," said that; but now Ahab was suspicious of such words from the prophet and demanded the truth. Micaiah said, "I saw all Israel scattered upon the mountains, as sheep that have no shepherd."

Ahab then said to his cohort, in effect, "See, I told you so!" Micaiah continued, saying that his vision asked, "Who will entice Ahab" to go to battle? The answer was, "a lying spirit in the mouth of the prophets."

Ahab went disguised into battle, but was killed anyway, as Micaiah had prophesied.

MICHAEL – *Who is Like unto God?*

Daniel 10:13, 21; 12:1; Jude 9; Revelation 12:7.

The guardian angel of Israel, referred to in Daniel as "one of the chief princes"; in the Book of the Revelation as one of the four archangels of "Apocalyptic"; in Jude as "contending with the devil."

Michael was thought of as the leader of the hosts of heaven against the hosts of Satan. He is thought of also as the guardian angel of the Church Militant as he was of the old Israel.

Ten men named Michael are mentioned in the Bible, but none needs be mentioned here.

MICHAL – *Who is Like unto God?*

I Samuel 14:49; 18:17ff.; 25:44; II Samuel 3:13f.; 6:16ff.

Saul's daughter who was held out as an incentive to David, as indeed was her older sister Merab, to go more and more into battle with the Philistines. The king's purpose was to promise son-in-law status to David in exchange for service in battle, in the hope that by having David strain himself to achieve that status he would be killed. Michal loved David and that fact helped Saul's purpose indirectly; for he now promised Michal in exchange for 100 Philistine foreskins. David brought him 200, and Saul, having given Merab to another man, now had to keep his promise.

Michal saved David's life on one occasion by helping him escape a team of Saul's assassins. She let David out of a window of his guarded house, and put a bolster in his bed foiling the knives of the killers. When the messengers from Saul questioned her, she claimed David was sick; and when Saul himself questioned her, she said the trick was David's, not hers, and that he had threatened to kill her.

When David was outlawed,

MILCOM

Saul gave Michal to a man named Palti. David demanded her return before settling with Abner and Ishbosheth after Saul's death.

Later, when David, as king, brought the ark of God into Jerusalem and danced ecstatically before it, Michal thought him undignified and rebuked him for his vulgar, shameless conduct. It is likely that in his ecstatic dance he had torn off his clothes. David's response to her bitter words was to put her away for the rest of her life.

MIDIAN, MIDIANITES – Contention.
Genesis 25:2-4; Exodus 2:15f.; 3:1; 4:19; 18:1; Numbers 22: 4; 25:15, 18; Judges 6:1f.; 7:1f.
Genesis lists Midian as a son of Abraham by Keturah. When Moses fled to the wilderness from Egypt he was cordially received by Jethro, a priest of Midian, whose flocks he tended and whose daughter, Zipporah he married. Jethro was very understanding and helpful to Moses; but, as the story in Judges indicates, relations with Midian were not always peaceful.

It is said that the Midianites were merchants, perhaps the first to use camels.

MILCAH – Counsel.
1. Genesis 11:29; 22:20-23; 24:15, 24.
Milcah was a daughter of Haran, brother of Abraham. She became the wife of Nahor and mother of Bethuel, who was Rebekah's father. Her eight sons were regarded as ancestors of the tribes in Northern Mesopotamia; and it is thought that she was considered the eponymous ancestress of one of the tribes.
2. Numbers 26:33; 27:1; 36: 11; Joshua 17:3.
One of the daughters of Zelophehad, a man who had no sons. His daughters claimed an inheritance since there were no men in the family, and their claim was acknowledged. Had the claim been denied, their father's properties would have gone to his brothers and their descendants. The daughters, five of them, asked that their father's "name" be kept alive through them.

MILCOM – Counsellor, King.
I Kings 11:5, 33; II Kings 23:13.
"The abomination of the Ammonites" for the worship of which Solomon built a temple on the Mount of Olives when he acquired a wife from among the Ammonites. Josiah had it de-

stroyed. Milcom, Moloch, Molech are varying names of the same diety. A principal characteristic of Milcom's worship was human sacrifice. Topheth—"the fireplace"—a high place in the Valley of Hinnom, the "valley of slaughter," was the center of such worship. Manasseh offered his son to Molech or Milcom. The reforms of Josiah failed to hold firm; for references are made again and again after his reign to the fact that worship was offered to the heathen gods, of which Milcom was certainly one.

MIRIAM – *Fat, Thick, Strong. Bitter?*
Exodus 15:20f.; Numbers 12:1ff.; 20:1; 26:59; Deuteronomy 24:9; Micah 6:4.
The sister of Aaron and sister, or possibly half-sister, of Moses, thought to be eldest of the three. In the "E" source of the Pentateuch she and Aaron are said to be the children of Amram and Jochabed. It might have been Miriam who stood guard over the child Moses hidden in the rushes and who, when he was discovered by Pharaoh's daughter, offered to call a nurse for him and called "his mother."

After the crossing of the Red Sea "Miriam the prophetess, the sister of Aaron, took a timbrel . . . and all the women went out after her with timbrels and dancing . . ." She led in a song of victory, probably accompanied by the wild dancing of the women, in celebration of the crossing.

Numbers 12 shows Miriam standing with Aaron in protest of Moses' marriage to a Cushite woman. They began to question his authority over them, reminding each other that they, too, had the power of prophecy. As tension mounted, the Lord called them into the "tent" and there described the difference between them by saying that he spoke "mouth to mouth" to Moses, to them only in visions. After this "murmuring" against Moses and after the council in the "tent," the cloud of the Lord's presence left the "tent" and Miriam was found to be a leper. She, thus, was exposed as the chief complainer. On the appeal of Moses to Yahweh, her leprosy was removed and her period of "uncleanness" limited to a mere seven days. She died during the time the Israelites "tarried" at Kadesh. There is no doubt that she was a "strong" and influential woman, perhaps a "bitter" one, as well.

MNASON – *A Searcher, A Seeker, A Suitor, A Remembrancer.*
Acts 21:16.
An "early disciple," a native of Cyprus. St. Paul lodged with him during his last visit to Jerusalem. From his Greek name it might be inferred that he was a Gentile convert, and the language suggests that Paul's stay with him was pre-arranged, possibly because Paul might not have been welcome among Jewish Christians.

MOAB – *Water of* or *from a Father?*
Genesis 19:37; Exodus 15:15; Numbers 21:11-36:13; Deuteronomy 1:5; 2:8; 29:1; Joshua 13:32; 24:9; Judges 3:12-30; 10:6; 11:15-25; Ruth 1:1ff.; etc.
The Book of Genesis makes Moab the issue of an incestuous relationship between Lot and his elder daughter, as well as the "father" of the people bearing his name. Thus did a late Hebrew writer express contempt for a neighboring people too close and too strong for comfort.

When the Joseph tribes escaped from Egypt, Moses and the people in their song of triumph referred to the "trembling" of the leaders of Moab at what they had heard about the defeat of Pharaoh's chariots. It was Balak, king of Moab, who employed Balaam to produce a curse on the Israelites; it was with the people of Moab that the Israelites "yoked" themselves and they began also to worship Baal Peor, a Moabitish deity—otherwise known, probably, as Chemosh—so that Moses ordered all the chiefs of the people who had "bowed down" to Baal Peor to be hung. Even this drastic measure did not rid the Hebrews of the effects of contact with Moab; for in later times Israel worshipped often at the shrines of Chemosh.

In a time of famine Naomi and her family went into the land of Moab, where her sons married and where they and their father died. Ruth, a Moabitess, the wife of one of Naomi's sons was later married to Boaz, and it was from this union that the fathers of David were said to have come.

Thus, relations between Israel and Moab were sometimes close and harmonious, sometimes bitter and savage. The prophets—Amos, Isaiah, Jeremiah, Ezekiel, Zephaniah—called again and again for the judgment of God on the Moabites. The kings—Saul, David, Omri, Ahab, Jehoram—had trouble keeping them in line. Indeed, II Kings 13:20 states that Israel was regularly invaded by Moab ("in the spring of the year"), which gave trouble to all the rising powers until subdued at last by Nebuchadnezzar, c. 600 B.C.

The "Moabite Stone," discovered in 1868, is the most informative single document yet found beyond the Bible itself having to do with Iron Age events in Palestine. In it Mesha, king of Moab refers to Omri and his son Ahab (not mentioned by name) as opponents: Omri took certain lands from Moab which, after "forty years," were re-taken. Reference is made to the building of "walls" and "gates," "towers" and "reservoirs," "highways" and cities. The Moabites were an interesting people, deserving of thoughtful and careful study. See MESHA, OMRI, AHAB.

MORDECAI – *A Little Man, Bitter, Bruising? Dedicated to Marduk.* More likely the latter.

The Book of Esther.

He was the cousin of Esther the Jewess and raised her as his own daughter. After she had become queen, so says the story, Morde-cai learned of a plot on the life of King Ahasuerus and told Esther of it. She in turn informed the king and a record of the incident was made, giving Mordecai credit for having saved the king's life. Mordecai brought trouble to the Jews in the city for his refusal to do obeisance to Haman, the king's favorite courtier, and Haman made elaborate plans to destroy Mordecai and with him all the Jewish people. When Esther heard of the plans being devised by Haman she boldly sought the king's presence, risking disfavor and banishment, even possible death, to ask that she might be allowed to prepare a great banquet to honor him and Haman. Meanwhile, as preparations for the dinner were in progress, Haman was persuaded to build a gallows on which to hang Mordecai, having been assured that he might do as he pleased with his enemies.

As this was going on, King Ahasuerus, being sleepless one night, called for a review of the records of the kingdom, and learned that Mordecai had not been rewarded for his loyalty in saving the king from assassination. He therefore ordered Haman, of all people, to see that Mordecai was provided with all the honors and dignities proper to one who had saved a king's life.

At the great banquet Esther revealed herself as a Jewess and as the "daughter" of Mordecai. She also exposed Haman as the enemy of herself and her people, with the result that Haman was hanged on the gallows prepared for Mordecai, and Mordecai was given all the honors once accorded Haman.

Mordecai is, of course, a fictional character. See ESTHER.

MOSES – Meaning uncertain. *Drawn from the Water?* Possibly derived from an Egyptian word meaning *Son, Child,* probably of some unnamed god. Whatever the meaning, the name is probably Egyptian.

The Book of Exodus; Leviticus; Numbers; Deuteronomy; Joshua 1:1ff.; Judges 1:16, 20; 3:4; 4:11; I Samuel 12:6-8; I Kings 2:3; 8:9, 53, 56; St. Matthew 8:4; 17:3f.; 19:7f.; 22:24; 23:2; St. Luke 2:22; 16:29-31; 20:28; 24:27, 44; St. John 1:17; 3:14; 5:45f.; 7:19-44; 8:5; 9:28f.; 13:39; Romans 5:14; 9:15; 10:5ff.; I Corinthians 9:9; 10:2; II Corinthians 3:7ff.; II Timothy 3:8; Hebrews 3:2ff.; 7:14; 8:5; 9:19; 10:28; 11:23f.; 12:21; Jude 9; Revelation 15:3; etc.

The principal sources for the stories of Moses are the "J" and "E" documents of the Pentateuch, both of which contain much legendary material and which have been worked over by later writers and editors Thus the exact details of his life cannot be presented with certainty; yet there was a Moses, the main outlines of whose life we know. It is likely, moreover, that many of the details which add flesh to the skeletal outline have their origin in oral tradition lying well and solidly behind the written documents. Without raising too many questions about details, without attempts at analysis of the sources, we shall try to sketch the main features of the story of one of the great characters in history.

Moses was born to Levite parents (said to be Amram and Jochabed) at a time when the "Joseph tribes" of the Israelites, in Egypt, were becoming so numerous as to be a threat to the Egyptians. The new Pharaoh condemned all male Hebrews to death at birth. When Moses was born, he was hidden three months at home; then he was placed in a basket-boat, perhaps to be found, as indeed he was, by someone like Pharaoh's daughter who took him for her own and gave him the advantages of Pharaoh's household. It is said that he was reared a prince.

At maturity Moses began to identify himself with his own people. He killed an Egyptian who was beating a Hebrew, got involved in a quarrel between two Hebrews who snarled at him as a murderer; and, with the news of his action in the ears of Pharaoh, he fled Egypt for his life.

His flight took him to Midian where he was befriended by Jethro (or Hobab or Reuel?), "a priest of Midian," whose daughter Zipporah he married.

Moses tended the flocks of Jethro and learned much about the country through which he was later to take the Israelites. It was in the wilderness of Midian that he received from the God, Yahweh, a revelation manifested in a bush which burned but was not consumed. In the same revelation Moses received a call from Yahweh to return to Egypt for the deliverance of Israel. He did not care to accept the call.

But return to Egypt he did. With the help of Yahweh he persuaded his brother—or half-brother—Aaron to work with him in gathering the elders of Israel to prepare for the struggle ahead. Moses and Aaron approached Pharaoh—probably Rameses II, 1301-1234 B.C.—with, first, a request for the people to hold a sacrificial feast in the wilderness. The answer was not permission to go but more work, making more bricks, now "without straw" provided. There followed a contest between Pharaoh and Moses, who with divine assistance produced a series of plagues, each more horrible than its predecessor, and at last the terrible "Passover," which took the first-born from every house in Egypt, but "passed over" the homes of the Israelites marked with the blood of the lamb. Great preparation was made for a long journey; all the people were poised for flight. When death struck the Egyptians, Pharaoh told Moses to take the people away. They were ready. In leaving they took to the wilderness to avoid war, possibly with the Philistines; for they were not yet ready for war with anyone. Their course led them to the Red Sea (the Sea of Reeds) where they crossed dry, favored by a strong east wind, and when the wind changed Pharaoh with his armies pursuing in heavy chariots were drowned. After the crossing songs of triumph were sung, with feasting and dancing. War with Amalek was unavoidable, but successful.

Hunger, thirst, fear of a new way of life, disappointment, and the creation of a strong people out of a mob of ex-slaves were problems to be faced in the wilderness. Moses' troubles with his people were too numerous to be recounted here. He "went in and out before the Lord" constantly, consulting him about his troubles with a rebellious or an apathetic crowd of people. With divine guidance he saw that they were fed, watered, healed of plague and snake-bite, and in time provided with a religion and the rudiments of a civil and criminal law. Jethro appeared to act as guide and to give good advice.

At Mount Sinai (or Seir, or Horeb?) where the Hebrews remained an extended period, the tradition states that the laws of Yahweh were given and the frayed edges of the mob were sharpened for the long and bitter struggles to be endured as Israel hammered its way, bit by bit, tribe by tribe, into the "promised land" of Canaan. On the plain below Sinai, Aaron allowed the people to build the golden calf, which Moses destroyed on his return from the Mount—an unpleasant interlude, but typical of the occasions which elicited from Moses the cry: "What shall I do with this people?" In spite of these many difficulties, Moses under divine impulse led his people into a "Covenant" relationship with Yahweh, which in the minds of the several writers was the most important single fact in the history of the people. The "Covenant," sealed in blood, was at once a touchstone and a lodestone for a people whose fortunes were never very great, whose hopes in material and political terms were never quite fulfilled. The law, given initially in elementary form at Sinai, became a mark of the people, who in time were known as the people of the Covenant and the Law.

From Sinai, led by the Glory of the Lord in the form of a cloud by day and a pillar of fire by night, Israel journeyed on to Kadesh.

At one point, Aaron and Miriam, jealous and restive under the authority of Moses, used Moses' marriage to a Cushite woman as an excuse to criticize him and to set themselves up as a counter authority. The result was leprosy for Miriam and a clear "statement" from Yahweh that his relationship to Moses was unique, "mouth to mouth," face to face. On Moses' appeal, Miriam was cleansed, but she died in Kadesh. The incident set the stage for the decline of Aaron's influence as spokesman, priest and leader. Eventually, he was stripped of office and was sent off to die apart from his people.

As the position of Aaron declined, that of Joshua, long a "minister" to Moses, grew in importance. An excellent judge and leader in military affairs he was carefully groomed for and eventually consecrated as Moses' successor.

Moses sent spies into the land of Canaan who reported a good land before them, but one well defended. A plan of attack was worked out, but the people, impatient and fearful, tried a plan of their own without Moses' leadership, and were badly defeated by the Amalekites and Canaanites.

Moses, deliverer, leader, lawgiver, judge, prophet and father to his people, led them to the borders of the new land, but was not himself allowed to enter. His, however, was the work, the faith, which produced a people with a memory of both slavery in Egypt and freedom under God, a people with a point of view, primitive though it was, of remarkable quality and distinction.

In evaluating the place of Moses in Israel it is necessary to say only that so highly was he regarded by his own disobedient and recalcitrant people that, when they began to think of the Messiah, the one anointed of God, to come, they spoke of him as "one like unto Moses." It was hard, perhaps impossible, to think of a greater leader than he. His influence overflowed the small people for whom, in the words of the Epistle to the Hebrews, he chose to "suffer afflictions"; and words about him from Deuteronomy seem quite appropriate: "And there has not arisen a prophet since in Israel like Moses, whom the Lord knew face to face . . ." See AARON, JETHRO, JOSHUA, MIRIAM, ZIPPORAH.

N

NAAMAH – *Pleasant.*

1. Genesis 4:22.

A daughter of Lamech by Zillah, and a sister of Tubal-cain.

2. I Kings 14:21, 31;
II Chronicles 12:13.

Naamah was an Ammonitess wife of Solomon. Her son, Rehoboam, was successor to Solomon.

NAAMAN – *Pleasant, Pleasantness.*

II Kings 5; St. Luke 4:27.

A general in the Syrian army whose leprosy was miraculously cured when he obeyed Elisha's command to bathe daily for seven days in the River Jordan.

It was from a Hebrew captive maiden that Naaman learned of the powers of the God of Israel and of his prophet Elisha.

Naaman sent to ask that the power of the prophet be used in his behalf. The message went to the king of Israel from the king of Syria, and Elisha heard that Israel's king was practically in mourning over the task assigned him of seeing to it that Naaman was cured. Elisha was incensed and bade the king send the leprous Naaman to him. When, without even seeing the prophet, Naaman got word of the simple prescription, he, in turn, was annoyed and refused to accept it seriously until his attendants persuaded him at least to try so easy a thing as to bathe seven times in Jordan. Having tried it as directed, he found himself wondrously cured. He was so impressed with the power of Israel's God—yet still of the belief that Yahweh could be powerful only on his own ground, so to speak—that he took home two loads of earth, so that he might worship this God of power in Damascus.

Naaman offered gifts to Elisha who refused them. Gehazi, Elisha's servant, took the gifts cryptically and found himself cursed with Naaman's leprosy.

Three other people called by this name are of no importance. See ELISHA, GEHAZI.

NABAL – *Fool, Foolish.*
  I Samuel 25:3ff.; 27:3; 30:5; II Samuel 2:2.

In this case the name reveals the man. David had been kind to the men who kept Nabal's flocks, and being in need of provisions he sent to Nabal asking for hospitality on a certain feast day. Nabal, "churlish and ill-behaved," sent David an insulting answer in the negative. David then "girded on his sword," intending to deal handily with Nabal.

But Abigail, Nabal's wife, heard of the incident and, taking provisions secretly, she went to David with apologies for her husband. So charming was she that not only did she talk David out of his wrath toward Nabal, but further, when a few days la-

ter Nabal died of apoplexy at the news of his wife's conduct, Abigail became David's wife. See DAVID, ABIGAIL.

NABOTH – *Fruits? Prominence?*
  I Kings 21; II Kings 9:21, 25f.

A citizen of Jezreel whose vineyard Ahab tried to buy or acquire by trade. His refusal to sell or trade disturbed the king, made him "sullen."

When Jezebel, Ahab's Sidonian wife, learned of the trouble she promised to obtain the vineyard for him, telling him to think no more of the matter and to leave it to her. She hired "two base fellows" to swear they had heard Naboth curse God and the king, after he had been showered with favors presumably by the king. So accused, he was stoned by an indignant mob and the vineyard was confiscated. Jezebel's tricks were effective.

But that was far from the end of the matter; for Elijah the Tishbite heard of it, came boldly before Ahab and laid a curse on him, saying, "In the place where dogs licked up the blood of Naboth shall the dogs lick your own blood."

Ahab was thus never able to enjoy the vineyard taken from Naboth. See ELIJAH, JEZEBEL.

NADAB – *Generous, Noble.*
1. Exodus 6:23; Leviticus 10: 1ff.

The eldest son of Aaron, who was appointed priest but who also died on the day of his appointment, consumed with his brother by the "unholy fire" they used in their censers. Nadab and Abihu apparently used an unauthorized, an unblessed, flame; or it might be that they were involved in some rite alien to the worship of Yahweh. At any rate, being childless, they were thus blotted out from the lists of the priesthood, and their younger brothers Eleazar and Ithamar were elevated to the priesthood in their places.

2. I Kings 14:20; 15:25.
A short-lived king of Israel. The son of Jeroboam, his reign (c. 901-900 B.C.) was curtailed by resort to murder on the part of Baasha, a general of the army.

NAHASH – The name comes from the word meaning "hiss," as a *Serpent.* Thus Nahash might mean, simply, "the snake," or "dedicated to the snake-god," etc.
1. I Samuel 11:1f.; 12:12.
A king of Ammon who was asked to make a treaty with the townspeople when he beseiged Jabesh-gilead. He answered that he would do so on condition that he gouge out all the right eyes of the men and so put all Israel to disgrace. The people asked for seven days to consider the matter, and sent out messengers to the tribes. Saul, plowing with his oxen, received the message. He killed a pair of oxen and sent pieces to all the tribes with the threat that any who would not come to the defence of Jabesh-gilead would find their oxen cut to bits. The men of Jabesh returned to Nahash saying that on the seventh day they would give themselves up. But Saul and his angry army slipped into the camp of Nahash and "cut down the Ammonites." It was Saul's first victory, and Nahash was responsible for it and the subsequent rise of Saul.

2. II Samuel 10:2; 17:27; I Chronicles 19:1f.
Another Ammonite king who dealt "loyally" with David, but whose son Hanun despitefully cut off half the beards of David's agents sent to console the son on the father's death. Hanum also cut off their garments—up to the hips. See HANUN.

NAHOR – From a word meaning "nostril, snort." Perhaps he had a prominent proboscis, or he might have pierced his nose. The relationship of the name to the root word is "obscure."

1. Genesis 11:22ff.; I Chronicles 1:26.

Nahor was the grandfather of Abraham.

2. Genesis 11:26ff.; 22:20ff.; 24:10, 15, 24, 47; 29:5; 31:53; Joshua 24:2.

Nahor was a son of Terah and brother of Abraham; he was father of Bethuel, Rebekah's father. A city was known by his name.

NAHUM – *Comforter.*
The Book of Nahum.

Nahum's prophecy gives no clue as to his own identity beyond the statement that he was "of Elkosh," and that his words are an oracle about Nineveh. Scholars think his prophecy is therefore to be timed between 667 B. C., the date of the fall of Thebes and 612 B.C., the fall of Nineveh.

The purpose of his oracle is to comfort Israel with a word on the fall of Assyria, of which Nineveh was the throne city. The wrath and vengeance of God, so often turned in times past on sinful Israel and Judah, now will be directed at equally sinful Assyria. For though the Lord is "slow to anger . . . he

will by no means clear the guilty" whether the guilty be "Israel," Assyria, or any other nation. Nahum's language is vivid and sometimes savage in its joy over the fall of Nineveh; but his concept of God as in charge of the affairs of all the nations is impressive.

NAOMI – *Pleasant.*
Ruth 1:2ff.

The mother-in-law of Ruth the Moabitess, who was given new lease on life after the death of her husband and sons. Times were not good in Moab, to which she had gone with her family to escape famine conditions in Bethlehem, and Naomi resolved to return to her own land and people.

As she prepared to leave she gave the daughters-in-law opportunity to remain with their people even as she was returning to hers. Orphah, the widow of Mahlon, decided to remain, but Ruth "clung to her," saying, "entreat me not to leave you . . . for where you go I will go . . . your people shall be my people, and your God my God."

At Bethlehem where Naomi was remembered and greeted by name, she replied that her name was no longer "Naomi," meaning "pleasant," but "Mara," meaning "bitter"; for, she said, she had gone away full and returned empty.

In time, however, through the love and obedience of Ruth, renewed interest in life was provided for Naomi. Ruth had a son by Boaz, and Naomi's neighbors declared that Ruth had been more to her than seven sons. Ruth's son, whom Naomi gladly nursed, was Obed, father of Jesse, grandfather of David. Naomi, in her patient and skillful assistance in dealing with Ruth and in helping to arrange for her second marriage, might be called the ideal mother-in-law. See RUTH, BOAZ, ELIME-LECH, MAHLON, CHILION, OR-PHAH.

NAPHTALI – *Wrestling.*
Genesis 30:7ff.; 35:25.

Jacob's son by Rachel's maid, Bilhah, and progenitor of the tribe of Naphtali. The tribe was assigned territories rich but hard to hold because of their strategic importance to traders whose routes passed through the area. Even so, Naphtali seemed to do well. Naphtali was one of the tribes to respond to the call of Barak and Deborah. Indeed, Barak was himself one of the tribe, which was war-like and strong, like "a hind let loose."

In later times, subjected to constant pressure from Syria the people of Naphtali lost any belligerence they might have had, and finally lost their lands to the Syrians, and their freedom as well.

NATHAN – *Giver, Gift.*
1. II Samuel 5:14; I Chronicles 3:5; 14:4.

One of David's sons who was born to him in Jerusalem.

2. II Samuel 7:2ff., 17; 12:1-25; I Kings 1:34.

Nathan was a fearless prophet of high integrity who was both friend and critic of David. It was he who agreed first that David should build a temple to house the ark of God and then returned to the king to say that not he but his successor should build it.

When David got himself involved with Bathsheba and had Uriah her husband killed to cover his crime of adultery, Nathan went to the king with a pitiful story of a rich man who had taken a poor man's ewe lamb, his only lamb, rather than one of his own plentiful flock, to offer in hospitality to a wayfarer. David was enraged at such injustice and declared that the rich man should be made to repay four-fold. Nathan, pointing his finger at the king said: "Thou art the man!" Bathsheba was, of course, the ewe-lamb and Uriah the poor man robbed and killed.

Nathan remained the friend of the king and of Bathsheba, in spite of his criticism of David. He helped her in the maneuvering which in David's last days placed Solomon on the throne and crushed the rebellion of Adonijah. It was Nathan who anointed Solomon as king.

Nine other men named Nathan are of little importance.

NATHANAEL – *Gift of God.*
St. John 1:45ff.; 21:2.
Philip told Nathanael about Jesus, describing him as "him of whom Moses in the law and also the Prophets wrote." Nathanael, a man "of Cana of Galilee," jested in reply: "Can anything good come out of Nazareth?" And Philip said: "Come and see."

Jesus called Nathanael an "Israelite in whom is no guile." He said this before introductions were made, and Nathanael was amazed. Jesus told him he had seen him under a fig tree, watching, even before Philip invited him to join the group. Nathanael then confessed: "Thou art the son of God! Thou are the King of Israel!"

Nathanael is said to be the same person as Bartholomew. See BARTHOLOMEW.

NEBUCHADNEZZAR (NEBU-CHADREZZAR) – *"Nebo, Defend the Boundary,"* or *Border.*
II Kings 24-25; Jeremiah 21:2, 7; 27-28; 37-39; 46:2-26; 49: 28; 50:17; etc; Ezekiel 26:7; 29:18f.; 30:10; Daniel 1ff.
King of Babylon who defeated Pharaoh Necho, king of Egypt, and extended his kingdom considerably; a great military man and a good administrator who was responsible for the grandeur of ancient Babylon. The Old Testament refers to him as the warrior who, after three campaigns, finally reduced Jerusalem to a heap of rubble and carried off the bulk of its citizenry to Babylon in 586 B.C.

NEBUZARADAN – *Nebo has an Offspring.*
II Kings 25:8, 11, 20; Jeremiah 39:9ff.; 40:1, 10; 43:6; 52:12, 15f., 26.
A captain of the guard of King Nebuchadnezzar who was appointed to carry out the destruction of Jerusalem. He was re-

sponsible for the burning of the Temple, the king's house, and all the great houses in the city; he broke down the walls and carried the people into exile, except for the "poorest of the land." However, he was instructed to treat the prophet Jeremiah with constraint and courtesy.

NEHEMIAH – *Yahweh is Comfort.*
The Book of Nehemiah, 1-7; 8:9; 10:1; 12:46f.

The Jewish cupbearer to King Artaxerxes of Persia, who wept on hearing from a traveller from Jerusalem of the state of affairs there and, eventually in c. 446 B.C., received permission and powers from the king to go to the city and rebuild it.

When he arrived he found the walls of the city in ruins, no place in or around the former king's palace to shelter even his beast. With the king's letters as authority and with spirited leadership he gathered crews for a quick rebuilding of the walls. The Samaritans and the Arabs ridiculed his efforts at first, then when it was about half done, they tried to stop it altogether. Nehemiah divided his crews into fighters and workers. He armed the workers and de-

ployed the guard about the city in stragetic spots so that work could go on in shifts. At last the job was done. Attention then had to be given to dwellings for the people, to the setting up of officers for the government of the city and officials for the conduct of worship. These things Nehemiah did in due course, so that Jerusalem was once more an organized community.

Only the leaders of the people lived in the new city at first. As housing was made available, one person in ten, chosen by lot, was brought in from the surrounding towns and villages to live in the new Jerusalem.

In 444 B.C. the walls were ready, organization of new life was completed, and with great ceremony the walls were thankfully dedicated.

And the Law was read. In the reading it was noted that Moabites and Ammonites were not to be members of the congregation. At Nehemiah's suggestion, indeed his insistance, Jews began to separate themselves from the surrounding peoples, not an easy thing to accomplish. Families were broken up, but only with great difficulty. Nehemiah went to Babylon for a space of twelve years. On his return to Jerusalem he found that much of his work of reform needed to be done over—with "curses" and beatings and hair pullings. He had to throw out Tobiah and all his furnishings from a luxurious apartment he had appropriated to himself in a temple chamber intended for a storehouse. Tobiah was an Ammonite. Eliashib, the high priest, was the son-in-law of Sanballat the troublesome Horonite. Nehemiah "chased him" away. Sabbath observance was lax and he had to inaugurate a set of "blue laws" to insure its proper observance. He shut the gates of the city at dark on the evening before the Sabbath to keep traders and hawkers from violating the Sabbath with commerce. He threatened to "lay hands on them" if they tried to sneak in at any time during a Sabbath. He whipped the Levites into order, insisting that they "purify themselves," that they keep guard over the place of worship, and otherwise perform their duties in good style.

It is well to note carefully the fact that Nehemiah was a layman whose faith and dedication and perseverance were all important to the accomplishment of a vast enterprise. Under him

the stage was set for a new kind of life for the people of Israel.

The Books of Ezra-Nehemiah should be read under the direction of a good, modern commentary. See EZRA.

NER – *Light.*
I Samuel 14:50f.; 26:5, 14; II Samuel 2:8, 12; 3:23-25; I Kings 2:5, 32; I Chronicles 8:23; 9:36, 39; 26:28.

There is some confusion as to the relationship between Ner and Saul. On the one hand it would seem that Ner was Saul's uncle; on the other that he was Saul's grandfather. Be that as it may, Ner was the father of Abner, the great commander of Saul's armies. See ABNER, ISHBOSHETH.

NERIAH – *Yahweh is Light.*
Jeremiah 32:12, 16; 36:4, 8, 14, 32; 43:3, 6; 45:1; 51:59.

Neirah was father of Baruch, Jeremiah's secretary and messenger.

NETHANEEL – *God Gives.*
Numbers 1:8; 2:5; 7:18, 23; 10:15.

Nethaneel (also spelled Nethanel) was the leader of the tribe of Issachar who stood beside Moses as the people were numbered. When the tabernacle was set up, he offered for his people one silver plate of considerable weight and a silver basin, both filled with fine flour "mixed with oil," one golden dish, "full of incense," and so on—a splendid offering.

NETHANIAH – *Yahweh Gives.*
II Kings 25:23-25; Jeremiah 40:8-15; 41:1-18.
The father of one Ishmael who, as one of the old royal family, refused to accept Gedaliah as governor of Judah for the Chaldeans, and who killed Gedaliah and his Chaldean compatriots at Mizpah.

NICANOR – *Conqueror.*
Acts 6:5.
One of the seven men "of good repute, full of the Spirit and wisdom," nominated by the congregation at Jerusalem to the Apostles for appointment and ordination to the diaconate. Nicanor's name appears third on the list. Nothing more is known of him.

NICODEMUS – *Champion of the People.*
St. John 3:1ff.; 7:50; 19:39.
A Pharisee and ruler of the Jews who wanted to know more of Jesus, but was afraid to be associated with him openly. He therefore sought Jesus by night to discuss with him various matters of importance. He was well aware, as he said, that Jesus was a "teacher come from God," because the things he was said to have done only God can give the power to do. But what more was he?

Nicodemus was not finally convinced that Jesus was Messiah until the Crucifixion, although as "one of them" secretly, he spoke on behalf of Jesus in the councils of the Sanhedrin. After the Crucifixion he helped with the burial of Jesus and so, with Joseph of Arimathea, he belatedly declared himself. See JOSEPH.

NICOLAS – *Conqueror of the People.*
Acts 6:5.
Like Nicanor, above, Nicolas was one of the seven chosen to serve tables, in order to give the Apostles freedom to preach the word of God. Nicolas was a "proselyte of Antioch."

NIGER – *Black.*
Acts 13:1.
The surname of Simeon, one of the prophets and teachers at Antioch. He was one of the group

gathered when the Spirit moved them to "set apart" Saul and Barnabas for "the work to which I have called them."

NIMROD – Meaning wholly unknown. *Mighty? Strong?*
Genesis 10:8-12.

The son of Cush, grandson of Ham, who became known as a "mighty hunter before the Lord," the first of the "mighty men," who was said to have been the founder of the ancient Assyrian peoples, builder of Nineveh.

NIMSHI – *Yahweh Reveals? Drawn Out?*
I Kings 19:16; II Kings 9:2, 20; II Chronicles 22:7.

There is some uncertainty as to whether Nimshi was father or grandfather of Jehu, whom Elijah appointed to be anointed king of Israel. See ELIJAH, JEHORAM, AHAZIAH.

NOAH (NOE) – *Rest.*
Genesis 5:29-9:29; Isaiah 54:9; Ezekiel 14:14, 20; St. Matthew 24:37f.; St. Luke 3:36; 17:26f.; Hebrews 11:7; I Peter 3:20; II Peter 2:5.

Noah, son of Lamech, in the midst of corruption found favor with God because he was a righteous man, "blameless in his generation." The implication of the story is that he was the only righteous man and, for this reason, was chosen, together with his family, to survive the catastrophic flood which God would send to destroy his sinful creation.

Noah was commissioned to build an ark "of gopher wood" in which—with his family and two creatures "of every living thing" —to ride out the flood which raged for forty days and nights, covering "all the high mountains." After a hundred and fifty days the waters had receded and the ark came to rest on Mount Ararat. In another version of the story, Noah sent out first a raven, then twice a dove, to test the waters. On the second try the dove returned with an olive branch and on the third test the dove did not return.

The flood over, God established with Noah a covenant never again to destroy the earth by water. The rainbow was to be a sign of the covenant.

One story makes Noah the first tiller of the soil and the first to make wine and to become intoxicated.

NUN – Meaning doubtful, perhaps *Be Established, Endure?*
Exodus 33:11; Numbers 11:28; 13:8, 16; Joshua 1:1; 2:1, 23; Judges 2:8; I Kings 16:34.

Nun was an Ephraimite, the father of the famous Joshua. There is some possibility that the name Nun is intended as a clan name rather than the designation of a person.

NYMPHAS – *A Bridegroom, A Bride?*
Colossians 4:15.

A man—or a woman—in whose house the Church had been planted in Laodicea. St. Paul sent to this person, and to those who met with him in the house, greetings from prison in Rome. The name is also spelled Nympha.

O

OBADIAH – *Servant, Worshipper, of Yahweh.*

The Book of Obadiah.

The prophecy of the Book of Obadiah predicts the destruction of the wily Edomites with whom Israel had been at odds in tradition since the days of Jacob and Esau, and who had been among those gloating over the casting of lots for the spoils of Jerusalem, after its fall to the Chaldeans in 586 B.C. High mountain strongholds will not be enough "in that day," for, said the prophet, the "Day of the Lord is near upon all the nations. As you have done, it shall be done to you . . ." It is a book filled with notes of hatred, revenge and retaliation. The prophet cannot fully express his happiness over the fact that now it appears that the allies of Edom are to turn and destroy her. Perhaps those allies were the Nabataeans who drove the Edomites before them in c. 312 B.C., and by that time were masters of the land. The dates, however, are uncertain.

Almost nothing is known of the writer, who sees after general destruction, concentrating on Esau, a few who will rebuild the "house of Jacob" in Mount Zion and will give the new kingdom to the rule of the Lord.

Another Obadiah was the chief steward in Ahab's household, and he hid and fed a hundred prophets of the Lord when Jezebel ordered them "cut off" to make a place for her own priests of Baal. See I Kings 18: 3ff. See also ELIJAH, AHAB, JEZE-BEL.

OBED – *Serving.*
Ruth 4:17ff.; St. Luke 3:32.
Ruth's son who was the father of Jesse, the father of David.

OG – *Giant.*
Deuteronomy 3:1ff; Numbers 21:33; Joshua 2:10; 9:10; 12: 4; 13:12ff.; Psalms 135:11; 136:20.
King of Bashan, whose iron bedstead, nine cubits long by four cubits wide, marked him as a giant. The fact that it was made of iron might have been as impressive as its size. The Hebrew hordes took all his cities and put the inhabitants to the sword. He was an Amorite, king of the northern group, as Sihon was king of the southern band of the Amorites. See AMORITES, SIHON.

OMRI – *Worshipper of Yahweh.*
I Kings 16:16ff.; II Kings 8:26; Micah 6:16; II Chronicles 22:2.
A general in the army of Israel who became king when Elah, son of Baasha (q.v.), was murdered by Zimri. While Zimri was called king by one party, Omri's soldiers put him up as king and within seven days suc-ceeded in putting him on the throne. Zimri saw that his stronghold would fall and set fire to the king's house, with him-self in it. Omri thus emerged as king with sufficient power to hold the title. He defeated Moab and made foreign treaties which he hoped would help extend the kingdom, but the Assyrians would not be defeated. The war which began with them in Om-ri's time and continued, inter-mittently, until Ahab was finally beaten and killed was more than Israel's resources could carry. Both Omri and Ahab, however, gave good account of themselves in the long contest with the As-syrians. Omri reigned twelve years, in the last six of which his position was uncontested.

Although little space is given to him in I Kings and even less in II Chronicles, Omri was a king of considerable stature: It was Omri who bought and built the city of Samaria. His was a pros-perous reign (c. 877-869 B.C.) and he made no small impres-sion on his neighbors as a mili-tary leader and as administrator. He is mentioned with deference on the Moabite Stone, and As-syrian records refer to Israel, long after his death, as the "land of Omri." He was founder of a dynasty which survived for more than fifty years, and of customs and commercial relations with others which brought prosperity to his kingdom. It was probably an objection to these alien customs and cordial relations with others which caused the writers of Kings and Chronicles to give him so little attention. See MOAB, AHAB.

ONESIMUS – *Profitable.*
  Philemon 1:10.
Onesimus was a runaway slave, the property of Philemon, who was sent back to his owner with a letter from Paul asking Philemon to treat him now not as a slave but as a beloved brother in Christ. This he asked, commanded indeed, on the ground that both now were Christians. Onesimus had been converted after his escape. Paul explained that Onesimus had been of great service to him in prison, so much so that he had come to regard him as a son. Paul declared that in sending Onesimus back to his master he was sending his "very heart." Onesimus was, thus, the occasion for the Epistle to Philemon.

ONESIPHORUS – *Bringing Advantage, Profitable.*
  II Timothy 1:16; 4:19.
A Christian from Ephesus who

"was not ashamed" of Paul's chains, and sought him out in the prison in Rome and "refreshed" him. Paul referred, also, to his good service at Ephesus.

OREB – *Black,* e.g. "as a Raven."
  Judges 7:25; 8:3; Psalm 83:11.
Two princes of Midian, Oreb and Zeeb, were taken in the struggle of Israel with the Midianites, and at the command of Gideon they were killed. The Ephraimites brought Gideon their heads, having beheaded Oreb "at the rock of Oreb," and Zeeb "at the winepress of Zeeb."

ORNAN – *Quick, Joyful, Glad.*
  I Chronicles 21:15ff.
The name given by the Chronicler to the Jebusite from whom David bought a threshing floor on which to erect an altar. The writer of II Samuel calls him Araunah. In both cases the suggestion to buy the threshing floor, on a hillock, it seems, was made by Gad. See ARAUNAH.

ORPAH – Meaning doubtful, but possibly from a word suggesting "to turn one's back on," to "give the back of the neck."
  Ruth 1:4, 14.
A daughter-in-law of Naomi, the

Moabite wife of her elder son, Mahlon. When Mahlon died, and Naomi decided to return to Bethlehem, Orpah remained with her own "mother's house" in Moab. Orpah is described in the story as having "turned back" to "her people and to her gods." See NAOMI, RUTH.

OTHNIEL – Meaning doubtful, but *God is Force* has been suggested.

Joshua 15:17; Judges 1:13; 3:9-11.

The younger brother of Caleb, son of Kenaz, to whom Caleb gave his daughter and lands in reward for his defeat of Kiriath-sepher, or Debir. When the young woman came to him she told Othniel to ask her father for a favor. When Caleb agreed, his daughter specified her wish for springs to go with the lands. Othniel was a warrior and "judge."

P

PARMENAS – *Faithful, Steadfast.*

Acts 6:5.

One of the seven disciples selected to serve tables, so that the Apostles might be free for "prayer and the ministry of the word." Parmenas was therefore one known to be "full of the Spirit and of wisdom."

PAUL (SAUL) – *Little, Small, Rest.*

Acts 7:35; 9ff.; Galatians 1-2; etc.

Until his conversion the Apostle to the Gentiles was a Jew of the Jews, a Pharisee of the Pharisees. He was a Benjamite, born in Tarsus of Cilicia to a well-to-do family who were able, at any rate, to send their son, Saul, to study with Gamaliel, the foremost Rabbi of his time. Further, the family had acquired Roman citizenship—not the possession of every Jew. Since St. Paul earned his living as a tentmaker, it is logical to suppose he had learned the trade from his family.

He appears in the New Testament as one most incensed over the events in Jerusalem for which Jesus and his disciples were responsible. A man of some promise among the Pharisees, as he admitted, Saul was determined to stamp out this brand of "heresy." Approvingly he held the coats of those who stoned Stephen, the first Christian martyr. Later, armed with authority by the chief priests, he started for the city of Damascus intending to do his utmost to rid the Jewish community there of the Christian infection.

On the Damascus road, however, there occurred to him an experience which turned him around, converted him to Christ and changed the course of history. In a vision he saw the Christ so clearly that he was blinded to everything else. To his question, "Who art thou, Lord?" the answer given was: "I am Jesus, whom you are persecuting." He was told to go on into the city and to obey such instructions as would be given him there. Blind, he was led into Damascus to the home of a man named Judas, where Ananias, also instructed by a vision, came hesitantly to lay his hands on Saul to restore his sight. Soon he was baptized and began to preach in the synagogues that Jesus is the son of God—to the amazement of everybody.

It was not long before Jerusalem heard of this surprising turn of events and the persecutor became the persecuted. Friends helped him escape from Damascus by lowering him over the wall in a basket. He went, says the Book of Acts, to Jerusalem where he attempted to join the disciples; "and they were afraid of him, for they did not believe that he was a disciple." Barnabas took his part and helped ease him into the company. He began to preach "boldly in the name of Jesus" in Jerusalem; and again fear for his safety led his friends to slip him out of the city. He was sent to Tarsus.

In Galatians we are told that after the escape from Damascus (but we do not know how long after), Saul went for three years into Arabia, no doubt to pray and to think; and that he then returned to Damascus. After a time spent probably in and around Tarsus he was sought out by Barnabas who brought him to Antioch, where the disciples were first called "Christians" and where, too, a good many Gentiles were converted and accepted in the Church.

The course of Saul's life and ministry was now set. He began to claim right to the title "apostle" on the ground that he did not receive the Gospel from man but directly, "through a revelation of Jesus Christ." He claimed also that the Lord had committed to him the mission of Christ to the Gentiles. Both these claims were contested, but Saul won out in the dispute his claims aroused; and with the "right hand of fellowship" he and Barnabas were sent to evangelize the Gentiles while "Peter and the others" were to specialize on the mission to the Jews. It is hard to believe, however, that he was wholeheartedly supported in Jerusalem on either of his claims; for many references in the Epistles show that the Jerusalem, or "Jewish," party caused trouble in the churches he established. St. Peter tried to support his work, and St. Paul did his part in trying to show his devotion to the Jerusalem Church by bringing gifts from his congregations in time of famine. He seemed eager to be at one with Jerusalem when he might well have cut himself off from the Church there.

The Book of Acts narrates three "missionary journeys" which carried St. Paul into many cities and through incredible adventures. He (still called Saul at this time) and Barnabas were "set apart" by the Church at Antioch and sent out with John Mark as assistant on a trip which took them to cities in Pisidia and Lycaonia where the Gospel was preached and small congregations organized. Saul, whose name was changed to Paul on this journey, developed the technique of starting his work in the synagogues where he had a natural group to evangelize. Usually he was well received at first by the Jews, then "contradicted" by them. When opposition appeared he gathered his few converts, and such Gentiles as were interested, into a new group, taught them carefully, helped them organize for the new life in Christ, stayed as long as he felt he could, and moved on to another place—all too often with the assistance of the irate Jews. At Iconium he was stoned and dragged away as if dead. Mark left him and Barnabas at Perga. The journey over in extent, the missioners revisited some of the churches, returned to Antioch and gave a full report of their work to the congregation. The main point of the report had to do with the fact that God through them had "opened the door of faith to the Gentiles." The Church at Antioch was greatly pleased with the good news.

But the Church at Jerusalem was not happy to hear that Gentiles were being received without first having them become Jews. It was decided that Paul and Barnabas should go to Jerusalem to confer with the "apostles and elders about this question." Peter and James spoke in behalf of the work of Paul and Barnabas, and the decision noted above was announced.

The second journey started again at Antioch. This time Silas (or Silvanus) was Paul's companion, and Luke joined them at Troas. At Troas, too, Paul received the vision of the call to Macedonia, which took him to Philippi, Thessalonica, and Corinth, then back to Antioch by way of Jerusalem. On this journey, St. Paul insisted that Timothy, a Greek convert, be circumcised because there were so many strict Jews in the congregation at Lystra. At Philippi Paul and Silas were beaten and thrown in prison. They were delivered from prison by an earthquake, and were thereafter asked to leave the city. St. Paul refused to do so on the ground that as Roman citizens they had been beaten and imprisoned without trial and now would do as they pleased. Also visited was Athens, where St. Paul had rather a difficult time on Mars Hill.

The third journey was largely a revisiting of churches in Galatia and Phrygia, and finally a visit to Ephesus where he found disciples of John with whom he worked and to whom he gave the gifts of the spirit.

The Apostle then proposed to go to Jerusalem. His fellow-workers urged him not to go because of the dangers involved. He did go, however, stopping along the way at various places. With him went representatives of the churches, particularly from Caesarea. A report was made to James and the elders. St. Paul took one of his converts to the Temple, and shortly afterward he was charged with having taken a Gentile into the holy place.

Thus began the long series of events which ended with Roman imprisonment and death. The charge against him started a riot, for the strict Jews intended to kill him. The Roman tribune sent soldiers to save his life, but he felt obligated to hold him for questioning. He was bound and flogged in the hope of finding out the cause of the riot. St. Paul claimed Roman citizenship and the right of trial. Many appearances before tribunals, councils, governors ensued. At last his "appeal to Caesar" developed into the long trip to Rome, involving shipwreck along the way.

It is well established that at Rome his missionary activity continued. It appears that he was given considerable freedom and that friends and associates were with him constantly. Some scholars have opined that after "two full years" in prison at Rome he was released for a time, then re-taken and finally martyred. Perhaps he was only given privileges of the town. The question is not to be answered with certainty. The last events of his life are not recorded and the conflicting traditions leave a story far from clear.

It is clear, however, that the influence of St. Paul on the development and spread of Christianity is incalculable. His epistles have been guides and source documents earnestly pored over by every generation of Christians from his own day to ours. St. Paul's words on every matter of importance to the Church must be weighed with utmost care by every student, and should be carefully read by every member of the Church.

PEKAH – *Yahweh has Opened* (my eyes?), *Yahweh Watches.*
II Kings 15:25-16:5; Isaiah 7:1ff.
The son of a captain in the army of Israel who, with fifty Gileadites, formed a group of assassins and killed King Pekahiah in his own house. Having taken the throne in this way Pekah was able to keep it for a period variously estimated at from three to twenty years, probably only three years. During his reign, however, the throne became almost an empty thing, for the Assyrians, under Tiglath-pileser, took from him seven important cities and carried away captive large numbers of people. Pekah left the throne as had his predecessor, for Hoshea and a group of conspirators killed him, "struck him down and slew him." Isaiah 7:4, referring to Rezin and Pekah as "two smoldering stumps of firebrands," is regarded as perhaps a slur on Pekah's ancestry. The dates of his reign are given as approximately 737-732? B.C.

PEKAHIAH – *Yahweh has Opened* (my eyes?), *Yahweh Watches.*
II Kings 15:22-26.
King of Israel killed by Pekah and his assassins after a reign of only two years. A picture of the conditions of life in Israel at about this time is given in Hosea. See PEKAH.

PELEG – *Division.*
Genesis 10:25; 11:16-19.
The first son of Eber. During Peleg's time "the earth was divided." His name became a by-

word for anyone with many sons and daughters.

PELETH – *Flight, Haste.*
Numbers 16:1.
A Reubenite whose son, On, was associated with Dathan and Abiram in an uprising against Moses. See DATHAN.

PENINNAH – *Pearl, Red Coral.*
I Samuel 1:2-4.
A wife of Elkanah, the father of Samuel. It was the fruitfulness of Peninnah which so depressed the barren Hannah, who finally became the mother of Samuel and of other children as well. Peninnah probably made life miserable for Hannah, for although Peninnah had children it was Hannah who was loved.

PERES (PHAREZ) – *A Breach.*
Genesis 38:29; Ruth 4:12.
The son of Tamar by Judah. He had so many children that his name became associated with a "full quiver" or a "full house." To say, as the elders did to Boaz about Ruth, "May your house be like the house of Perez," was to wish for him a large family. Perez was said to be an ancestor of David. See RUTH, NAOMI, BOAZ.

PERSIS – *That Which Divides, Persian* (The Hebrew word

for Persia means "chop up, rend, divide").
Romans 16:12.
Although her name suggests division, the woman in Rome to whom greetings were sent, together with a special commendation for her hard work, was referred to as "the beloved Persis."

PETER SIMON, CEPHAS – *A Stone, A Rock.*
St. Matthew 4:18; 8:14; 10:2; 14:28f.; 15:15; 16:16ff.; 17:1ff.; 18:21; 19:27; 26:33ff.; St. Mark 3:16; 5:37; 8:29ff.; 9:2ff.; 10:28; 11:21; 14:29ff.; 16:7; St. Luke 5:8; 6:14; 8:45ff.; 9:20ff.; 12:41; 18:28; 22:8ff.; 24:12; St. John 1:40; 6:8; 13:6ff.; 18: 10ff.; 20:2ff.; 21:2ff.; Acts 1:13, 15; 2:14, 37, 38; 3:1ff.; 4:8ff.; 5:3ff.; 8:14ff.; 9:32ff.; 10:5ff; 11:2ff.; 12:3ff.; 15:7ff.; Galatians 1:18-2:21; I Peter 1:1; II Peter 1:1.
Simon Bar Jonah, that is, the son of Jonah, was a fisherman in partnership with his brother Andrew, who brought him to see Jesus—according to the story in the Fourth Gospel. All the Gospels show him "leaving the nets" to follow Jesus, henceforth "to catch men," and John's Gospel promises that Simon will be

called Cephas or Peter, "the rock."

Peter was one of the first to follow Jesus and became one of the "inner circle" of the disciples. He and Andrew made a team sent out by Jesus to spread the Gospel. He and James and John were often together, as for example, on the Mount of the Transfiguration. Jesus was in Peter's home and healed his wife's mother of a fever.

St. Peter was a quick, perceptive, and impulsive man, given to bursts of enthusiasm—and depression. He recognized his own unworthiness of his Lord's faith in him. It was Peter who first declared that "Jesus is Christ." At the Transfiguration it was he who blurted out the wish to build three tabernacles as a memorial of the occasion. It was also he who denied his Lord at the trial, after saying vehemently that he would die first. He might well have been ready to die, but not at all ready to see his Lord die.

After the Resurrection, Peter ran first to the sepulchre—but dared not enter. Jesus's words to Mary were, "Go tell the disciples and Peter," as if he knew well the difficulties Peter, especially, faced.

Quickly, after the Ascension,

St. Peter became a strong, "rock-like" leader, ready, eager to face anything for his Lord.

He became the spokesman for the group of the Apostles. He and James were involved in several miracles of healing, and Peter raised Dorcas from the dead. The word about Peter and the others was such that many sick and troubled souls hoped only to have the shadow of them fall in blessing; for they were known "to have been with Jesus."

The transition from Judaism to the full acceptance of Christ's teaching was not easy for Simon Peter. Rock-like when convinced, he was equally strong and stubborn before the notion that Samaritans and Gentiles could be Christians without first becoming Jews, without first being circumcised. A direct vision was required to make him understand that the Lord's saving work was performed for all who would believe in him. Once convinced, however, he tried to stand with Paul on the question of admitting Gentiles to the Church. St. Paul felt that he was not always consistent about it, for in Antioch St. Peter ate with Gentiles until "certain men" came from Jerusalem, men who would be critical of any such breach of Jewish custom.

Peter endured persecution and imprisonment with great spirit. If we are to believe the tradition that he is directly behind the Gospel of Mark, he was also a humble man whose shortcomings, clearly apparent to himself, he did not hesitate to declare openly.

In the Book of Acts, St. Peter is presented as a kind of "bellwether" of the Church, one whose now solid character, tested by adversity and imprisonment, was a source of strength and inspiration to all.

Tradition speaks markedly of his having gone to the great hub-city of Rome where, with St. Paul, he shares the honor of having established the Church. It speaks also of his courage in the persecutions there and of his quiet submission to martyrdom, of his having requested to be crucified upside down as a means of making special witness to the Lord Jesus.

Scholars are not at one on the subject of the epistles bearing his name. It is now thought that he is very closely associated with the First Epistle, though probably not directly its author. Serious doubts are held with regard to his having had any hand in the Second Epistle. Of course, the apocryphal Gospel of Peter is just that. Whatever his relation to the books bearing his name, or to the Gospel of Mark, of which he is said to be the apostolic source, one cannot think very much about the Christian Church without coming to a consideration of St. Peter, "The Rock," who before the Resurrection was not one to be counted on, and after it was the spark which, taking flame from Pentecost, set the Church in motion.

PHALTI (PALTI, PHALTIEL) – *Yahweh Causes to Escape.*
I Samuel 25:44.

As the man to whom Saul gave Michal, David's wife, Phalti must have felt the need for help from Yahweh to escape David's vengeance when, after David became king, he demanded that she be returned to him. Phalti must have loved Michal, for (II Samuel 3:16) as she was returned to David "her husband went with her, weeping all the way," until Abner roughly sent him home.

PHANUEL – *Vision of God.*
St. Luke 2:36.

A woman "of the tribe of Asher" whose daughter, Anna, was a prophetess in the temple at Jerusalem at the time of the purification of Mary and the presentation of Jesus. She was advanced in age.

PHARAOH – Originally, *The Great House,* i.e., "the King's House;" later it meant *The King.*
Genesis 12:15; 37:36; Exodus 1:11; 2:15; 3:10-18:10; I Kings 3:1; 11:1, 18-22; Jeremiah 25:19; 44:30; II Kings 18:21; 23:29ff.; Ezekiel 17:17; 29-32.
Pharaoh was the title of the kings of Egypt, several of whom appeared in the affairs of the people of Israel. Tradition associates one with Abram, Joseph, Moses (perhaps three), Solomon, Hezekiah. Pharaoh was mentioned in the prophecies of Isaiah, Jeremiah and Ezekiel. References are too numerous and of too little importance to be treated in detail.

PHILEMON – *Friendly, Affectionate.*
The Epistle to Philemon.
A convert in Colossae who offered his home as a place of meeting for the Church. He seems to have been somewhat well-to-do and generous with his means as well as with his home. The letter from St. Paul to him had to do with a runaway slave, Onesimus, whom the Apostle was sending back to his master. He gave Philemon the twice good news that the former slave had been converted to Christ and that he had served Paul well. In view of this he suggested that Onesimus be treated as a brother in Christ and promised Philemon that in Christ service now to be given by his slave would be gladly offered, not grudgingly as in former times. The Apostle wrote as if he felt he might have kept Onesimus with him in Rome without incurring the anger of the master; but said that he wanted to do the right thing. The tone of the letter indicates respect and friendship on the part of each for the other. While Paul does not ask that Onesimus be emancipated, the language of the letter is such as to hint that he had it in mind; and it is quite possible that Philemon got the point.

PHILETUS – *Beloved, Amiable.*
II Timothy 2:17.
This letter to Timothy warns against the teaching of Philetus who had "swerved from the truth by holding that the Resurrection is past already," that is, that it is to be thought of as a spiritual change coming with conversion rather than a hope and pledge of everlasting life.

PHILIP – *Lover of Horses, Warrior.*

1. St. Matthew 10:3; St. Mark 3:18; St. Luke 6:14; St. John 1:43ff.; 6:5-7; 12:21ff.; 14:8f.; Acts 1:13.

Philip the Apostle was called by Jesus shortly after the response of Andrew and Simon Peter. Like them Philip was from the town of Bethsaida. We are not told anything about his occupation. It was Philip who called Nathanael, saying to him, "We have found the Messiah . . . come and see!"

He seems to have had a practical nature, for when Jesus was thinking of the feeding of the thousands he asked Philip, "whence shall we buy bread, that these may eat?" In that miracle Philip seems to have been chosen to be a "first assistant." It was he who at Jerusalem brought a group of Greeks to speak to Jesus.

The Fourth Gospel speaks of Philip's intense listening to the words of Jesus concerning the relationship of the Son to the Father, but he was puzzled. He said to Jesus, "Show us the Father, and we shall be satisfied." Jesus' answer was a question: "Have I been so long with you, and yet you do not know me, Philip? He who has seen me has seen the Father . . ."

More about Philip, than that he was listed with the Eleven in Acts, we do not certainly know. It is thought that he went to Asia Minor and was buried at Hieropolis after a long ministry.

Philip the Apostle and Philip the Evangelist have been confused to the point of identification. Both Polycrates, Bishop of Antioch c. 190 A.D. and Clement of Alexandria, also c. 190 A.D., refer to Philip the Evangelist as Philip the Apostle. (See below).

2. Philip the Evangelist—Acts 6:5; 8.

In the list of the seven who were set apart as "deacons" Philip is named after Stephen, and his story follows in Acts after that of the first martyr. He was chosen as one "full of wisdom and of the Holy Spirit" to assist in administrative affairs, but he is soon seen in action as a preacher of the Gospel at Samaria, where many were converted, including a magician called "Simon Magus." It was his work here which was completed after his departure by Peter and John, who went down from Jerusalem to bestow the Holy Spirit by the "laying on of hands." This story suggests that Philip the Evangelist was not one of the Twelve and so did not have the authority of the laying on of hands. He baptized, but did not give the Spirit.

Leaving Samaria he went to Gaza by way of Jerusalem. On the desert road he met, converted and baptized a eunuch of Ethiopia who had been to Jerusalem to worship.

From this experience he went on to Caesarea where he settled and later entertained St. Paul as he was en route to Jerusalem. In this passage in Acts (21:8-14) we learn that Philip had four unmarried daughters "who prophesied." Here it was also that a prophet named Agabus came in and bound St. Paul's hands and feet with his own girdle, prophesying thereby the imprisonment of the Apostle.

3. Philip the Tetrarch—St. Luke 3:1; 19:12ff.; St. Mark 6:17.

One of the sons of Herod the Great, a just man, the best of the Herods. He was an active builder. His time of authority was long, from 4 B.C. to 34 A.D.

PHILISTINES – Meaning uncertain, *Immigrants?*

Genesis 21:32-34; 26:1-18; Exodus 13:17; Judges 3:3, 31; 10:6ff.; 14:1-16:30; I Samuel 4:1ff.; 5:1, 8-11; 6:1-7:14; 17:

1ff.; 31:1ff.; II Samuel 5:17ff.; 8:1; 21:12ff.; 23:9-16; Isaiah 2:6; 9:12; 11:14; Jeremiah 25: 20; 47:1-4; Ezekiel 16:27, 57; 25:16f.; Amos 1:8; 6:2; 9:7; etc.

The Philistines were a people, Aryan in origin, possibly from Crete, who were the chief opponents of the Israelites as they began to consolidate their position in the land of Canaan, and who eventually gave their name to the land, Palestine. Occupying the coastal plains and being a sea-faring people, they were troublesome to Israel as an ever-present threat even to the days of David and Solomon, who managed to keep them in bounds but never to subdue them completely.

These people moved into their areas as the ancient Hittite empire began to fall apart, and from the Hittites they learned something of the use of iron, a Hittite monopoly. I Samuel 13: 19-22 shows how they kept the Israelites from making or even from sharpening swords and spear tips. "There was no smith to be found throughout all the land of Israel; for the Philistines said, 'Lest the Hebrews make themselves swords and spears.'" Thus when Saul met the Philistines at Michmash, he defeated them with an army supplied mostly with farm tools. No doubt the most prized spoil of that battle was the captured armory.

David, often involved with the Philistines in guerilla warfare, was also befriended by them during his outlaw days. Except for the suspicion of the Philistine commanders he might have been involved in the battle of Mount Gilboa, in which Saul and Jonathan were killed.

The major cities of the Philistines were Gaza, Gerar, Ashdod, Ashkelon, Ekron, Ziklag which was given to David, and Joppa.

PHINEHAS – *Oracle?*

1. Exodus 6:25; Numbers 25: 7, 11; 31:6; Joshua 22:13; Judges 20:28; Ezra 8:33.

The son of Eleazar and grandson of Aaron, Phinehas was thus regarded as in the succession to the office of high priest. On one occasion he caused the death of two persons who were introducing alien religious practices picked up from the Midianites. His act was regarded as saving Israel from the plague (possibly venereal disease), and for it his sons were given perpetual title to the priesthood. Phinehas is named as the priest who carried the sacred vessels with the army in the war against the Midianites.

After the exile a group of priests claimed descent from him and based their claims to the priestly office on the right of succession as "his sons."

2. I Samuel 1:3; 2:34; 4:1ff. The younger son of Eli, the priest of the famous sanctuary at Shiloh. Phinehas and his brother Hophni were killed when the ark of God being carried by them in battle was captured by the Philistines. When news of the death of his sons was delivered, Eli fell from his seat and broke his neck from the shock, and the wife of Phinehas gave birth prematurely to a son whom she named Ichabod, meaning "The glory has departed from Israel." The reference was to the capture of the ark rather than to the death of Phinehas. Later writers attributed the death of Eli, Hophni, and Phinehas to the evil ways of Eli's sons, who were said to be greedy and contemptuous of their duties and overly intimate with women worshippers. See HOPHNI, ELI, ICHABOD.

PHLEGON – *Burning, Zealous.*
Romans 16:14.
One of those at Rome to whom St. Paul sent greetings. He was

grouped with Hermes, Patrobus, and Hermas and "the brethren who are with them," as if they might have been associated in some special way.

PHOEBE (PHEBE) – From a Greek word meaning *Pure, Bright, Radiant,* title of Artemis-Diana.

Romans 16:1.

One who is called a "deaconess" in the Church at Rome. Paul commended her as one who because she had been a "helper of many and of myself as well," should be received with cordiality, "as befits the saints."

PHYGELUS – *Fugitive.*

II Timothy 1:15.

In this Epistle to Timothy the writer states, "You are aware that all who are in Asia turned away from me." One of the Asiatics named was Phygelus. No reason is given for the "turning away."

PILATE – *One Armed with a Dart, Thrusting.*

St. Matthew 27:2, 13ff.; St. Mark 15:1ff.; St. Luke 3:1; 13: 1; 23:1ff.; St. John 18:29ff.; Acts 3:13; 4:27; 13:28; I Timothy 6:13.

Nothing is certainly known about the parentage, place, or date of birth of Pontius Pilate, who was "procurator" of Judaea from A.D. 26-37. Although a man of good experience as his position indicates, he was singularly inept in his dealings with the Jews. Rome, for example, had long respected the Jewish horror of images of all sorts, even to the point of removing in Jewish territory figures of the Emperor customarily borne on military standards. Pilate insisted on carrying—by night— the standards with Emperor-images into the city of Jerusalem. The pleas of the Jews he ignored and he threatened to kill any of the people who raised further disturbance about the matter. But so many of the people of the city surrounded the standards in fanatical protest that he could not afford to kill all of them, and he had to give in. In this two facets of his character were exhibited: a calloused attitude toward the people and their customs not generally approved by Roman officialdom, and a weakness in the use of the threat.

Further, according to Josephus, he used temple funds to build an aqueduct, and broke up the ensuing riot by planting disguised soldiers in the crowd. Relations between Pilate and the Jews were so bad that at the time Jesus was brought before him Pilate was in a position of needing to please them. He could find no substance in the charge against Jesus as reported to him by the Sanhedrin. Blasphemy meant nothing to the Roman, and Jesus' refusal to speak in his own behalf impressed him. To the question: "Are you the king of the Jews?", Jesus' answer, "*You* have said so," was satisfactory. Pilate was quite ready to release him, since he found in the conflicting testimony no real evidence of sedition against Rome, his only real concern with the whole matter.

St. Matthew's Gospel states that Pilate's wife warned him of danger in the handling of this case and that he was alert to the possibility of prejudice. Thus when he found no "cause" he washed his hands of the whole affair. St. Luke says that Pilate sent Jesus to Herod, as Tetrarch of Galilee, and that Herod, finding nothing wrong, sent him back to Pilate who joined Herod in stating his innocence. St. John's Gospel suggests that Pilate was about to release Jesus, for the Jews cried out, "If you release this man, you are not Caesar's friend!" This was an implied threat toward Pilate

who, in a moment of weakness, acquiesced in their demand and ordered the crucifixion of an innocent man. St. Mark writes that Barabbas, a common robber and murderer justly accused, was released instead of Jesus, in accord with the custom that at "the feast" a prisoner, "whom they would," should be set free.

After this historic moment Pilate failed again to please the people under his command, this time the Samaritans, and was relieved of duty and called home. Tradition and legend about him give a wide variety of stories— that he committed suicide; that he was convicted and stood trial in the Lord's own tunic which served as a prophylactic against the wrath of Tiberius; that his body was thrown into the Tiber and attracted so many evil spirits as to produce unholy fear amongst the people; that it was removed and walled up in a pit in the Swiss Alps. Some think of him as a weak man who tried but failed to befriend the Lord; others rank him as a prince of the devils; still others consider him an unfortunate instrument of the Lord to accomplish the divine purposes. Perhaps it is on such a theory that Pilate is regarded by the Coptic

Church as a saint, whose day is observed on June 25!

PILDASH – *Flame of Fire.*
Genesis 22:22.
Abraham's brother, the sixth son of Nahor.

PIRAM – *Wild, Roving.*
Joshua 10:3.
An Amorite king who combined with four others to try to stop the invasion of the Israelites after the battle for the city of Ai.

PORCIUS
Acts 24:27. See FESTUS.

POTIPHAR – *Gift of the Sun God?*
Genesis 37:36; 39:1.
The Egyptian of high position, captain of Pharaoh's guard, who bought Joseph from the Ishmaelite slave-traders. Joseph served him well and became a sort of "executive director" of Potiphar's many enterprises. Potiphar's wife, however, after failing to seduce her husband's slave, kept a garment he lost in escaping from her and accused him falsely of trying to attack her. Potiphar, of course, believed her and Joseph was thrown into prison—where he met Pharaoh's baker and butler,

through whom he was brought into the king's own house.

POTIPHERA – *Gift of the Sun God?*
Genesis 41:45, 50; 46:20.
The father of Asenath, Joseph's wife. Potiphera was a priest of On, or Heliopolis, and served the sun god Re.

PRISCILLA, PRISCA
Acts 18:2.
See AQUILA.

PROCORUS – **Possibly from the Latin, *procor*, meaning *Ask, Entreat;* or from the Greek, *Leader of the Company* (chorus).**
Acts 6:5.
One of the Seven chosen by the primitive Church in Jerusalem to serve tables so that the Apostles might be free to preach the Gospel. Nothing more is said of him.

PUBLIUS – **A Roman forename suggesting relations to the state, the public.**
Acts 28:7f.
"The chief man of the island" of Malta who was kind and hospitable to Paul and his shipwrecked company. Paul healed his father.

PUDENS – *Shamefaced.*
II Timothy 4:21.
A Christian in Rome who sent greetings to Timothy.

PUL
II Kings 15:19; Isaiah 66:19.
See TIGLATH-PILESER.

PUT, PHUT – *Bow.*
Genesis 10:6; Ezekiel 27:10; Nahum 3:9.
The third son of Ham, whose descendants were mercenaries of Tyre and Thebes, according to the prophecies of Ezekiel and Nahum.

Q

QUARTUS – *Fourth.*
Romans 16:23.
A disciple who sent his greetings to friends in the Church at Rome.

R

RAAMAH – *Trembling.*
Genesis 10:7; I Chronicles 1:9.
The fourth son of Cush. The
name is also given to a city referred to in Ezekiel 27:22, which
was on the Persian Gulf.

RABMAG – *Head of the Magi.*
Jeremiah 39:3.
An officer and possibly a prince
of Babylon, whose name was
Nergalsharezer. He and other
princes and officers "came and
sat in the middle gate" after the
fall of Jerusalem in 586 B.C.;
and when king Zedekiah of
Judah tried to escape, they captured him and sent him to Nebuchadnezzar who killed his sons
before his eyes, then put out his
eyes, and sent him to Babylon.

RABSARIS – *Head of the Eu-
nuchs.*
Jeremiah 39:3.
A Babylonian officer. See RAB-
MAG, above.
There was also an officer of
Sennacherib, king of Assyria,
named Rabsaris. See II Kings
18:17ff., and RABSHAKEH, below.

RABSHAKEH – *Head of the
Cupbearers.*
II Kings 18:17ff.; Isaiah 36:
2ff.
When Hezekiah of Judah rebelled against Assyria, "the great
king" of Assyria sent Rabshakeh
to warn Hezekiah that his alliance with Egypt, as proposed,
was reliance on "a broken reed
of a staff," and to state that it
was the Lord himself who was

on the side of Assyria. In the name of Sennacherib he said: "The Lord said to me, Go up against this land and destroy it." The representatives of Hezekiah tried to keep Rabshakeh from speaking directly to the people, but Rabshakeh shouted out his words to the "men sitting on the wall" of the city, in an attempt to separate the people from their king. His trick did not work, and Sennacherib's army was beaten by "the angel of the Lord" in the night.

RACHEL – *A Lamb.*
   Genesis 29:6-31:34; 33:1ff.; 35:16f.; 46:19-22; 48:7; Ruth 4:11; I Samuel 10:2; Jeremiah 31:15; St. Matthew 2:18.
The younger daughter of Laban with whom Jacob fell in love almost at sight. He worked for her for seven years—and was given Leah instead by the tricky Laban. But within a week he had Rachel also, in exchange for the promise of another seven years of work. Rachel's sons were Joseph and Benjamin. She died as Benjamin was born. Rachel was much frustrated by the fact that she had no children while Leah was bearing four sons. When at last Joseph was born to Rachel she was overjoyed.

As Jacob left Laban's house and service, he appealed for and received Rachel's loyalty. Not only did she agree to go with her husband but also she stole Laban's household gods and sat on them while he searched Jacob's tents for them. Jacob's explanation of the reasons for leaving Laban (Genesis 31) makes good reading. See JACOB, LABAN, LEAH.

RAHAB, RACHAB – *Breadth, Broad.*
   Joshua 2:1; 6:17ff.; Hebrews 11:31; James 2:25.
A harlot of Jericho who housed and hid Joshua's spies who had been sent to "view the land." The king of the land learned of their arrival and ordered Rahab to give them over to him. It was her idea that the Hebrews would take the land, and she hid the spies instead of turning them over to the king. Having hid them well she sent the searchers on a blind pursuit; then she appealed for protection from the ravaging Hebrews when they should come to take the city. The spies promised protection and told her to bind a scarlet cord in her window as a sign of immunity to attack. Jericho was destroyed, but Rahab and her family were saved

and absorbed into Israel. See
JOSHUA, CALEB.

RAM – *High.*
1. Ruth 4:19; I Chronicles 2:9.
The grandson of Perez and
great-great-grandfather of Boaz,
Ruth's second husband.
2. I Chronicles 2:25, 27.
The son of one Jerameel, the first
son of Hezron, alleged to be a
descendant of Judah.
3. Job 32:2.
The head of the family of Elihu,
the young man whose long and
angry speech is inserted into the
Book of Job.

**RAMESES (RAAMSES, RA-
MESSES)** – *Son of the Sun.*
Genesis 47:11; Exodus 12:37;
Numbers 33:3ff.
Eleven pharaohs were named
Rameses. It was Rameses II (c.
1301-1234 B.C.) who was pharaoh during the days of the Exodus of the Israelites under Moses.
It was this pharaoh who moved
the capital of Egypt to the great
Delta region and who built some
of Egypt's greatest monuments.
The great hall at Karnak and the
colonnade at Luxor were constructed in his time, and his ego-
tism is indicated by the number
of great statues of himself and
the substitution of his own alleged exploits for those of his
predecessors on the records of
the country.

RAPHA – *Fearful.*
II Samuel 21:16ff.; I Chronicles 20:4ff.
Translated as Ishbibinob, one of
the "descendants of the giants,"
Rapha was himself a giant
whose "spear weighed three
hundred shekels of bronze, and
who was girded with a new
sword," and who, further,
"thought to kill David." Instead,
however, he was killed by Abishai. After this episode, David's
men urged him not to go again
into battle.

RAPHAEL – *The Healing of
God. God Heals.*
The Apocryphal Book of Tobit, 3:17; Revelation 8:3 (?).
The angel of healing sent to the
assistance of Tobias who was
married to a widow whose seven
previous husbands had been
killed on the wedding day by
Asmodaeus, an evil spirit. The
widow, Sarah, having been re-
proached by her father's maid-
servants about the loss of seven
husbands, prayed to be allowed
to die or to be relieved of the
Asmodaean curse. Raphael was
then sent to remove the curse, to
scale away the "white films from
the eyes of Tobit," the father of

Tobias, "and to bind the evil spirit." Tobit tried to pay the angel for his services, not knowing who he was; but Raphael said, in refusing: "Those who perform deeds of charity . . . will have fulness of life . . ."

The reference to Raphael in the Book of Revelation is uncertain.

REBECCA, REBEKAH – Meaning uncertain, but *Stall, Stalled,* in the sense of being well-fed, content.
Genesis 22:33; 24:15ff.; 25: 20ff.; 26:7f.; 27:5ff.; 49:31.

Daughter of Bethuel and the wife of Isaac, who was selected for him by the trusted servant of Abraham. She was chosen when, in drawing water for the emissary of Abraham, she offered also to water the camels, and so gave the sign the servant had prayed for. Meekly she went with him to marry Isaac. To them were born Jacob and Esau. Rebecca favored Jacob and was not a bit meek in arranging things to have him take Esau's blessing by trickery. She cooked for Jacob the meal Isaac has asked of Esau and she helped Jacob disguise himself with animal skins in order to deceive his father. See ISAAC, JACOB, ESAU, ABRAHAM.

RECHAB – *A Rider? A Band of Riders?*
II Samuel 4:2ff.

One of two brothers who were captains of raiding bands under the command of Ish-bosheth, Saul's son. Rechab and Baanah, his brother, on learning of the death of Abner thought they might gain position with David by killing Ishbosheth. They killed him while he slept, brought his head to David, and were themselves put to death at David's order. David was anxious not to be associated with the death of any of Saul's family. See ISHBOSHETH, ABNER.

RECHAB,   RECHABITES – *Rider, Riders.*
Jeremiah 35; II Kings 10:15, 23.

A group of tent-dwellers, nomads, "purists," probably Kenites, who rigidly obeyed the command of "Rechab, our father, not to drink wine or to build cities or houses or to sow seed." The Lord told Jeremiah to force them to drink wine, as a symbolic act. They refused. Then their obedience to the command of their father was used to show in bold relief the disobedience of the people of Judah and Jerusalem to the command of their God.

The Rechabites were a group within Israel who resisted valiantly the change from nomadic to settled agricultural life, thinking that the latter was the road to decadence and separation from the true laws of God.

REHOBOAM – *Freer, Enlarger of the People?*
I Kings 11:43-12:24; 14:21ff.
Solomon's son and successor. He was hard and brittle, and apparently incapable of taking good advice. His reign was constantly threatened by civil war, and the internal confusion created by his own poor management laid the nation open to Egyptian attack. Shishak of Egypt took the treasures of the Temple and the palace. After this disaster shields of bronze to protect the king were substituted for the shields of gold used in the days of Solomon. In Rehoboam's time a cult of male prostitutes was tolerated as well as all the "abominations" Solomon's wives had introduced to the country. His failure to deal effectively with the complaints brought to him by Jeroboam resulted in the division of the kingdom. When asked to lighten the yokes laid on the people by Solomon, he stated his intention to increase them; and he said that whereas his father had beaten them with whips he would beat them with scorpions. See JEROBOAM, SOLOMON.

REHOBOTH – *Wide Spaces.*
Genesis 36:37.
A King of the Edomites; also the name of a well dug by Isaac's servants (Genesis 26:22).

REHUM – *Pity, Merciful.*
1. Ezra 2:3; Nehemiah 12:3.
One of the chief men who returned to Jerusalem with Zerubbabel. He is referred to as Nehum in Nehemiah 7:7.
2. Ezra 4:8f., 17, 23.
A Persian chancellor of Artaxerxes.
3. Nehemiah 3:17.
A son of Bani, a Levite, who helped repair the wall of Jerusalem.
4. Nehemiah 10:25.
One of the Levites who sealed the convenant with Nehemiah.

REI – *Yahweh is Friend.*
I Kings 1:8.
A friend of David, one of his "inner circle" of the court, who remained loyal in the revolt of Adonijah.

REKEM – *Friendship.*
Numbers 31:8.
One of the five kings of Midian

who formed a combination against the invasion of the Israelites under Moses and Phinehas. All five of the kings were killed, along with Balaam, who had been hired to invoke a curse on Israel. See BALAK, BALAAM, PHINEHAS.

REMALIAH – *Yahweh Increases.*
II Kings 15:25-37; 16:1, 5; II Chronicles 28:6; Isaiah 7:1-9; 8:6.

Remaliah was a Gileadite whose son, Pekah, a captain in the army of Israel, killed king Pekahiah and "reigned in his stead." See PEKAH, PEKAHIAH.

REUBEN – *"See, a Son?" Wolf? Seen,* or *Cared for by God?*
Genesis 29:32; 30:14; 35:22f.; 37:21-29; 42:22, 27; Exodus 1:2; 6:14; Numbers 1:20; Deuteronomy 11:6.

Jacob's first son by Leah. At maturity he was involved with his father's concubine and disinherited. Reuben, in the Joseph story, would not allow Joseph to be killed by his brothers, although he agreed that something had to be done about "the dreamer." He intended to rescue Joseph from the pit into which he had been thrown. Joseph was sold to the Ishmaelite slavers

without Reuben's knowledge or consent.

The tribe of Reuben did not fare well and gradually fell away from any attempt at leadership or tribal pride of strength. See JACOB, JOSEPH.

REUEL (RAGUEL) – *God is Friend.*
See JETHRO.

REZIN – *Dominion.*
II Kings 16:5-9; Isaiah 7:1-9; 8:6; 9:11.

The king of Syria who was allied with Pekah of Israel in war against Ahaz. They laid seige to Jerusalem but could not take the city. Their attack, however, forced Ahaz to seek an alliance with Assyria. After receipt of moneys from Ahaz, Tiglath-pileser's army took Damascus, capital of Syria and killed Rezin.

REZON – *Prince, Noble.*
I Kings 11:23ff.

A fugitive from Hadadezer of Zobah, who in the time of Solomon gathered a band of marauders and, going to Damascus, became king of Damascus. "He was an adversary of Israel all the days of Solomon," and as king of Syria he accomplished much "mischief" against Israel, which he "abhorred."

RHODA – *A Rose.*
Acts 12:13.

When Peter was miraculously released from prison, "he went to the house of Mary, the mother of John whose other name was Mark," and knocked at the gate. His knock was answered by Rhoda, a maid in the house, who recognized Peter's voice and, in her excitement, ran to tell the people gathered for prayer without opening the door. The people could not believe her words, but when Peter continued to knock, "they opened, they saw him and were amazed."

RIZPAH – *Variegated?*
II Samuel 3:7; 21:8-14.

Rizpah was a concubine of Saul with whom Ishbosheth accused Abner, his father's great general, of having improper relations. It was Ishbosheth's attitude toward this incident that caused Abner to give his support to David.

Rizpah's two sons by Saul, together with five sons of Merab, Saul's daughter, were handed over to the Gibeonites who wanted revenge on Saul's family because of his massacre of the Amorites years before. The men were hanged and left exposed. Rizpah covered herself with sackcloth and sat on a prominent rock for all to see, until David buried their bones with those of Saul and Jonathan. Thus were both the Gibeonites and Yahweh appeased.

ROBOAM
See REHOBOAM.

RUFUS – *Red.*
St. Mark 15:21; Romans 16:13.

His father was Simon of Cyrene, who was compelled to help Jesus carry the Cross.

A Christian in Rome who was remembered in the Epistle to the Romans.

Could this man, "eminent in the Lord," and whose mother was "his mother and mine," be Rufus, the son of Simon?

RUTH – *Friendship.*
The Book of Ruth; St. Matthew 1:5.

The Moabite daughter-in-law of Naomi who preferred the company of her mother-in-law to her father's people, after the death of her husband. When Naomi returned to her own home in Bethlehem, Ruth went with her. There she met and married Boaz, a man remarkable in his wisdom and restraint. To Ruth and Boaz was born Obed, father of Jesse, whose son was David. The ancestry of Jesus was thus traced to this woman of Moab.

The Book of Ruth is an "historical romance," written not in the days of the Judges but after the Exile. Its purpose was to protest the rigid laws of Ezra and Nehemiah against mixed marriages and intolerance. What better way to protest than to show that the great David was himself the son of a woman of Moab?

S

SABA, SABAEANS – *An Oath, A Covenant.*

Isaiah 45:14; Ezekiel 23:42; Job 1:15; Joel 3:8; I Kings 10:1-13. Also SHEBA.

The Sabaeans might have been descendants of Seba, a son of Cush, or of Sheba, his grandson; or of Joktan a son of Eber; or of Abraham by Keturah, his second wife. In any case they were known as traders with access to rich goods—spices, gold, gems, slaves—which they might have acquired as much by robbery as by trading.

Job was told, for example, that the Sabaeans "fell upon" and "took" his servants; in Ezekiel they are shown as having bracelets and crowns to bring in "from the wilderness"; in I Kings the Queen of Sheba is said to have visited Solomon with many rich gifts. She asked him questions, testing his reputation for wisdom, and remained with him for an elaborate entertainment. Undoubtedly, the Queen and Solomon had some commercial venture under way; and tradition says that the Queen bore Solomon a son, Menelek, having become a wife of Solomon, and that Menelek went to Ethiopia where he established a kingdom of his own.

SALATHIEL, SHEALTIEL – *"I Have Asked of God."*

I Chronicles 3:17; Ezra 3:2, 8; 5:2; Nehemiah 12:1; Haggai 1:1, 12, 14; 2:2, 23; St. Matthew 1:12; St. Luke 3:27.

A son of Jeconiah, or perhaps his grandson, who was father of Jehoiakim, king of Judah. He is listed in all these places not as of importance in himself, but rather as the father of Zerubbabel who led the first group of exiles to return to Jerusalem. See ZERUBBABEL.

SALMON, SALMA – *Strength, Firmness.*
Ruth 4:20f.; I Chronicles 2:11; St. Matthew 1:4-6; St. Luke 3:32.

The father of Boaz, Ruth's husband, and grandfather of Obed, whose son, Jesse, was the father of David, according to the genealogy in the "historical romance," the Book of Ruth, and the Chronicler.

SALOME – *Peace* (Feminine form of Solomon).
St. Mark 15:40; St. Matthew 27:56.

The wife of Zebedee, mother of James and John, who was also the sister of Mary, the mother of Jesus. Salome, in the First Gospel, was said to have come with James and John to ask for places for her sons on the right and left of the Lord in his kingdom. She was present at the Crucifixion and was with the Marys when they visited the tomb on the day of the Resurrection.

Although no name is given in the stories (St. Mark 6:22ff.; St. Matthew 14:6ff.) it has been said that the dancing daughter of Herodias, whose performance before the king ultimately cost the head of John the Baptist, was named Salome.

SAMLAH – *Garment.*
Genesis 36:36f.; I Chronicles 1:47f.

One of the kings of ancient Edom, "before any king reigned over Israel." His city was Masrekah. This genealogy is from the source of the Pentateuch known as "S" and said to be of Edomitic origin.

SAMSON – *Distinguished, Strong.*
Judges 13-16.

Samson, son of the Danite Manoah, was the Hebrew "strong man," comparable in many ways to the Philistine Goliath, to Hercules of the Greeks, and to the Norse Siegfried. He was born "of promise" to parents who were instructed carefully to see that he was raised a Nazarite—kept, that is, from strong drink and ritually unclean foods and from the use of a razor. The angel who first appeared to Manoah's wife with the promise of a son came again, on supplication, to make matters perfectly clear to the prospective father, disappearing from view in the flame of the burnt offering of thanksgiving made by Manoah and his wife.

When the legendary Samson grew to manhood he wandered "down to Timnah," where he became enamoured of a Philistine woman. Over his parents' protest he married her, and took his parents to the marriage feast. There he proposed a riddle to the thirty young men, his guests, with high stakes riding on the answer. The men got the answer by having Samson's wife, under threat, prod it out of Samson himself after seven days of weeping and nagging. Samson paid the price by killing thirty Philistines and handing over their goods to the young men.

This is characteristic of Samson's use of his great strength. He was no leader, and his war with the Philistines was a personal matter of vengeance. None of the folktales of Israel's strong man tell of any benefit to the people from Samson's strength. Yet the people seemed to enjoy such discomfiture as he was alleged to have inflicted on the Philistines. They might have enjoyed quite as much the fact that their rustic hero got into trouble because of his unsuccessful relations with women, and because of his pride and vanity.

Angry at his wife's sharing of his secret, he went home in a huff, and the woman's parents gave her to the best man at the wedding. Samson cooled off and went back to claim his bride, but her father refused to let him in the house. In reaction Samson put torches to the tails of three hundred foxes and burned out the crops and orchards of the Philistines, who then burned Samson's "wife" and "father-in-law." Samson then "smote them hip and thigh with great slaughter."

The Philistines, of course, retaliated, and Samson was bound for them by his own people, but escaped and killed 3000 Philistines with the "jawbone of an ass."

In Gaza, he fell in love with a harlot, Delilah who, in time and for money, ferreted out the secret of his strength, cut his hair and handed him over to her townsmen. They bound him, blinded him, and made sport with him in their temple. As his hair grew his strength returned, and his last act was that of pulling down the temple of Dagon on himself and some 3000 Philistines gathered for sacrifice.

A sorry use he made of his

great strength. The story, sordid as it is, probably was intended as a warning against mixed marriages, the pride of strength, the fruits of luxury, and light attitudes toward religious vows. Samson the strong man, amounted to little, though in the folk-stories he was called a "judge" in Israel.

SAMUEL – *Name   of   God, Heard of God.*

I Samuel 1-12; 15-16:13; 25:1; 28:3-20; I Chronicles 6:28; 9: 22; Psalm 99:6; Jeremiah 15:1; Acts 3:24; 13:20; Hebrews 11: 32.

Samuel was the "grand old man" among the judges. Both judge and priest, he tried to hold Israel to the ancient ways, to prevent the development of a monarchy. Finally he felt he must yield to popular pressure and, still protesting, he discovered and anointed Saul as Israel's first king. For a time he was in the position of "elder statesman" to Saul; but as the king's power and popularity grew with his victories over the Philistines, Samuel's influence diminished.

The time came when Samuel could no longer support the king. He warned Saul that because he failed to destroy "utterly" the Amalekites and all their possessions, because of his pride and greed which produced disobedience, the Lord "has rejected you from being king over Israel." Then, acting on an oracle of God he filled his horn with oil and went to Jesse the Bethlehemite and, after offering sacrifice, demanded to see Jesse's sons. Having seen all of them but David, a youngster in the fields with the sheep, Samuel sent for David. When he arrived, the Lord told Samuel, "Arise and anoint him, for this is he," the man to be king in Saul's place.

This done as a last great act in behalf of his people, Samuel retired to his home and school for prophets at Ramah. When he died somewhat later, "all Israel assembled and mourned for him."

Of his birth and early years little has been said. He was born as a child of prayer, to Hannah and Elkanah, and "devoted" by his mother to the Lord, in the care of Eli the priest at Shiloh. In his lifetime vast changes developed in the life of his people. Samuel was largely responsible for the strength and unity needed to develop a "nation" out of the tribes, for he himself was for long the leader, and as circumstances changed he chose new and strong leadership of the right sort to consolidate Israel's gains and to meet the new life—even though he disapproved of what he saw in that way of life.

As he relinquished his place to Saul, he addressed the people with these questions: "Whose ox have I taken? Or whose ass have I taken? Or whom have I defrauded? Whom have I oppressed? Or from whose hand have I taken a bribe to blind my eyes with it?" The people answered: "You have not defrauded us or oppressed us or taken anything from any man's hand." See HANNAH, ELI, SAUL, DAVID, KISH.

SANBALLAT – *The Moon God has Enlivened, Given Life.*

Nehemiah 2:10; 4; 6:2; 13:28; A Horonite leader who was "greatly displeased" at the appointment of Nehemiah as rebuilder of Jerusalem. Sanballat organized a group to destroy the work on the walls of the city, after his ridicule had failed to dissuade the workers under Nehemiah. Some of the Jews living in the area heard Sanballat's plot to destroy the half-raised walls and gave Nehemiah word of it. Nehemiah placed armed guards in low spots behind the walls and organized his people into guard units and work units. He armed the workers as well as the guards and went on with the project. Work went more slowly because of Sanballat, but it did not stop.

When he saw he could not stop the work, Sanballat then tried to lure Nehemiah into a conference outside the city. When that trap failed he sent out rumors that Nehemiah intended to lead his people in revolt against Persia.

But when the walls were completed and the Temple reconstruction was under way, and while Nehemiah was on his trip to Shushan, Sanballat, whose son-in-law was a son of Jehoida the priest, tried to use his position to find a soft spot for himself in the new city. In due time Nehemiah "chased him from me."

SAPPHIRA – *Sapphire.*

Acts 5:1ff.

The wife of Ananias, who joined her husband in making a half-empty gesture of generosity in selling their land and giving the proceeds to the Church. In keeping back some of the money they sealed their own fate, for Peter exposed the lie, and Sapphira, shortly after her husband, died of shame.

SARAH, SARAI – *Princess, Yahweh is Prince.*
Genesis 11:29ff.; 12:4ff.; 16: 1-8; 17:15-21; 18:6ff.; 20:1-21: 14; 23:1ff.; 24:36, 67; 25:10, 12; 49:31; Isaiah 51:2; Romans 4:19; 9:9; Hebrews 11: 11.

The wife (and half-sister) of Abraham whose name first was Abram; hers was first Sarai. The names were changed with the promise of the birth of Isaac, when both were old. In their travels Abraham twice used deception in an effort to conceal the fact that Sarai was his wife. He tried to pass her off as a sister, thinking to protect her (and himself) that way. She was commandeered for the harems of the kings of Egypt and Gerar and saved only by divine intervention. The two incidents are thought to be merely different versions of the same story, which is told also of Isaac and Rebekah involving the same king of Gerar.

Sarah was accounted to be 90 years of age when Isaac was born. Childless until now, she had given Abraham her maid, Hagar, to bear him children. Ishmael was born to Hagar. After Isaac's birth Sarah became jealous of Ishmael and Hagar, and she forced Abraham to drive them out into the wilderness. Sarah was buried in the "cave at Macpelah," the famous cave to which many were said to have been taken for burial.

SARGON – *The Established, the Legitimate, King.*
Isaiah 20:1.

Sargon was a king of Assyria who lived c. 772-705 B.C. Ruling as Sargon II, son of Shalmaneser V and father of Sennacherib, he was the greatest king of the greatest empire yet to be established in the Middle East. It was he who finally captured Samaria, after the three year struggle for it under Shalmaneser, and so produced the downfall of the kingdom of Israel in 721 B.C. The kingdom of Judah paid him tribute. Although he is mentioned by name only once, he is the king of Assyria intended in II Kings 17:5ff.

SAUL, SHAUL – *Asked, Inquired* (of).
1. Genesis 36:37f.; I Chronicles 1:48f.

This Saul, or Shaul, was one of the kings of ancient Edom, whose capital city was Rehoboth, "on the Euphrates."

2. I Samuel 9:2-27; 10:11-11; 13:1-19:24; 20:25-21:11; 22: 6ff.; 23:7-27:1.

The handsome son of the wealthy Kish, a Benjamite, who was tall and powerful as well as handsome. Kish sent Saul to search the hill country of Ephraim for a herd of lost asses. Failure to find them after a long search brought them to a city in the land of Zeph where a "man of God" was known to be. There they found that man to be Samuel. To the surprise of Saul and his servant, their arrival was expected, for Samuel had had a vision about a man of Benjamin who would become a hero of the people. When Saul appeared, the Lord told Samuel, "Here is the man who shall rule over my people." This meeting ended with the anointing of Saul and with Saul's joining a band of prophets at Gibeah in an ecstatic experience.

Another version of Saul's selection tells of Samuel calling an assembly of the tribes and choosing the tribe of Benjamin and then Saul by lot. Saul was not present for the festivities, for he had modestly hidden himself in the baggage.

His first act of valor after the anointing was the rescue of certain of his people from Nahash the Amorite, who had agreed to a treaty with the men of Jabesh which included the gouging out of their right eyes. Saul heard of the plight of these men and, cutting a yoke of oxen to bits, he sent the leaders of the tribes a rallying call—with the threat of death to their own oxen if they failed to obey the call. Nahash was defeated and the men of Jabesh delivered.

He then defeated the Philistines at the garrison town of Geba, and was on his way to a solid position as king. Jonathan, his son, was now at his side, a good warrior in his own right. Battles were fought with plowshares, mattocks, axes and sickles, for the Philistines would not permit a smith or smithy to exist amongst the Hebrews.

As Saul's influence spread, and he became more king than tribal leader, his pride grew also, and he violated the word of the Lord as spoken through Samuel to destroy the Amalekites completely. Agag the king was saved —and later slain by Samuel, who went berserk—and some of the spoil of battle was preserved. Saul tried to prove that he meant to offer the spoils to "Samuel's God," but Samuel rejected the excuse and Saul with it.

Rejection by Samuel seems to

have preyed on Saul's mind, for thereafter he was described as being "tormented" by an evil spirit. Samuel selected David to succeed Saul. Knowledge of this and David's might in battle kept the king in constant depression. His last years were spent more in trying to dispose of David than in following up his opportunities against the Philistines and others. He even tried to kill Jonathan because of his friendship for David, and he did command Doeg the Edomite to slaughter the priests at Nob who had befriended David.

Meanwhile Samuel died and Saul, worried sick, went to a "witch" to conjure up the spirit of Samuel to ask his counsel. From Samuel's shade he received no comfort at all, rather the certain fact that now the Lord had turned from him and would give the kingdom to David, and him and his people to the Philistines. "Tomorrow," said Samuel's apparition, "you and your sons shall be with me."

The next day Jonathan and two brothers were killed in battle and Saul, trapped, fell on his own sword to escape capture and torture at the hands of the Philistines. His head, and the heads of his sons were taken as trophies, and their bodies were pinned to the wall of Bethshan until rescued and burned by the men of Jabesh, those whom Saul had rescued in his first military action.

3. For the third man named Saul, see PAUL. See also DAVID, JONATHAN, SAMUEL, ABNER, MICHAL, KISH.

SCEVA – From a Greek word meaning to "Prepare," to "Dress"; possibly meaning "one who wears a priest's attire."
Acts 19:14.
A Jewish priest with seven sons at Ephesus tried to cast out a demon in the Name of Jesus. The evil spirit answered: "Jesus I know, and Paul I know; but who are you?" Then the evil spirit caused the demented man to attack and overpower all of them, so that "they fled . . . naked and wounded."

SECUNDUS – Second, After, Following.
Acts 20:4.
One of a group of companions of St. Paul as he left Macedonia for Syria. Secundus was a Thessalonian.

SEGUB – Might, Protection.
I Kings 16:34.
The unfortunate youngest son

of Hiel of Bethel, who rebuilt Jericho. An ancient custom in Canaan was that of offering a human sacrifice at the building or re-building of a city, even of an important house. At the laying of the foundation of the new Jericho, Abiram, the first son of Hiel, was offered, and his bones probably were laid in a hole in the stone. When the gates were placed, Segub was sacrificed.

There is evidence to suggest that the Hebrews once observed the custom.

SENNACHERIB – *Sin* (the Moon God) *Multiplied Brothers.*
II Kings 18:13-19; 19:16-20, 36; Isaiah 36:1ff.

Son and successor of Sargon II, king of Assyria. The son carried on the military program of his father and defeated an allied army of Egypt and Judah. He took all the fortified cities of Judah except Jerusalem and exacted heavy tribute from Hezekiah, which stripped the Temple treasury, including gold from the doors and posts. Some 200,000 prisoners were said to have been taken.

When he was ready, Sennacherib sent an army to Jerusalem. Rabshakeh, the commander, taunted Hezekiah over the defeat of Egypt, Judah's ally, and the weakness of Judah. "Do you rely on the Lord?" he asked. Then boastfully he said, "I am the agent of the Lord." He went on to ask what god of what people had been able to deliver his people from the king of Assyria. Hezekiah "rent his clothes" and consulted Isaiah the prophet. Isaiah soothed him by saying that Yahweh would put a spirit in Rabshakeh so that he would "hear a rumor and return to his own land." Hezekiah went to the Temple to pray and Isaiah sent him an oracle of deliverance. That night the "angel of the Lord slew 185,000 Assyrians in camp and the army broke camp and went home."

Domestic problems kept Sennacherib off balance for a time; probably these as much as the miraculous slaying of his hosts forced his return to Nineveh. He gathered all his forces for a mighty attack on Babylon and laid it in ashes.

Sennacherib was killed as he was at worship in the temple of Nisroch, his god. See HEZEKIAH, SARGON, RABSHAKEH, ISAIAH.

SERAIAH – *Yahweh is Prince.*
1. II Samuel 8:17.
A scribe of David important

enough to be named with the priests.

2. II Kings 25:18; I Chronicles 6:14; Ezra 7:1; Jeremiah 52:24.

When Nebuchadnezzar took Jeusalem, Seraiah, the son of Azariah, was chief priest.

3. II Kings 25:23; Jeremiah 40:8.

Gedaliah, Nebuchadnezzar's governor of Judah, advised Seraiah and other leaders in the community to remain quietly in the city and not to fear the Chaldean officials; and "It shall be well with you," he said.

4. I Chronicles 4:13f.

Seraiah was the father of Joab, David's great general.

5. Ezra 2:2; Nehemiah 10:2; 12:1, 12.

A priest who went to Jerusalem with Zerubbabel from the Exile.

6. Nehemiah 11:11.

A son of Hilkiah, a priest, who remained in Jerusalem after the Exile and who was known there as "ruler of the house of God."

7. Jeremiah 36:26.

Seraiah was sent by king Jehoiakim to seize Jeremiah and Baruch after the king had read and in contempt burned the scroll the prophet and his secretary had written, but "the Lord hid them" from Seraiah.

8. Jeremiah 51:59-61.

Seraiah the son of Neriah went to Babylon with the defeated king of Judah. He was given a book of warnings to read to Zedekiah, and told him that once it was read, it should be thrown into the Euphrates River, weighted with a stone, as a symbol of the fact that Babylon would sink under the weight of evil to be brought on her by the Lord.

SERGIUS – A Roman family or clan name, of Sabine origin. Acts 13:7ff.

Sergius Paulus was pro-consul at Cyprus, who being with one Bar-Jesus, a false prophet, summoned Paul and Barnabas to speak to him the word of God. Even though he was said to be "a man of intelligence," it was the magician's idea that Sergius would be able to resist whatever they might say. But Paul saw the magician for what he was and caused him to be blinded "for a time." Whereupon, Sergius "believed."

SHADRACH
See ABEDNEGO.

SHALLUM – Related to a word meaning, *Requite, Recompense, Retribution.*

1. II Kings 15:10ff.
The murderer of King Zechariah of Israel. Shallum was king for one month before he, in turn, was killed by Menahem.

2. I Chronicles 3:15; Jeremiah 22:11.
The son of Josiah, king of Judah, who is not mentioned in II Kings.

3. II Kings 22:14.
The husband of Huldah the prophetess consulted by Hilkiah the priest about "the book of the law" found when the Temple was repaired under Josiah, c. 621 B.C.

4. I Chronicles 9:17ff.
A Levite gatekeeper of the "threshold of the tent" as this was set up after the return from the Exile in Babylon. The legend was that his fathers had been in charge of the entrance of the "tent of meeting" in olden times.

Ten other men so named are mentioned in the Old Testament.

SHALMANESER – *Shulman is Chief.*
Five Assyrian kings were named Shalmaneser, but only two are mentioned in the Old Testament. The name is also spelled Shalman.

1. Shalmaneser III, although not mentioned directly in the Old Testament, figured nevertheless in the affairs of Ahab who, according to "a historic rock record . . . on the upper Tigris," sent some 2000 chariots and 10,000 men into battle against him. It appears that Ahab formed an alliance with Ben-hadad of Syria to check the rising influence of Shalmaneser. Non-biblical records indicate, further, that Jehu of Israel paid tribute to Shalmaneser, whose long reign (c. 859-824 B.C.) saw the rise of the Assyrians to the place of power in the area.

2. II Kings 17:3; 18:9.
Shalmaneser V, c. 727-722 B.C., received tribute from Hoshea, the last of the kings of Israel; and when Hoshea, in an alliance with Egypt, tried to throw off the burden of Assyria, Shalmaneser made him a prisoner and laid siege to Samaria. The siege lasted three years, and Shalmaneser died before Samaria fell to his successor, Sargon II, in 722-1 B.C.

SHAMGAR – *Cupbearer, Fleer, Deliverer.*
Judges 3:31; 5:6.
Shamgar was listed as the third of the judges in Israel after Joshua. He was noted for having "delivered" Israel from Phi-

listine oppression by killing six hundred of them with an ox-goad. The Song of Deborah refers to his days as being times when normal caravan travel ceased, when "travelers kept to the byways." Shamgar's efforts probably relieved that situation to some small degree.

SHAMMAH – *Fame, Renown.*
1. Genesis 36:13, 17.
A son of Reuel, and grandson of Esau; he was a leader of one of the Edomite tribes.
2. I Samuel 16:9; 17:13.
The third son of Jesse who was with his older brothers in the camp of Saul in the campaign against the Philistines.
3. II Samuel 23:11ff., 33.
A Hararite in the time of David who stood alone at Lehi against a band of the Philistines and killed them. Later he was given a place of responsibility in David's list of thirty-seven body guards. Another Shammah, a Harodite, might be the same man, although he is listed separately, II Samuel 23:25.

SHAPHAN – From a word meaning a "rock-badger." Possibly, *Sly? Elusive?*
1. II Kings 22:3ff.; II Chroni-cles 34:8ff.; Jeremiah 36:10ff.
A scribe in the reign of Josiah to whom Hilkiah the priest gave the newly discovered "book of the law." Shaphan was told to deliver it to the king. He read it first to himself and then to King Josiah. He then took the book to Huldah the prophetess, as the king commanded him to do. Thus, in this important episode in the life of the people, Shaphan was chief messenger and reader.
2. II Kings 22:12; 25:22; II Chronicles 34:20; Jeremiah 26:24; 39:14; 40:5; 41:2; 43:6.
The father of Ahikam, an officer in Josiah's court. He might be the same person as the above.

SHAPHAT – *He Has Judged.*
1. Numbers 13:5.
A Simeonite, son of Hori, who was sent with the spies to look over the land of Canaan. As did all but Caleb, he liked what he saw but urged caution in trying to take the land.
2. I Kings 19:16.
The father of Elisha, the great prophet.
Three other men named Sha-phat need not be considered.

SHAREZER – *Protect the Prince?*

II Kings 19:37; Isaiah 37:38. Sharezer and his brother, Adramelech, sons of Sennacherib, murdered their father while he was at worship in the temple of "Nisroch his god" at Nineveh. He and and his brother escaped "into the land of Ararat."

SHAVSHA – (He) *Persists?*

I Chronicles 18:6.
A scribe or secretary in David's court who was entrusted with state papers and records. He might be the Seraiah in II Samuel 8:17, and the Shisha in I Kings 4:3.

SHEAL – Probably related to a word meaning, *Ask, Request.*

Ezra 10:29.
One of the group of priests, a son of Bani, who had taken a foreign wife and, on hearing the law, agreed to put her away.

SHEALTIEL

See SALATHIEL

SHEAR-JASHUB – *A Remnant Returns,* or *Shall Return.*

Isaiah 7:3.
Isaiah used signs and symbols to give greater point to his prophecies. Thus he named his son Shear-jashub, "the remnant shall return," to keep before the people his message that God would finally redeem Israel through a "remnant" of the faithful.

SHEBA – *An Oath, A Covenant.*

II Samuel 20:1ff.
"A worthless fellow" who thought mistakenly that when Absalom revolted the power of David was broken. Using Absalom's action as a cue, Sheba led the men of Israel in a simultaneous revolt. Judah remained loyal to the king, unexpectedly. David was willing to look lightly upon the rebellion of Absalom, though it drove him out of Jerusalem; but when Absalom was killed, David sent Abishai and Joab with full strength to put down Sheba, who, he said, "Will do us more harm than Absalom," for he represented the northern tribes not wholly united to David. Joab pursued Sheba to a fortified city intending to rout him out. A wise woman of the city intimated that the battle and siege were not necessary—if Sheba were all he wanted from the town. Joab heard her suggestion. The next day Sheba's head was thrown over the wall of the

city and Joab returned to Jerusalem, his mission accomplished.

SHEBA, THE QUEEN OF

I Kings 10:1ff.; St. Matthew 12:42; St. Luke 11:31.

The independent, spirited and lovely ruler of the Sabaeans who, when she heard of his fame and wisdom, visited Solomon "to test him with hard questions."

It is likely that her visit was also a diplomatic and commercial mission. The writer of I Kings would have it that she came as one among other rulers to do homage to a wise and powerful king. Her country was well populated by traders with extensive interests in gold, spices, and fine cloths. Trade agreements were therefore liable to be among "all that was in her mind."

Tradition suggests that Solomon added her to his collection of wives. If so, he did not keep her long, for having "given her all that she desired" in addition to the customary "bounty" of presents, he saw her return to her own land. Tradition persists, also, that a son was born to this queen as a result of her visit to Solomon, and that the son became king of the Ethiopians or the Abyssinians.

In the New Testament the Queen of Sheba is called the "queen of the South." See SABA, SABAEANS, SOLOMON.

SHEBNA – *Youthfulness.*

II Kings 18:18, 26, 37; 19:2; Isaiah 22:15; 36:3.

Secretary to Eliakim, who was head of the household of Hezekiah. According to Isaiah, Shebna was "feathering his nest." II Kings suggests that Eliakim out-ranked Shebna; but Isaiah's outburst against Shebna speaks of him as "hewing out a habitation," a tomb, for himself in a place from which the Lord would dislodge him and give his robe and girdle and authority to Eliakim.

SHECHEM – *Shoulder.*

Genesis 33:18-34:31.

Although Shechem is better known as the name of a city, Shechem the son of Hamor was the man who, having raped Dinah, the daughter of Jacob, wanted then to marry her. So desirous was he to marry her that he submitted to the demand that he be circumcised, along with all his father's male people. Then, while they were "sore," Simeon and Levi took them by surprise and killed them all.

SHEM – *Name, Renown.*
Genesis 5:32; 6:10; 7:13; 9:23-10:1; 10:21f., 31; 11:10f.
The first son of Noah. Shem was with Noah aboard the Ark. He and his brother Japheth covered their father's "nakedness" as he lay intoxicated, uncovered and helpless under the influence of the wine he had learned to make.

Shem was remembered as the ancestor of Elam and the Elamites, of Asshur and of Aram, among others.

SHEMAIAH – *Yahweh is Fame.*
I Kings 12:22; II Chronicles 11:2; 12:5ff.
Twenty-five men named Shemaiah may be found in the Old Testament; only one of them is of any real importance.

Shemaiah was the prophet who advised Rehoboam to allow the revolt of Jeroboam to proceed. He persuaded Solomon's son and heir to think that the revolt was the will of the Lord and therefore not to be resisted. See REHOBOAM, JEROBOAM.

SHEMER – *Watchman, Overseer, Guard.*
I Kings 16:24.
The owner of "the hill of Samaria" which he sold to King Omri for two talents of silver. The latter fortified the place and made it his capital city.

SHESHBAZZAR – *Sun God Protect the Lord,* or *the Son?*
Ezra 1:8, 11; 5:14, 16.
The governor of Jerusalem when Cyrus sent the vessels of Israel back to the city from which they had been taken. Ezra 5:16 states that it was he who laid the foundations for the new Temple. He is otherwise known as Zerubbabel.

SHIMEI – *Yahweh is Fame.*
II Samuel 16:5-13; 19:16-23; I Kings 2:8ff.
Nineteen men were named Shimei; but only two will be mentioned here.

One of the two was an officer of David who remained loyal to him as Adonijah revolted; and the other, curiously, threw stones and curses at David when Absalom was in rebellion.

As David fled from Jerusalem in Absalom's revolt, any number of would-be leaders and disgruntled men raised their hands and tongues against the king. Shimei, probably related to Saul, heard of David's hasty departure and came out to curse him. Abishai, riding beside the king, asked permission to "take off his head," but David forbade it.

After the fall of Absalom, however, when David was again in Jerusalem, Shimei "made haste" and "fell down before the king," begging as a coward would do for his miserable life. David again held Abishai's sword.

But David did not forget the curse of Shimei. He warned Solomon of the presence and danger of Shimei and suggested that he should not be "held guiltless." Solomon forced Shimei to build a house in Jerusalem and to stay in the city. One day, somewhat later, Shimei left the city ostensibly to search for runaway slaves. The search took him to Gath. On his return Solomon called him in, revealed his knowledge of the disobedience, informed him of the consequences and sent Benaiah to strike him down.

SHISHAK, SHESHONK
I Kings 11:40; 14:25; II Chronicles 12:2ff.
The king of Egypt who gave refuge to Jeroboam after his revolt against Solomon. Later, during Rehoboam's reign, he took and plundered the city of Jerusalem and the surrounding territory.

SHOBI – *Yahweh is Glorious.*
II Samuel 17:27.
The Ammonite prince who provided David with "beds, basins, and earthen vessels," and food for his retinue during his flight from Absalom.

SHUNAMMITE, SHUNEM – A Place-name.
Two Shunammite women left a mark in the Old Testament.
1. I Kings 1:3, 15; 2:17-22.
A maiden of Shunem named Abishag was appointed to keep the aged David warm. See ABISHAG.
2. II Kings 4:12-36.
A woman of Shunem noticed that Elisha, "a holy man," passed her way often and she provided food and shelter for him. Elisha, in turn, prayed that she might be given a child. A son was born to her. Later the son died, and the woman sought the prophet who, with prayer and touch, restored the child to life. A brilliantly told story of a truly noble woman. See ELISHA.

SIHON – *The Great, Bold One.*
Numbers 21:21-24; Deuteronomy 1:4; 3:2; 31:4; Judges 11:19; Psalm 135:11; 136:19.
King of the Amorites whose refusal to allow the Israelites led by Moses to pass through his

lands which he had recently taken from the Moabites; and whose attack on Israel led to his death and the dispossession of the Amorites from the land. So savage was the destructive power of Israel released on Sihon that Og, king of Bashan, and Balak of Moab were badly frightened.

Sihon seems to stand in later literature of the Old Testament as a symbol of the futility of resisting the people of God. See OG, BALAK, BALAAM.

SILAS, SILVANUS – From the Latin, referring to the *God of the Forests, the Country, Woodsman.*

Acts 15:22-40; 16:19-29; 17:4-15; I Thessalonians 1:1; II Corinthians 1:19; I Peter 5:12. One of the "leading men" in the Church at Jerusalem who was sent with Judas Barsabbas, Paul, and Barnabas to Antioch to convey the decision of the "Council of Jerusalem" on the question of admitting Gentiles to the Church without first having them become Jews.

He seems to have been a Roman citizen and also a spirit congenial to St. Paul, for he was one who made the second missionary journey, replacing Barnabas. He was thrown into prison with Paul at Philippi. They were delivered by an earthquake which occurred as they prayed and sang hymns.

The first Epistle of Peter refers to Silas (Silvanus) as the bearer of that letter to the exiles in Pontus, Galatia, Cappadocia, Asia, and Bithynia. See PAUL, BARNABAS, BARSABAS.

SIMEON – Meaning doubtful, but it is suggested that the name is related to Leah's statement that he was born "Because the Lord has heard"; another suggestion, also doubtful, *Offspring of a Hyena and a Wolf.*

1. Genesis 29:33; 34:25-31; 35:23; 42:24ff.; 43:23; 46:10; 48:5; 49:5; Exodus 1:2; 6:15; etc.

The second son of Jacob and Leah, whose tribe seems to have fared badly in warfare. The tribe of Simeon, under the protection of Judah, in time lost its identity to Judah. Simeon was not prominent in the biblical stories. He and his brothers, Reuben, Levi and Judah, lashed out at Shechem for the rape of their sister, Dinah; and when Joseph in Egypt sent his brothers to bring Benjamin, Simeon was held as hostage. Otherwise, little is said of Simeon.

2. St. Luke 2:22-34.

Simeon, "righteous and devout," had had word by revelation that he would not die before he had seen the Lord's anointed, the Christ. When Jesus was brought to the Temple for "presentation," Simeon took him in arms, blessed him and Mary and Joseph, and uttered the beautiful words now known as the *Nunc dimittis*. Having seen the Christ and recognized him, Simeon was ready to "depart" this life "in peace."

3. Acts 13:1.

"Simeon who was called Niger" is named, after Barnabas, as among the "prophets and teachers" in the Church at Antioch.

SIMON – *Hearing*.

Several men named Simon appear but few details are available for discussion of them. Simon Peter is listed herein under the name PETER, by which the apostle is better known.

1. St. Matthew 26:6; St. Mark 14:3.

Simon the Leper, in whose home in Bethany Jesus was entertained. Some think he might have been related to Mary and Martha. He was cured by Jesus, and Jesus was "anointed" in his home.

2. St. Mark 6:3; St. Matthew 13:55.

Simon, the "brother of Jesus."

3. St. John 6:71.

The father of Judas Iscariot.

4. St. Mark 15:21.

Simon the Zealot, one of the Twelve.

5. Acts 9:43.

Simon the Tanner, at whose home in Joppa St. Peter stayed "many days." It was in his home that Peter had the vision of the sheet containing all kinds of animals and the command, "Rise, Peter, kill and eat!"

SIMON MAGUS – Simon "the Great."

Acts 8:9ff.

A magician in Samaria converted and baptized by Philip. He had called himself "the great one." Later, when Peter and John went to Samaria and conferred the gifts of the Spirit by the laying on of hands, Simon was greatly impressed and offered to buy the apostolic powers thus exhibited. The Apostle's rebuke, and scorn for his money, frightened him so that he begged their prayers to avoid what he thought was a curse.

From this man and this incident comes the term "simony," meaning any attempt to buy the power and position usually given in the Church for devotion and ability.

SISERA – Meaning unknown, but perhaps *One Who Arrays* (an army?); *One Who is Unrestrained, Not Controlled?* Judges 4:2ff.; 5:20ff.; I Samuel 12:9; Psalm 83:9.

Sisera was military commander of the army of Jabin, king of the Canaanites, whose army with "nine hundred chariots of iron" was defeated by the armies of Deborah and Barak which had no chariots. As the hosts of Jabin under Sisera gathered for battle on the plain of Esdraelon, a mighty storm made a morass of the plain, and the "brook" Kishon became a torrential stream. Under these conditions the chariots of Sisera were useless, and the army of Barak ripped through Sisera's forces to what seemed a miraculous victory. Sisera himself escaped the plain on foot and sought refuge with Heber the Kenite. He should have been well received in Heber's tent; but in Heber's absence (was he attached to Sisera's army?) Jael, Heber's wife, invited Sisera into the tent and gave him refreshments; as he was beginning to relax, she hit

him with a mallet and drove a tent peg through his temple. With the destruction of Jabin's army and the death of Sisera, the Canaanitish domination of Israel was broken, "and the land had rest for forty years." See BARAK, DEBORAH, JAEL.

SO – Meaning Unknown. II Kings 17:4ff.

A King of Egypt to whom King Hoshea of Israel appealed for help against his overlord, Shalmaneser, king of Assyria. Hoshea had been paying tribute to Shalmaneser, but thinking to gain the help of Egypt he failed to pay, with the result that Shalmaneser's armies laid siege to Samaria for three years and took Hoshea captive. There is uncertainty as to who So was, precisely, for no king of Egypt of that name appears in the lists of the Pharaohs. It is possible that he was a prince of Egypt, or merely a high official.

SOLOMON – *Peace, Peaceable.* II Samuel 12:24; I Kings 1:10-12:23; 14:21, 26; I Chronicles 3:10; 22:5-19; 28:5-29:30; II Chronicles 1:1-11:17; Psalm 72, 127 (titles); Proverbs 1:1; 10:1; St. Matthew 1:6f.; 6:29; 12:42; etc.

David's son by Bathsheba. By the connivance of his mother and Nathan the prophet he became king and successor to the mighty David.

Solomon is popularly known as "the wise man." In some ways he was indeed wise. By a certain astuteness in handling internal affairs, by putting up what moderns would call a "good front," and by making strong alliances and sound trade agreements, he managed to consolidate his position both at home and abroad.

Many alliances, however, were sealed by marriage to women who brought strange customs, strange religions with them. Solomon tolerated the whims and fancies of his women. To keep up the front proved costly. Forced labor crews commandeered by the king for his building program (and ultimately loaned out to others) proved irritating to the people. Toleration of peoples and ideas proved debilitating and confusing. Departure in his middle and later years from the covenant with the Lord proved disastrous.

Vanity, and indulgence where he should have been strict, leniency where he should have been positive, rigidity where he

should have been lenient—these brought the wise man's kingdom to losses and divisions from which it never recovered. Thus, in spite of his associations and trade agreements with such people as the Pharaoh, Hiram king of Tyre, and the Queen of Sheba, in spite of his great building program and his reputation for wisdom, leaders like Jeroboam the son of Nebat, and Hadad the Edomite and Rezon of Damascus began, during his reign, to set the stage for the division of the kingdom he had inherited from David. When Solomon died, Jeroboam returned from Egypt and tried to effect a reconciliation with Rehoboam, Solomon's son; but Rehoboam, with visions of glory exceeding those even of his father, refused to hear the complaints of the followers of Jeroboam, so that all the tribes except Judah withdrew to form the Kingdom of Israel.

The legend of the gift of wisdom in answer to Solomon's prayer persisted, so that various books of the Hebrew "Wisdom Literature" were attributed to him, although he did not write them.

Solomon's reign, c. 960-922 B.C., during a time when both Egypt and Assyria were weak and not very aggressive, was the high point of the development of Israel as a nation; and Solomon himself was a man who could make the most of his opportunities. Judgment on Solomon should not, perhaps, be too harsh; for it is likely that deep, traditional differences between the tribes of the north and the south, buried under Saul and David to meet the Philistines, were too great to be overcome by any leader in that place, at that time.

SOPATER, SOSIPATER – *The Father Saves.*

Acts 20:4; Romans 16:21.

A companion of St. Paul through Macedonia on his journey to Jerusalem with gifts and representatives from the Churches. Sopater was from Berea. He might have been the same person as Sosipater, a "kinsman" of the author of the "postscript" to the Epistle to the Romans.

SOSTHENES – *Well "Put,"* *Well Made* (by God); or from the word "to Save," *Saviour?*

Acts 18:17; I Corinthians 1:1.

At Corinth Paul tried to testify to the Jews that "Christ was Jesus." They opposed and "reviled" him and he "shook out his garments" saying, "From now on will I go to the Gentiles." One Jew, Sosthenes, the ruler of the synagogue, apparently was converted. When an attack on Paul which brought him before Gallio, the Proconsul, was dismissed as mere quibbling, the Jews took out their rage on Sosthenes. They beat him before the tribunal of Gallio, presumably to show the Proconsul the great intensity of their feelings toward anyone friendly to Paul. The Apostle referred to Sosthenes as "brother." Sosthenes was a man of integrity and courage.

STACHYS – *An Ear of Corn?*

Romans 16:9.

A friend of St. Paul in Rome; he was called "beloved."

STEPHANAS – *A Crown.*

I Corinthians 1:16; 16:15-17.

The first person, together with his family, to be baptized by St. Paul, and mentioned as the "firstfruits" of his preaching in Achaia. Stephanas, with Fortunatus and Achaicus, visited Paul in Ephesus. These three might have brought a letter from Corinth which elicited in response the first letter to the Corinthians, and they might have been bearers of that letter to the Church at Corinth.

STEPHEN – *A Crown.*

Acts 6:5-8:3; 11:19; 22:20.

Stephen was one of the "seven men of good repute, full of the Spirit and of wisdom" chosen and set apart to assist the apostles in the distribution of alms at Jerusalem. The work to which he was appointed in this way was expected to accomplish the healing of a division in the Church between the Hebrews and the Hellenists over what seemed to be neglect of the widows in the latter group.

But Stephen was not confined to that duty alone. "Full of grace and power," he did wonders and signs and became an effective apologist. So successful was he in the art of disputation that his opponents felt they must dispose of him, even if somewhat shady methods were necessary. False witnesses accused him of speaking against the law of Moses and blasphemous words against God; saying, they charged, that Jesus would destroy the Temple and change the customs of Moses. He was brought before the Council and asked, "Is this so?"

Stephen's defense was fearless. He argued, as reported in the Book of Acts, that they, not he, were the offenders, and described them as "stiff-necked and uncircumcised in heart and ears," lawbreakers, killers of the prophets and, finally, of the "Righteous One."

On hearing these things from Stephen the members of the Council were outraged and "rushed on him" and stoned him to death. Stephen prayed as he died that the accusers might be forgiven. Saul of Tarsus "was consenting to his death," as he stood by minding the garments of those who threw stones. It is likely that Stephen's defense and his death left a deep impression on Saul. With Stephen's death a serious persecution of the Church in Jerusalem began and many of the disciples were scattered. As they went to places of relative safety, they preached the Word and many were converted to the faith.

Stephen, the first "Christian Martyr," became in death, as in life, a strong light in the development of the Church, a high example of fidelity to the cause of the Lord.

SUSANNA – *Lily.*

1. St. Luke 8:3.

One of the women who gave of her means, and other assistance, to Jesus and the disciples as they "went on through cities and villages, preaching and bringing the good news of the kingdom of God."

2. The Story of Susanna in the Apochrypha.

Susanna, a woman of very "great refinement and beautiful," was also the virtuous wife of a Jew prominent among his people in Babylon. Two elders coming often to his house saw Susanna and lusted after her. They caught her bathing in the garden and threatened that unless she gave herself to them, they would accuse her of entertaining a young man. She decided that she would throw herself on the Lord rather than allow herself to fall into the hands of the unscrupulous elders. She therefore cried out, and the elders accused her, as they said they would do, and hailed her before the assembly, in which they themselves were among the judges. As it appeared that Susanna would be put to death, the Spirit moved young Daniel to cry out for justice, for further examination. He demanded the right to examine the accusers, and getting each one by himself asked under what tree he had seen the virtuous Susanna in intimacy with a young man. Each elder gave a different kind of tree, and Daniel, of course, quickly showed them to be the culprits. Susanna was vindicated and Daniel earned great respect from the incident.

The short story of Susanna is an addition to the Book of Daniel, appearing in the Greek at the beginning of the book and in the Vulgate as Daniel 13.

SYNTYCHE – *A Happy Chance, A Happy Event.*
Philippians 4:2.
Syntyche and Euodia were two women in the Church at Philippi who had allowed some disagreement to come between them. Paul appealed to the congregation to help them, for, as he said, "They have labored side by side with me in the Gospel . . ."

SYRIA, SYRIANS – From a word root meaning, *Citadel, Castle, Stronghold, Palace.*
Genesis 25:20; 28:5; 31:20, 24; Deuteronomy 26:5; II Samuel 8:5-13; 10:6-19; I Kings 20:20-29; 22:11, 35; II Kings 5:2, 20; 6:9; 7:4-16; 8:29; etc.; Isaiah 9:12; Jeremiah 35:11; Amos 9:7; St. Luke 4:27.
The Syrians were thought of as the Aramaean branch of the Shemitic tribes, their patronymic having stemmed from the name of Aram, who was the fifth son of Shem. The lands of

the Syrians varied from time to time; but in general, as stated in Isaiah 7:8, "the head of Syria is Damascus," a land more productive than that of Palestine, one toward which the Israelites ever looked with envy. So desirable was it that it was conquered by most of the rising powers. The richness of the land might be suggested by reference merely to the "cedars of Lebanon," to "Damascus" fabrics and steel. It is thus to be expected that Syria was a strong influence on the Israelites. The city names of Syria—Damascus, Tyre, Sidon, Berea, Carchemish, Antioch, for example—are often seen in the Bible, as are the names of Syrian leaders such as Hadadezer, Ben-hadad, Hazael, Hiram, and Rezin.

Syrian religious influences were also felt constantly within Israel, as might be expected. Many gods were worshipped in Syria, including the familiar Baalim and the fertility goddesses, as Astarte; so that Israel felt religious as well as economic pressure from Syria.

T

TABEAL – *God is Good.*
Isaiah 7:6.
Tabael was the father of the man whom Rezin of Syria and Pekah of Judah wanted to place on the throne of Judah in the place of Ahaz, c. 735 B.C. The name is also spelled Tabeel.

TABITHA – *Gazelle.*
Acts 9:36, 40.
See DORCAS.

TAHPENES
I Kings 11:19f.
The queen of Egypt in the days of Solomon. Her sister was given as wife to Hadad of Edom, one of Solomon's adversaries.

TAMAR – *Palm, Date Palm.*
1. Genesis 38:6, 11, 13, 24;
Ruth 4:12; I Chronicles 2:4.

The wife of Er, the first son of Judah. Tamar was the mother of Pharez, and therefore an ancestor of David and Zerah.

When her husband died, she was given to his younger brother, Onan; but Onan refused to have children for his deceased brother, and the "Lord slew him also." Judah told Tamar to wait until his son Shelah grew to manhood. But when Shelah was grown, Judah failed to keep his promise. Tamar then, disguised as a harlot, tricked Judah into her tent and obtained his signet ring as a pledge. Pregnant by Judah, she showed the pledge to prove it. Her sons, thus, were Judah's sons.

2. II Samuel 13:1ff.
Tamar was the daughter of David who was raped by her

half brother, Ammon. Absalom, her full brother, killed Ammon and was banished.

3. II Samuel 14:27.
Absalom had a daughter named Tamar, named possibly for his beautiful sister, whom he loved tenderly.

TATNAI – *A Teacher?*
Ezra 5:3, 6; 6:6, 13.
A governor of "the province Beyond the River" under the king of Persia, who tried to stop the work of Zerubbabel on the rebuilding of the Temple in Jerusalem. Thinking that they were at work without proper authority, Tatnai (also spelled Tattenai) wrote to Darius the king giving him a full report on the situation as he saw it. Darius searched the records, found a decree of Cyrus authorizing the work, and wrote of that fact to his governor.

TERAH – Meaning uncertain, but *A Wanderer? One Who Turns About?*
Genesis 11:24ff.; Joshua 24:2.
A son of Nahor who was the father of Abraham, Nahor, and Haran. A native of the Chaldean city of Ur, he migrated to Haran where he died at a great age.

TERTIUS – *"The Third."*
Romans 16:22.
It is possible that Tertius was the secretary to whom the Epistle to the Romans was dictated, for he slips in a little personal note, referring to himself as "I, Tertius, the writer of this letter . . ." It has been suggested that he was Silas.

TERTULLUS – Diminutive of *Tertius*. See above.
Acts 24:1ff.
A lawyer employed by the Jews to present their case against St. Paul to Felix, the Roman governor. He was an orator who called the Apostle "a pestilent fellow, an agitator."

THADDAEUS – Meaning possibly akin to Theudas. See below.
St. Matthew 10:3; St. Mark 3:18; St. Luke 6:16; Acts 1:13.
The Gospels of Matthew and Mark list Thaddaeus as one of the Twelve. He is probably the same man as Judas the son of James, as listed in St. Luke and in Acts. He was also called Lebbaeus. Little is known of him; tradition speaks of his work in Egypt and Syria, and of his having been buried in Beirut after he was crucified.

THEOPHILUS – *God Loves, Dear to God, Highly Favored of God.*

St. Luke 1:3; Acts 1:1.

The Gospel of St. Luke and The Acts are directed to Theophilus, who might have been a Roman official converted to the Christian faith. It is possible that the name Theophilus was his Christian name, not his Roman name. He might not have been a Christian at all; but rather one to whom Luke wrote hoping that he could help gain for Christians in Rome the freedom accorded to devotees of other religious points of view. This latter seems unlikely, however, for the writer refers to his having had previous information, perhaps "instruction," in the facts under consideration.

THEUDAS – Possibly a contraction of *"Theodoros," a Gift of God.*

Acts 5:36ff.

When the Apostles were brought before him, Gamaliel referred to a certain Theudas who gathered some four hundred men about him, and "gave himself out to be somebody," but really amounted to nothing. He was killed and his band was dispersed. The great Rabbi suggested that the disciples of Jesus, if allowed to work unmolested, might disband and amount to nothing now (as he thought) that their leader was no longer with them.

THOMAS – *A Twin.*

St. Matthew 10:3; St. John 14:1-7; 20:24ff.

The name "Thomas" means "a twin"; but as the man among the Twelve who was most difficult to convince he has often been called "the doubter." As Jesus spoke obliquely of himself as "the way," Thomas spoke up to say that since he did not know where the Lord would go he could not, of course, know the way. After the Resurrection, Thomas, who had not been present when Jesus appeared to the others, declared that until he had touched the nail wound and the spear thrust in Jesus' hands and side he could not believe him risen from the dead. Some days afterward Jesus appeared again and offered Thomas the opportunity to feel his hands and side. Still later he appeared to Thomas and others of the disciples at the Sea of Galilee.

Tradition tells us that Thomas became a missionary to Parthia and India, and an apocryphal gospel is attributed to him.

TIBERIUS CLAUDIUS NERO – Tiberius is a Roman Imperial title, probably having reference to the River Tiber. Nero is a name associated with the Claudian family, from the Sabine word, "brave."

St. Luke 3:1.

Tiberius came to the imperial rank in Rome, after four others nominated by Augustus died, in 14 A.D. For a time he reigned with Augustus before he came to full power as Emperor. He was a good military leader and a good ruler, on the whole, although he did maintain his power by the execution of a number of persons who might have got in his way. It was in the fifteenth year of his reign that John Baptist began to preach repentance and the coming of the kingdom of God. He was Emperor when Pontius Pilate was procurator of Judaea.

TIGLATH – PILESER.

II Kings 15:29; 16:7-10; I Chronicles 5:6, 26; II Chronicles 28:20.

One of the most powerful kings and military leaders in ancient times, who conquered for Assyria, or exacted tribute, Babylon, Syria, Phoenicia, and Mesopotamia, among others. His appearance in II Kings was occasioned by the request of Ahaz, who needed help to defend himself against a confederation of Pekah of Israel and Rezin of Syria. Tiglath-pileser broke up the combination by killing Rezin and taking Damascus, and by carrying much of Israel into captivity. Isaiah had disapproved the confederacy. Tribute from Ahaz of Judah prevented any serious attention from Tiglath-pileser toward Jerusalem. Ahaz thus became his vassal, and the price for protection was very great.

Tiglath-pileser was the third of his name, and might be the same as PUL. His reign began in 745, ended in 727 B.C.

TIMAEUS – *Highly Prized, Honored.*

St. Mark 10:46.

The father of the blind man whose name was Bartimaeus, or son of Timaeus, and who sat by the side of the road at Jericho to beg. This was the Bartimaeus of whom Jesus asked: "What do you want me to do for you?" The answer: "Master, let me receive my sight."

TIMON – *Honorable.*

Acts 6:5.

One of the Seven chosen to serve

tables in the primitive Church at Jerusalem, along with Stephen and others. Nothing is said of Timon except that he was chosen and appointed by the laying on of hands for this special duty. All of the Seven were said to be men filled with the "Spirit and wisdom."

TIMOTHY, TIMOTHEUS – *Honored of God.*

Acts 16:1; 17:14f.; 18:5; 19:22; 20:4; Romans 16:21; I Corinthians 4:17; 16:10; II Corinthians 1:1, 19; Philippians 1:1; 2:19; I Thessalonians 1:1; 3:1-7; I & II Timothy; Philemon 1; Hebrews 13:23.

The son of a converted Jewess (Eunice) and a Greek father, Timothy was born at Lystra. He became a Christian and was recommended to Paul as a companion for the second of his missionary journeys. Because of the number of strict Jews in the places into which Paul planned to go, where the fact that Timothy's father was a Greek would be known, the Apostle had him submit to circumcision.

At Athens Paul sent Timothy on a special mission to Thessalonika, and asked him to bring back a report on the Church there. The report became the occasion for the Epistles to that Church. He was also sent to deal with troubles in the Church at Corinth, but was replaced there by Titus.

Timothy was left by Paul in Ephesus to care for the work there, and was one of a group who met the Apostle at Troas on his way to Jerusalem to bear gifts and to report.

When Paul was imprisoned in Rome he sent for Timothy. Little is known definitely of him beyond the fact that he did join Paul in Rome. Tradition refers to him as the first Bishop of Ephesus, as a close friend of John the Apostle, and as a martyr under Nero.

The Epistles to Timothy are a special study in themselves.

TITUS – A common Roman forename, often abbreviated simply, "T".

Galatians 2:1-3; II Corinthians 2:13; 7:6, 13f.; 8:6, 16, 23; 12:18; II Timothy 4:10; Titus 1:4.

When Paul went with Barnabas to report to the Church in Jerusalem on their activities among the Gentiles, he took Titus with him to let the Judaisers see for themselves, in Titus, what God had wrought in the world of the Gentiles; for Titus was a Greek. Paul declared that Titus had not been required to become a Jew (i.e. to be circumcised) before being admitted to the Church. With Titus as "exhibit A" the work of Paul and Barnabas among the Gentiles was approved by the Council of the Apostles.

Titus was a companion of Paul in his travels, and was sent to Corinth to accomplish what Timothy seemed unable to do there. He was also made agent in Corinth for collection of funds to be sent for relief of the Church in Jerusalem, hard-pressed by famine. Titus was left in Crete to establish the Church.

Close friendship with St. Paul made Titus hurry to Rome when he learned of the Apostle's imprisonment. He was called by St. Paul, "My true child in a common faith," and was entrusted with many responsibilities.

TOBIAH, TOBIJAH – *Yahweh is Good.*

1. II Chronicles 17:8.
King Jehoshaphat of Judah attempted to strengthen his kingdom and to do away with as much as possible of the religious practice contrary to the worship of Yahweh. He sent Levites to the several cities of Judah to teach the law, and priests to put it into practice. One of the Levites was Tobijah.

2. Ezra 6:20; Nehemiah 7:62.
Not everyone who returned from the Exile was able to prove "their fathers' houses or their descent, whether they belonged to Israel." Among such was one Tobiah. Since his name was not to be found among the genealogies, he had no rightful place to claim in the new community.

3. Nehemiah 2:10, 19; 4:3, 7; 6:1, 12ff.; 13:4-8.
Tobiah was an Ammonite who, with Sanballat, opposed the building of the new walls around Jerusalem. Yet when they were built in spite of jeers and active opposition, Tobiah, who had good connections both in Judah and elsewhere, used his influence to obtain for himself an excellent apartment in a building once used to store the various sorts of offerings received from the people. When Nehemiah returned from his long trip to Babylon, the capital, he found Tobiah comfortably ensconced in the apartment "in the courts of the house of God," and as he said, "I was very angry, and I threw all the house-

hold furniture of Tobiah out of the chamber."

TOBIAS – *Yahweh is Good.*
See TOBIT.

TOBIT – *Yahweh is Good,* (My Good).
The Apocryphal Book of Tobit.
A pious Jew exiled to Nineveh in the time of Shalmaneser, who tried to keep the law and who at great danger to himself made it his business to bury the dead among his people in accord with the law. While burying a Jew thus he was stricken blind and wished to die. Remembering a sum of money left with Gabael, a friend in another city, he sent his son Tobias to claim the money. On the way Tobias, with the aid of the angel Raphael, drove away the evil spirit from the maiden Sara (whose seven husbands had died on the wedding night under the influence of the evil Asmodeus) and married her. He went on to get the money from Gabael, and with Sara and Raphael (also called Azarius) returned to his father's house and saw the angel restore his father's sight. Tobit then continued in

his good works, more respected than before by his fellow Jews.

TROPHIMUS – *Nourished, Nourisher, Master of the House, Steward.*
Acts 20:4; 21:29ff.; II Timothy 4:20.
A Christian of Ephesus who went with St. Paul on his journeys into Asia. He was with Paul also when he took gifts to the Church in Jerusalem. While there it was thought that Paul had taken him, a Gentile, into the court of the Temple, and an uproar ensued. Paul was arrested by the soldiery to save his life, and allowed to speak to the crowd. At first the people listened, for he spoke in Hebrew, but when he said that the Lord had sent him to the Gentiles, the crowd shouted again, "Away with him!"

TRYPHENA – *Dainty, Effeminate?* Possibly *Proud.*
Romans 16:12.
A woman to whom greetings were conveyed through the Epistle.

TRYPHOSA – *Delicate? Broken?* Possibly *Pierced.*
Romans 16:12.
A woman in Rome to whom

greetings were sent by St. Paul, with the comment, a "Worker in the Lord."

TUBAL-CAIN – *"The Father of Copper and Iron Smiths," Smith, Artificer.*
Genesis 4:22.
The son of Lamech and Zillah who became a forger of "all instruments of bronze and iron." He was thus accounted the first "smith," and his shop the first smithy. He was probably regarded as the founder of the tribe of Kenites or at least associated with them, a people who knew how to work metal and whose traditional habitat was near the iron and copper mines in the Arabah.

Although it is not certain, it appears that the root behind the name "Tubal" indicates some underground activity such as that of a miner.

TYCHICUS – *Fortunate.*
Acts 20:4; Ephesians 6:21; Colossians 4:7; II Timothy 4:12; Titus 3:12.
A traveller with St. Paul to Jerusalem. He delivered the Epistle to the Colossians and possibly that to the Ephesians. He was to have been sent to Titus at Crete to help or to relieve him, but there is no account of his arrival.

TYRANNUS – *Kingly, Lordly, Imperious.*
Acts 19:9.
Tyrannus was a property owner in Ephesus in whose hall St. Paul argued daily for the Way for a period of perhaps two years. No mention is made of the status of Tyrannus with regard to the Way; but it is supposed that he was a Christian.

U

URBANE, URBANUS – *Belonging to a City, "Sophisticated?"*
Romans 16:9.
One of the Christians in Rome to whom St. Paul sent his regards as a "fellow worker in Christ."

URIAH – *Yahweh is Light* (My Light or Flame).
1. II Samuel 11:3-12:23; 23:29; I Kings 15:5.
Uriah was the victim of one of the few really dishonorable acts attributed to King David. The king had an affair with Bathsheba, Uriah's wife, while her husband was with Joab in a campaign against the Ammonites. When Bathsheba told David she was with child by him, the king sent for Uriah the Hittite on pretext of obtaining information about the campaign.

He then told Uriah to go home to his wife. But Uriah, a loyal soldier, refused to take privileges denied his fellow soldiers and "slept at the door of the king's house" instead. After another futile attempt to have Uriah go home, David sent word to Joab to put Uriah in the thick of battle and to withdraw so as to be certain that he was killed. He was killed and, after a proper time of mourning, Bathsheba was taken to the king's house as his wife.

Uriah the Hittite was one of David's "valiant men."
2. II Kings 16:10ff.
Although Uriah is here spelled Urijah, the name is the same.

Urijah was a priest in Jerusalem to whom king Ahaz gave the task of fashioning an altar like the one Ahaz had seen in Damascus.

3. Jeremiah 26:20ff.

Uriah the prophet whose words against Judah brought on him the wrath of King Jehoiakim. His words were startlingly like those of Jeremiah himself, and the king "sought to put him to death." Uriah fled to Egypt to escape the king's assassins, but Jehoiakim's agents were sent to Egypt and forced the return of the prophet. On arrival he was killed and his body thrown into the burial place of the common people.

Three other men named Uriah, all priests, need not be considered.

URIEL – *My Light is God* (El);
My Flame is God.

1. I Chronicles 6:24; 15:5, 11 and II Chronicles 13:2.

Two people named Uriel by the Chronicler are of little importance. One was a Levite in the family of Kohath in David's time, whose father was Tahath. Nothing more is said of him, except that he was one of several Levites allegedly appointed to carry the ark into the city after the first tragic attempt to do so some months before. The Chronicler attributed the death of a former bearer, Uzzah, to the

fact that he was not a Levite. This time the Levites "sanctified themselves" before their attempt to move the ark, presumably, from the house of Obed-edom to the place prepared for it in Jerusalem, and the trip was made with much ceremony. See UZ-ZAH, OBED-EDOM.

The other Uriel, mentioned in II Chronicles, was the father of Abijah's mother. Abijah was king of Judah; his grandfather was from Gibeah.

2. The Apocryphal Book of II Esdras 4:1ff.; 5:20ff.; 10:28ff.

Uriel was the name of the angel, usually regarded as one of the archangels, who as a special messenger from God interpreted for Ezra the signs of the times, the signs of the end of the age, and instructed him in the course of action proper for him under the circumstances.

UZZA, UZZAH – *Strong,*
Strength, Yahweh is (My)
Strength.

II Samuel 6:3ff.; I Chronicles 13:7ff.

One of the drivers of the new cart which bore the ark of God from Baalejudah, where it had been in the custody of Abinadab, to the new city of David—Jerusalem. As one of the oxen stumbled Uzzah put out his hand to touch and steady the ark. Instantly he died. His death was understood to be a sign of God's anger toward anyone who touched the ark without authority, and further, that Yahweh disapproved of the transfer of the ark at that time. But David was angry that Yahweh would allow his wrath to break forth in such a manner, and he was troubled, as well. He did not continue the trip into the city. The ark was housed with Obed-edom outside the city for three months and then brought in with great rejoicing. See ABINIDAB, OBED-EDOM.

UZZIAH – Meaning the same as for Uzza, above.
II Kings 14:21; 15:1ff.; II Chronicles 26:1ff.; Isaiah 1:1; 6:1; 7:1; Hosea 1:1; Amos 1:1; Zechariah 14:5.
It should be observed that Uzziah the son of Amaziah was also called Azariah. Uzziah (Azariah) ascended the throne of Judah c. 786 and reigned until c. 734 B.C. Records of his official acts are few in spite of the long time in office. His was thought of as a reasonably good rule, although he was cursed with leprosy and forced to give charge of the government to Jotham, his son. See AZARIAH, JOTHAM.

UZZIEL – *God is Strong.*
Exodus 6:18, 22; Leviticus 10:4; Numbers 3:19, 30; I Chronicles 6:2; 15:10; 23:12, 20; 24:24.
A son of Kohath, who was a son of Levi. Uzziel is mentioned more often than his works would seem to justify; but he was one of the chiefs of "houses" selected, according to the Chronicler, to bring the ark into the city of Jerusalem and to serve probably as a leader of song, music and dancing for the joyous occasion.
Five other men named Uzziel are of little importance.

V

VASHNI – *Yahweh is Strong.*

I Chronicles 6:28, 33(?).
Vashni is listed by the Chronicler as the first son of the prophet Samuel; but I Samuel 8:2 gives Samuel's first born as Joel.

VASHTI – *Beautiful.*

Esther 1:9-2:4.
The exceptionally beautiful but haughty wife of King Ahasuerus who refused to obey her husband's command to appear at a banquet in order to show her beauty to the people and the princes. Her refusal was considered not only an insult to the king and his guests, but also to all husbands. Her act of disobedience would "be made known to all women, causing them to look upon their husbands with contempt." A decree was therefore issued that Vashti should be put away and "another who is better than she" be found.

This opened the way for Esther, a Jewess, to become queen and heroine of her people. See ESTHER, MORDECAI, HAMAN.

W

THE WITCH OF ENDOR
I Samuel 28:7ff.

Although the text of the story calls the woman a "medium" or "the woman," she is popularly known as the "Witch of Endor."

Saul had attempted to put an end to the practice of magic and witchcraft among the tribes. He killed some who had "familiar spirits," and announced that sorcery would be punishable by death henceforth. Yet he was not convinced that divination by sorcerers and "mediums" should be wholly stamped out, and the practice went underground.

After the death of Samuel, Saul's troubles with the Philistines and his anxiety over the rising prominence of David re-duced him to a state of apathy. He "enquired of the Lord and the Lord answered him not, neither by dreams, nor by Urim, nor by prophets." Desperate, he disguised himself and at night sought out "a woman that hath a familiar spirit" to ask that she "bring up" the shade of Samuel, from whom he hoped to receive counsel and consolation.

The woman at Endor did call up Samuel's ghost, but Saul received no comfort, for Samuel confirmed the fact that the Lord had departed from Saul and predicted further that on the morrow "shalt thou and thy sons be with me."

Saul was "sore troubled" at the prediction and refused further ministrations from the woman until his servants insisted that he eat the meal she had prepared for them. She was afraid to have Saul in her house and anxious that from the meal he should re-ceive strength to be on his way before daylight; for, having recognized him, she knew that her life was "in his hands." See SAUL, SAMUEL.

Z

ZACCHAEUS – A combination of a Hebrew and a Greek word meaning, probably, *A Pure Staff* or *Rod? Upright man?*
St. Luke 19:2-10.
A "chief tax collector, and rich," who wanted to see Jesus but could not because of the crowd; he was a short man. He therefore climbed a sycamore tree in order to observe the events taking place. Jesus saw him in the tree, being probably amused at the unusual sight of a rich tax collector in such an undignified position, and calling him by name told him to come down; for, said Jesus, "I must stay at your house today." Zacchaeus stood before Jesus and declared that he would give half his possessions to the poor and restore fourfold any properties he had taken by false accusation. Jesus then said that "salvation" had come into the house of Zacchaeus. The strict Jews in the crowd criticized Jesus for being the guest of such a sinner as Zacchaeus.

ZACHARIAH, ZACHARIAS, ZECHARIAH – *Yahweh Remembers, is Renowned.*
No less than thirty-two men bore this name, which was spelled first one way, then another. Because the *Revised Standard Version* of the Bible, which has been used for quotations, uses the standard spelling, Zechariah, for all the people so named, we shall adopt that spelling for the five men to be identified herein.

ZECHARIAH

1. St. Luke 1:5ff.; 3:2.

The father of John the Baptist. Zechariah was a priest in the Temple at Jerusalem. He and his wife Elizabeth were "righteous before God" and "blameless," but they had no child and they were well along in years.

As he performed his duties of burning incense while the people were at prayer, an angel appeared to be standing before him on the right side of the altar of incense. The angel, Gabriel, calmed his fear and gave him the promise of a son, to be called John, a son who would be called also "great" because he would be "in the spirit of Elijah," and would prepare the way for the Messiah.

Zechariah was dubious and expressed his doubts. Gabriel then said that for his doubt he would be unable to speak until all the promised things concerning John were fulfilled. When John was born the question of naming him was debated within the family. Elizabeth said he should be named John and her statement was confirmed by Zechariah who, still speechless, wrote the name on a tablet. When he had finished the writing, his "tongue was loosed," and he praised God with the words now known and used as the *Benedictus*, a much loved canticle in the liturgy of the Church.

2. II Kings 14:29; 15:8-11.

The son of Jeroboam II, Zechariah was king of Israel for six months, c. 746-745 B.C. He was killed by Shallum the son of Jabesh, who held the throne for one month.

3. II Chronicles 24:20-22; St. Matthew 23:35; St. Luke 11:51.

Zechariah was the son of the faithful priest, Jehoiada, who had helped save young Joash from the murderous wrath of his grandmother and later had helped bring him to the throne. During Jehoiada's lifetime the old priest was a trusted and honored advisor to King Joash. When he died, however, the king turned to counselors who led him away from the policies of Jehoiada, and the people "forsook the house of the Lord," with the result that "wrath came upon Judah and Jerusalem."

At this point Zechariah "stood above the people" and rebuked them for their sins, saying, "Because you have forsaken the Lord, he has forsaken you." The people "conspired" against him, and at the king's command they stoned him to death. As he died, Zechariah said, "May the Lord see and avenge!"

The Gospels of Matthew and Luke refer to the death of Zechariah, obviously the same man although called the son of Barachiah, as having been "murdered between the sanctuary and the altar."

4. II Kings 18:2; II Chronicles 29:1.

The father of Abi (Abijah), who was the wife of Ahaz and mother of Hezekiah, kings of Judah.

5. Ezra 5:1; 6:14; Zechariah 1:1; 7:1, 8.

Zechariah the son of Berechiah, son of Iddo, was a prophet in Judah. His activities as a prophet may be dated as contemporaneous with the latter part of the work of Haggai, c. 520 B.C. and following.

Although Zechariah was much concerned to call the people to repentance, he intimated that repentance had been shown and that the purpose of the Lord in chastising the people had been accomplished. "As the Lord of hosts purposed to deal with us for our ways and deeds, so he has dealt with us." And that being so, the angel of the Lord said to Zechariah, "I have

returned to Jerusalem with compassion; my house shall be built in it . . ." Thus the "four horns" of Zechariah's vision, horns which had been used to scatter Israel, were now to be used to put down the nations which had done more than enough of the purpose of the Lord. The line in the hand of the "man" met by the prophet was a "measuring line" to be used in measuring Jerusalem for rebuilding. The call of the Lord was heard as "Ho! Escape to Zion, you who dwell with the daughter of Babylon."

Zechariah envisioned in Zerubbabel, called Joshua in chapter 3, the Messiah, who "Not by might, nor by power, but by my spirit" would rule the land and the people in the name of the Lord. Stealing and the bearing of false witness in the new kingdom would be so punished as to come to an end. Wickedness would be "thrust down" and borne away to the "land of Shinar." Zerubbabel who had laid the foundations of the new Temple would see it completed, and in the new regime the remnant of Israel would be prosperous and at peace—no longer a curse, but a blessing. The peoples of the nations would want to go with the Jews to their city to worship their God; for, they would say, "We have heard that God is with you."

The coronation of Zerubbabel, of course, failed to materialize. The Persian officers got wind of it, and Zerubbabel disappeared.

The prophet shows many similarities to Ezekiel, and a strength of hope in sharp contrast to the dour thoughts of many another prophet.

The Book of Zechariah, however, contains materials much later than those of the prophet himself. Chapters 9-14 consist of two "Oracles" from the Greek rather than the Persian period (9:13, e.g.). From these chapters several thoughts and phrases have been taken much to heart by Christians. For example, the story of the Triumphal Entry of Jesus into Jerusalem is phrased in words from Zechariah 9:9 (St. Matthew 21: 5); the thirty pieces of silver as the price of betrayal (St. Matthew 27:9f.) may be found in Zechariah 11:12ff.; the words of Jesus in St. Mark 14:27 ("I will strike the shepherd, and the sheep will be scattered") are a quotation from Zechariah 13:7; and the words in St. John 19:37, "They shall look on him whom they have pierced," are from Zechariah 12:10.

As chapters 1-8 reveal the influence of Ezekiel in many ways, so do chapters 9-14 show clearly the characteristics of the later apocalyptic style.

ZADOK – *Just, Righteous.*

II Samuel 8:17; 15:24-36; 17: 15; 18:19ff.; 19:11; 20:25; I Kings 1:8, 26, 32ff.; 4:2-4; I Chronicles 6:8, 53; 15:11; 16: 39; 18:16; 24:3-6, 31; 29:22; Ezra 7:2; Ezekiel 40:46; 43: 19; 44:15; 48:11.

Zadok was one of several prominent priests in Jerusalem in the time of David. Abiathar was another, as was his son Ahimelech. In the rebellion of Absalom, when David was forced out of his city, Zadok and Abiathar, together with their sons, were instructed to remain in Jerusalem to guard the ark and to act as informers for the king. Here it appears that Zadok and Abiathar were priests of equal status in the court, although II Samuel 8:17 states that "Zadok . . . and Ahimelech the *son* of Abiathar were priests . . ."

In the attempt of Adonijah to take the throne in David's latter days, Zadok took the side of Solomon, Abiathar the side of

Adonijah. When Nathan the prophet and Bathsheba prevailed on David to declare Solomon king and to have him crowned at once, it was Zadok who anointed Solomon and placed the crown on his head. The king then made Zadok chief priest and banished Abiathar to his home in Anathoth.

Zadok and his family became the first family of the priesthood in Jerusalem. When, under Josiah in 621 B.C., worship was centralized in the city, the "Zadokites," priests of the family of Zadok, were among the most influential people in all Israel. The position of the family was, of course, contested by other priestly families; but Ezekiel supports the Zadokites as having exclusive rights to the priestly office. Ezekiel was himself a priest of the line of Zadok. The Chronicler took care to trace Zadok to the elder of Aaron's sons and so to enhance the already secure position of his descendants.

ZALMUNNA – Meaning doubtful. ZEBAH – *Sacrifice, Victim.* ZEEB – *Wolf, Hyena.*
Judges 8:4ff.

Three kings of Midian who were killed by Gideon. Zeeb was killed at the "winepress of Zeeb," and another "prince of Midian" named Oreb was slain upon the "rock Oreb." Gideon and his three hundred men pursued Zalmunna and Zebah, "faint yet pursuing them," beyond the Jordan to Succoth. At Succoth Gideon asked for provisions for his weary men and, being refused, threatened to return and "tear your flesh with the thorn of the wilderness." At Penuel provisions were again refused and threats uttered. Having caught Zalmunna and Zeeb, Gideon returned to the two towns and carried out his savage reprisals. He "taught" the elders of Succoth with briars and completely destroyed the town of Penuel.

Gideon then commanded his son, Jether, to kill the two kings; but Jether, "yet a youth," was afraid to obey. The kings taunted Gideon until he himself "slew" them. See GIDEON, JETHER, OREB.

ZEBEDEE – *Gift of Yahweh.*
St. Mark 1:19f.; 3:17; 10:35; St. Matthew 4:21; 20:20; 26:37; 27:56; St. Luke 5:10; St. John 21:2.

The father of James and John, the disciples of Jesus. Zebedee's wife was Salome, sister of Mary the mother of the Lord. Zebedee was a fisherman, apparently a successful one, for he seems to have had others in his employ. When the sons left their work with him nothing more is said of Zebedee. See JAMES, JOHN, SALOME.

ZEBUL – *Gift, Dwelling.*
   Judges 9:28ff.
Zebul was a governor of the city of Shechem under Abimelech, an absentee king. After Abimelech had taken the city, a certain Gaal moved in and began to try to stir up the people against Abimelech. Zebul learned of Gaal's plottings and informed his master; and he gave Abimelech an idea for driving Gaal and his men out of the city. In the course of the proceedings Gaal had boasted that he had no fear of Abimelech. But when the king actually appeared and through Zebul's trickery was in command of the situation, he was not so eager. Zebul thoroughly enjoyed Gaal's humiliation.

ZEBULUN – *Dwelling.*
   Genesis 30:20; 35:23; 46:14; 49:13; Judges 1:30; 4:6, 10; 5: 14, 18; 6:35; 12:12; etc.
The sixth son of Jacob by Leah,

his tenth son. Three of the clans of nomads stem from Zebulun's sons—Sered, Elon and Jahleel. Judges 5, the Song of Deborah, counts the Zebulunites as among those responding to the call to arms. The wording of the song indicates that Zebulun contributed leadership to the cause, for they were said to "bear the marshal's staff."

ZEDEKIAH – *Yahweh is Might.*
   1. I Kings 22:11, 24; II Chronicles 18:10, 23.
A false prophet who, using a pair of horns to symbolize his words, told Ahab and Jehosphaphat that if they went to battle against the Syrians at Ramothgilead they would be victorious. With his horns of iron before him, Zedekiah said, "With these you shall push the Syrians until they are destroyed." Jehoshaphat was suspicious of the prophecy, however, and Micaiah was called to give an oracle. When Micaiah spoke favorable words, Ahab was suspicious, and finally Micaiah told him the truth as he saw it; namely, that the Lord had said, "Who will entice Ahab, that he may go up and fall at Ramoth-gilead?" In the conflict of prophecies in which Zedekiah was in effect called a liar by Micaiah, Zede-

kiah "struck Micaiah on the cheek."

2. II Kings 24:17-25:7; I Chronicles 3:15; II Chronicles 36:10; Jeremiah 1:3; 21:1-14; 24:8-10; 27:1-28: 1; 29:3; 32:1-5; 34:2ff.; 37: 1ff.; 38:5-39:10; 44:30; 49: 34; 51:59; 52:1-11.

The youngest son of Josiah who was appointed king of Judah under Nebuchadnezzar, 597 B.C. Originally his name was Mattaniah. The king of Babylon seems to have been involved in the change of names as well as in the appointment. Zedekiah took an oath of obedience to Babylon, but he joined a coalition of Moab, Ammon, and Tyre against Nebuchadnezzar after considerable hesitation and vacillation. In 588 B.C. there was open revolt. Egypt promised assistance, an important factor in the decision to rebel. Babylon laid siege to Jerusalem, but the siege was lifted when word came that Egypt's chariots were coming up. Jeremiah, who had urged submission to Babylon, was thrown into a cistern; but even from the cistern he contended that salvation for the city depended upon submission. Babylon renewed the attack and took Jerusalem in 586 B.C. Zedekiah tried to es-

cape but was captured and taken to Babylon where he was forced to watch the slaying of his sons, and then was himself blinded. He remained a captive in Babylon.

3. Jeremiah 29:21f.

A prophet in the time of Jeremiah who, because he aroused hopes for delivery of the city of Jerusalem from the Babylonian threat, was strongly opposed by Jeremiah. Zedekiah's prophecies played a part in the revolt against Nebuchadnezzar, which brought about the disastrous siege of Jerusalem and its final fall in 586 B.C. Jeremiah accused Zedekiah of immorality as well as false prophecies. For his part in stimulating the revolt Nebuchadnezzar put Zedekiah to torture by having him roasted in a fire.

ZELOPHEHAD – Meaning uncertain.

Numbers 26:33-35; 27:1-11; 36:2ff.; Joshua 17:3-6; I Chronicles 7:15.

This name is important as having a place in the development of thought amongst the Hebrews about the rights of inheritance. The story states that Zelophehad died leaving five daughters, but no sons. The daughters argued that because they had no man to claim their father's inheritance, it should pass to them. In Numbers it was Moses, in Joshua it was Joshua and Eleazar the priest, who heard their arguments and granted their claims, giving them part of the tribal inheritance of Manasseh. A long passage in Numbers, however, explains that in order to keep the inheritance of Manasseh from passing through marriage to other tribes, it was understood that these and any other women in similar circumstances would marry only men of their own tribe.

ZENAH, ZENAS – The Greek name "Zenas" is a poetic form of "Zeus," the chief god in the Greek Pantheon.
Titus 3:13.
A lawyer or law student of Crete whom St. Paul wanted to have come to him at Nicopolis, where he was to spend the winter. He asked that Zenah and Apollos, who was to travel with him, be provided well for the journey.

ZEPHANIAH – *Yahweh is Darkness.*
1. The Book of Zephaniah.
During the reign of Josiah, the prophet Zephaniah spoke of judgment to come upon his peo-

ple, and on all the peoples of the earth, because of the idolatry and immorality prevalent amongst them. The word of the Lord to him was that the earth would be "devoured with the fire of my jealousy," but afterward the "remnant in Israel," and through them other peoples, would turn "to a pure language." He said that the God of Israel, standing in the midst of the purified peoples, would hear their shouts of joy and praise and thanksgiving. Israel, after the holocaust, would be a "name and a praise among all the peoples of the earth."

Zephaniah, the son of Cushi, claimed royal ancestry through Hezekiah. Since many of the things condemned in his prophecies were changed to some degree by the reforms of Josiah in 621 B.C., it might be supposed that Zephaniah prophesied somewhat before that date.

2. II Kings 25:18; Jeremiah 21:1; 29:25ff.; 37:3; 52: 24ff.
Zephaniah was "second priest," i.e. next to the chief priest, in Jerusalem at the time of the fall of the city to Nebuchadnezzar. He stood with King Zedekiah against the idea of Jeremiah that the city should submit to the Chaldeans. He was employed

by the king to confer with Jeremiah in an effort to silence him or to persuade him to change his opinions. Jeremiah was adamant, both in his opinion as to the need to work with the Babylonians and also in his attitude as to the length of the exile.

Zephaniah, with many others, was taken to Riblah by the captain of the Chaldean guard. There they were taken to the king who had them executed.

ZERUBBABEL – *Offspring,* or *Shoot of Babylon.*
I Chronicles 3:19; Ezra 2:2; 3: 2ff.; 4:2f.; 5:2; Nehemiah 7:7; 12:1, 47; Haggai 1:1, 12ff.; 2: 2ff.; Zechariah 4:6ff.

The governor of Judah who was chosen as one of the group to return from exile and to rebuild the Temple in Jerusalem, by permission of Darius. He was largely responsible for the task and actually accomplished it, although he was forced by his opponents, first Rehum the commander and Shimshai the scribe, then Tattenai the governor, to appeal to the king for help. Zerubbabel was much respected and beloved by his associates, who regarded him somewhat as a saviour. Zechariah seems to have wanted him crowned as the Messiah. As the Book of Haggai closes, the prophet says: "In that day, says the Lord of hosts, I will take you, O Zerubbabel my servant, the son of Shealtiel, says the Lord, and make you like a signet ring; for I have chosen you, says the Lord of hosts."

ZERUIAH – *Balm* (of Yahweh).
I Samuel 26:6; II Samuel 2:13, 18; 3:39.

There is some uncertainty as to whether Zeruiah was the daughter of Jesse or of Nahash; but there is no question about the fact that her three powerful sons were known as her sons. Joab, Abishai, and Asahel were all known as sons of Zeruiah, rather than as the sons of their father. Possibly this unusual designation had to do with the fact that Zeruiah was an exceptional woman; or it might be the vestige of the ancient custom of tracing lineage through a maternal ancestor; or it might have been a means of connecting these stalwart warriors with the line of David.

ZIBA – *Strength? Crier, Yelper?*
II Samuel 9:1-12; 16:1-4; 19: 17ff.

One of Saul's household, possibly a slave at the time of Saul's death, who became wealthy and influential, and a counselor to King David. He informed David of the condition of the remaining members of Saul's family after David rose to power, and it was through Ziba that David was enabled to show kindness to Mephibosheth, Jonathan's crippled son. The king made Ziba the steward of all the lands to which Mephibosheth was entitled.

Later, as David fled Jerusalem in the uprising of Absalom, he met Ziba as he brought provisions for the retinue of the king. On inquiring for Mephibosheth he was told, slyly, that Jonathan's son stayed on in the city with the notion that now the kingdom would be returned to Saul's house. David then gave Ziba all Mephibosheth's possessions; but after Mephibosheth gave a good account of his actions caused by his lameness, half of his inheritance was returned to him. Ziba, former servant or slave in a king's house, thus became lord of half the dead king's private fortunes.

ZILLAH – *Protection, Screen.*
Genesis 4:19-23.
One of the wives of Lamech. Zillah was the mother of Tubal-

cain. See LAMECH, TUBAL-CAIN.

ZILPAH – *Myrrh Dropping.*
Genesis 29:24; 30:9f.; 35:26; 37:2; 46:18.
A handmaid whom Laban gave to Leah, Jacob's first wife. Leah later gave Zilpah to Jacob as a concubine, and she bore him two sons, Gad and Asher. See JACOB, LEAH.

ZIMRI – *Celebrated.*
Numbers 25:14.
"While Israel dwelt in Shittim the people began to play the harlot with the daughters of Moab," and to attend their sacrificial feasts. It appears that the people were smitten by "the plague," and Moses commanded that the chiefs of the people, and any who had been "yoked" with the women of the area, should be hung "in the sun." A man named Zimri deliberately brought a Midianite woman named Cozbi into his tent, "in the sight of Moses, and . . . the whole congregation." Phinehas the priest also saw it, and he went to the tent with spear in hand and pierced the two of them through. By rigid separation from the peoples of the place the plague was "stayed,"

although thousands died of it nevertheless.

ZIPPOR – *Sparrow, Bird.*
Numbers 22:2ff.; Joshua 24:9; Judges 11:25.
The father of Balak, king of Moab. See BALAK, BALAAM.

ZIPPORAH – *Little Bird.*
Exodus 2:21; 4:25; 18:2.
The daughter of Jethro, the priest of Midian. Zipporah became Moses' wife. Gershom and Eliezer were her sons. Moses "sent her away" from Egypt, and with her sons she returned to her father in Midian. In Exodus 4:24-26 there is an interesting story probably intending to account for the origin of circumcising infants instead of waiting, as in former times, until young men reached the age of puberty or until a time just before marriage. Moses had not been circumcised. He became ill and Zipporah thought this deficiency the cause of his illness. She circumcised her young son with a "flint" and touched Moses' "feet" to make the rite count for him as well as for her son.

This, as the story suggests, corrected the fault in Moses and saved his life. See JETHRO, MOSES.

ZOHAR – *Nobility, Distinction.*
Genesis 23:8.
Zohar was the Hittite father of Ephron, from whom Abraham bought the famous field of Ephron with the cave of Macpelah "at the end of it." Abraham bought it for a "burying place," and it is often mentioned as the last resting place of the patriarchs and their families.

ZOPHAR – *Hairy, Rough.*
Job 2:11; 11:1; 20:1; 42:9.
One of the solicitous "friends" of Job. He insisted that there were, in Job's inner life, faults which God could see, and that if only Job would confess and "set your heart right," he would forget his misery. He dwelt heavily on "the wicked man's portion from God"—wrath, terror, destruction. It was from the ministrations of such friends that Job appealed thus: "Have pity on me, have pity on me, O you my friends!" See JOB, BILDAD, ELIPHAZ.

Bibliography

Bibliography

Albright, W. F. *The Archaeology of Palestine*. Baltimore: Penguin Books, 1949.

Albright, W. F. *From the Stone Age to Christianity*. Baltimore: Johns Hopkins Press, 1940.

Anderson, Bernhard W. *Understanding the Old Testament*. Englewood Cliffs, N.J.: Prentice-Hall, 1957.

Baly, A. Denis. *The Geography of the Bible*. New York: Harper & Bros., 1957.

Barclay, William. *The Gospel of John* (2 vols.). Edinburgh: St. Andrew Press, 1955.

Barclay, William. *The Epistle to the Romans*. Edinburgh: St. Andrew Press, 1955.

Barclay, William. *The Mind of St. Paul*. New York: Harper & Bros., 1958.

Barclay, William. *The Master's Men*. New York: Abingdon Press, 1959.

Bewer, Julius A. *The Old Testament*. New York: Harper & Bros., 1949.

Bewer, Julius A. *The Prophets*. New York: Harper & Bros., 1952.

Black, Matthew. *The Scrolls and Christian Origins*. New York: Scribner's, 1961.

Bornkamm, Gunther. *Jesus of Nazareth*. New York: Harper & Bros., 1960.

Bouquet, A. C. *Everyday Life in New Testament Times*. New York: Scribner's, 1953.

Branscomb, B. Harvie. *Mark*. New York: Harper & Bros.

Bright, John. *A History of Israel*. Philadelphia: Westminster Press, 1959.

Brown, Driver and Briggs. *Hebrew and English Lexicon of the*

Old Testament (Corrected Impression). New York: Oxford Univ. Press, 1952.

Buber, Martin. *Moses.* New York: Harper & Bros., 1946.

Cannon, William R. *The Redeemer.* New York: Abingdon Press, 1951.

Carrington, Philip. *Our Lord and Saviour.* Greenwich: The Seabury Press, 1958.

Chase, Mary Ellen. *The Bible and the Common Reader.* New York: Macmillan Co., 1956.

Cruden, Alexander. *Cruden's Complete Concordance to the Holy Scriptures.* New York: Revell Co.

Cullmann, Oscar. *Peter.* Philadelphia: Westminster Press, 1958.

Davidson, B. *The Analytical Hebrew and Chaldee Lexicon.* New York: Harper & Bros., 1959.

Deissmann, Adolph. *Paul.* New York: Harper & Bros., 1912 (1957).

Dentan, Robert C. *The Holy Scriptures.* Greenwich: The Seabury Press, 1949.

Dentan, Robert C. *The Apocrypha, Bridge of the Testaments.* Greenwich: The Seabury Press, 1954.

Dibelius, M. and Kummel, W. G. *Paul.* Philadelphia: Westminster Press, 1953.

Dibelius, M. and Kummel, W. G. *Studies in Acts of the Apostles.* New York: Scribner's, 1956.

Dix, Dom Gregory. *The Claim of Jesus Christ.* New York: Cloister Press, 1951.

Dodd, C. H. *The Authority of the Bible.* New York: Harper & Bros., 1928.

Dodd, C. H. *The Interpretation of the Fourth Gospel.* New York: Cambridge University Press, 1953.

Dodd, C. H. *Romans.* New York: Harper & Bros., 1950.

Dodd, C. H. *Johannine Epistles.* New York: Harper & Bros., 1946.

Foakes-Jackson, F. J. *The Acts of the Apostles.* New York: Harper & Bros., 1931.

Gaster, Theodore H. *The Dead Sea Scriptures.* New York: Doubleday (Anchor), 1957.

Goodspeed, E. J. *Paul.* New York: Abingdon Press, 1947.

Goodspeed, E. J. *A Life of Jesus.* New York: Harper & Bros., 1950.

Grant, Frederick C. *An Introduction to New Testament Thought.* New York: Abingdon Press, 1950.

Grant, Frederick C. *How to Read the Bible.* New York: Morehouse-Gorham, 1956.

Grant, Frederick C. *Translating the Bible.* Greenwich: The Seabury Press, 1961.

Guthrie, Harvey H., Jr. *God and History in the Old Testament.* Greenwich: The Seabury Press, 1960.

Hastings, James, ed. *A Dictionary of the Bible.* New York: Scribner's, 1909.

Hastings, James, ed. *A Dictionary of Christ and the Gospels.* New York: Scribner's, 1909.

Interpreter's Bible, The. New York: Abingdon Press.

James, Fleming. *Personalities of the Old Testament.* New York: Scribner's, 1951.

Jewish Encyclopedia, The. New York: Funk and Wagnalls, 1916. (12 vols.)

Johnson, Sherman E. *Jesus in His Homeland.* New York: Scribner's, 1957.

Johnson, Sherman E. *Commentary on the Gospel According to St. Mark.* New York: Harper & Bros., 1960.

Kee, H. C. and Young, F. W. *Understanding the New Testament.* Englewood Cliffs, N.J.: Prentice-Hall, 1957.

Knox, John. *Chapters in a Life of Paul.* New York: Abingdon Press, 1950.

Knox, John. *Life in Christ Jesus.* Greenwich: The Seabury Press, 1961.

Kuhl, Curt. *The Prophets of Israel.* Richmond: John Knox Press, 1960.

Liddell and Scott. *Greek-English Lexicon,* New Edition. (2 vols.) New York: Oxford University Press, 1940.

Manson, William. *The Gospel of Luke.* New York: Harper & Bros., 1931.

Manson, William. *The Epistle to the Hebrews.* London: Hodder & Stoughton, 1951.

Meek, T. J. *Hebrew Origins.* New York: Harper & Bros., 1936.

Miller, Madeleine S. and J. Lane. *Bible Dictionary.* New York: Harper & Bros., 1952.

Neil, William. *Thessalonians.* New York: Harper & Bros., 1950.

Nelson's Complete Concordance to the Revised Standard Version of the Bible. New York: Thomas Nelson & Sons, 1957.

Nock, Arthur D. *St. Paul.* New York: Harper & Bros., 1930.

Noth, Martin. *The History of Israel.* New York: Harper & Bros., 1958.

Oesterley, W. E. and Robinson, T. H. *An Introduction to the Books of the Old Testament.* London: S.P.C.K., 1934.

Oesterley, W. E. and Robinson, T. H. *The Psalms.* London: S.P.C.K., 1953.

Oesterley, W. E. and Robinson, T. H. *An Introduction to the Books of the Apocrypha.* London: S.P.C.K., 1958.

Parker, Pierson. *Inherit the Promise:* Six Keys to New Testament Thought. Greenwich: The Seabury Press, 1957.

Pfeiffer, R. H. *Introduction to the Old Testament.* New York: Harper & Bros., 1941.

Pfeiffer, R. H. *A History of New Testament Times.* New York: Harper & Bros., 1949.

Pfeiffer, R. H. and Pollard, W. G. *The Hebrew Iliad.* New York: Harper & Bros., 1957.

Pritchard, James B., ed. *Ancient*

Near Eastern Texts Relating to the Old Testament. Princeton: Princeton University Press, 1955, 2nd ed.

Pritchard, James B., ed. *Ancient Near East.* Princeton: Princeton Univ. Press, 1959.

Rhys, J. and Howard W. *The Epistle to the Romans.* New York: Macmillan Co., 1961.

Rowley, H. H. *From Joseph to Joshua.* London: The British Academy, 1950.

Scott, E. F. *Pastoral Epistles.* New York: Harper & Bros.

Scott, R. B. Y. *The Relevance of the Prophets.* New York: Macmillan Co., 1944.

Seitz, Oscar J. F. *One Body and One Spirit:* A Study of the Church in the New Testament. Greenwich: The Seabury Press, 1960.

Selwyn, E. G. *The First Epistle of St. Peter.* London: Macmillan, 1955.

Simcox, C. E. *They Met at Philippi.* New York: Oxford University Press, 1958.

Simpson, C. A. *The Early Traditions of Israel.* Oxford: Blackwell, 1958.

Snaith, Norman H. *The Jews from Cyrus to Herod.* New York: Abingdon Press.

Taylor, Vincent. *The Gospel According to St. Mark.* New York: St. Martin's Press, 1959.

Taylor, Vincent. *The Person of Christ in New Testament Teaching.* New York: St. Martin's Press, 1958.

Taylor, Vincent. *The Life and Ministry of Jesus.* New York: Abingdon Press.

Thomas, D. W. *Documents from Old Testament Times.* New York: Harper & Bros., 1958.

Torrance, T. F. *The Apocalypse Today.* Grand Rapids: Wm. B. Eerdmans, 1959.

Wright, G. Ernest. *Biblical Archaeology.* Philadelphia: Westminster Press, 1960.

Wright, G. Ernest. *The Old Testament Against Its Environment.* Chicago: Alec R. Allenson, Inc., 1950.

Wright, G. E., and Fuller, R. H. *The Book of the Acts of God.* Garden City: Doubleday (Anchor), 1960.

Yerkes, R. K. *Sacrifice in Greek and Roman Religions and Early Judaism.* New York: Scribner's, 1952.

Young, Robert. *Analytical Concordance to the Bible* (22nd American Edition). Grand Rapids: Eerdmans, 1955.

The following titles in the Torch Bible Commentaries, London: S. C. M. Press:

Allan, J. A. *Galatians,* 1953.

Browning, W. R. F. *St. Luke,* 1960.

Cox, G. E. P. *St. Matthew,* 1952.

Cunliff-Jones, H. *Deuteronomy,* 1951.

Hanson, A. and M. *The Book of Job,* 1953.

Hanson, R. H. P. and A. *Revelation,* 1941.

Hanson, R. P. C. *II Corinthians,* 1954.

Hunter, A. M. *St. Mark,* 1948.

Hunter, A. M. *Romans,* 1955.

Knight, G. A. F. *Ruth and Jonah,* 1950.

Knight, G. A. F. *Esther, Song of Solomon, Lamentations,* 1955.

Knight, G. A. F. *Hosea,* 1960.

Marsh, John. *Amos and Micah,* 1959.

Neil, W. *Hebrews,* 1955.

North, C. R. *II Isaiah,* 1952.

Richardson, Alan. *Genesis I-IX,* 1953.

Richardson, Alan. *St. John.* 1959.

Synge, F. C. *Philippians and Colossians,* 1951.

Williams, R. R. *Acts,* 1953.